GHOSTS OF HIROSHIMA

BOOKS BY CHARLES PELLEGRINO

NONFICTION

Ghosts of Hiroshima

To Hell and Back: The Last Train from Hiroshima

StarTram: The New Race to Space
(with James Powell and George Maise)

The Californian Incident

Farewell, Titanic: Her Final Legacy

The Jesus Family Tomb (with Simcha Jacobovici)

Ghosts of Vesuvius

Ghosts of the Titanic

Return to Sodom and Gomorrah

Unearthing Atlantis

Chronic Fatigue Syndrome: The Hidden Epidemic
(with Jesse A. Stoff)

Her Name, Titanic

Chariots for Apollo
(with Joshua Stoff)

Darwin's Universe
(with Jesse A. Stoff)

Time Gate: Hurtling Backward Through History

STANDALONE NOVELS

Dust

The Killing Star
(with George Zebrowski)

Flying to Valhalla

STAR TREK: THE NEXT GENERATION

Dyson Sphere
(with George Zebrowski)

AS BILL SCHUTT AND J. R. FINCH

Hell's Gate

The Himalayan Codex

The Darwin Strain

GHOSTS OF HIROSHIMA

CHARLES PELLEGRINO

BLACK STONE
PUBLISHING

Copyright © 2025 by Charles R. Pellegrino
Published in 2025 by Blackstone Publishing
Cover design by Matthew Marley, incorporating design elements by Alenka Linaschke
Book design by Blackstone Publishing
Includes a modified photograph by Nick-D, composited
with other elements, cropped, and color corrected
Used under the Creative Commons Attribution-ShareAlike 4.0 International License
License details: https://creativecommons.org/licenses/by-sa/4.0/

All rights reserved. This book or any portion
thereof may not be reproduced or used in any manner
whatsoever without the express written permission
of the publisher except for the use of brief quotations
in a book review.

Printed in the United States of America

First edition: 2025
ISBN 979-8-228-30989-0
History / Wars & Conflicts / World War II / Pacific Theater

Version 1

Blackstone Publishing
31 Mistletoe Rd.
Ashland, OR 97520

www.BlackstonePublishing.com

To Tomorrow's Child

Either we live by accident, or we live by plan and die by plan. . . . Some say we shall never know and that to the gods we are like the flies that the boys kill on a summer day, and some say, on the contrary . . .
　　　　　　　　—Thornton Wilder, *The Bridge of San Luis Rey*

Our lives are not our own. From womb to tomb we are bound to others, past and present. And by each crime and every kindness, we birth our future.
　　　　　　　　—David Mitchell, *Cloud Atlas*

TABLE OF CONTENTS

Illustration of Hiroshima	viii
Illustration of Nagasaki	x
Author's Note	xi
Excerpt from *Hiroshima Nagasaki Download*	xiii
Prologue: By Accidental Connections, or by Spooky Action at a Distance?	1
Chapter 1: Sunrise	7
Chapter 2: Butterfly, Butterfly	21
Chapter 3: Profiles of the Future	53
Chapter 4: Neutron Star	75
Chapter 5: Surfing the Improbability Curve	105
Chapter 6: All This Has Happened Before; All This May Happen Again	133
Chapter 7: The Fallen Sky	163
Chapter 8: Is It Dusk Already?	179
Epilogue: Island in the Stream of Stars	251
The Shadow People Project	253
Appendix: Key Eyewitnesses (Alphabetical Guide)	257
Acknowledgments	263
Sources and Notes	267
Index	299

FURUMOTO
FARM (post-war)

LUM
MIL

SASAKI
HOUSE

MIZUHA

MRS. AOYAMA

KOI STATION

1000
150

MUNICIPAL OFFIC

TSUTOMU YAMAGUCHI

JOGAKUIN SCHOOL
for GIRLS

AKIRA IWANAGA

ARMY AIR FIELD:
DR. NISHINA'S
LANDING POINT
WITH MITSUO FUCHIDA

MITSUBISHI SHIPYARD
KENSHI HIRATA

Hiroshima, August 6, 1945. Principal survivors and their locations at Moment Zero. (Compiled from multiple field maps with survivor annotations [on the maps], and interviews.)

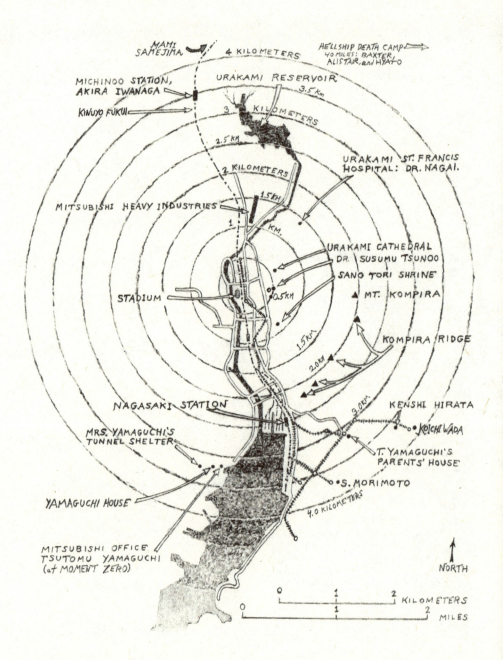

Nagasaki, August 9, 1945. Principal survivors and their locations at Moment Zero. (Compiled from multiple field maps with survivor annotations [on the maps], and interviews.)

The question of whether the atomic bombs should have been exploded over Hiroshima and Nagasaki is a subject for another time and for other people to debate.

This is simply the story of what happened to people and objects under the atomic bombs, and it is dedicated in the hope that no one will ever witness this, or die this way, again.

NOTE: Because many of the names encountered in this book may be unfamiliar to readers and occasionally may even sound alike, brief alphabetized biographies of major eyewitness participants are included for reference, beginning on page 257.

You could not make these landscapes up and have people believe it. Even as fiction, no one would believe [in] it. That is why, for over sixty years, I kept what I saw to myself... until the day others [who] spoke about it were called liars, [supposedly] because the atom bombs could not have happened that way. For people underneath an A-bomb to have become shadows on the wall, and charcoals, before they could fall to the ground, no one wanted to believe it. But it happened.

—Miyuki Broadwater (age 8),
Hiroshima Nagasaki Download

PROLOGUE:
BY ACCIDENTAL CONNECTIONS, OR BY SPOOKY ACTION AT A DISTANCE?

In 1948, a former Office of Strategic Services (OSS) agent named Walter Lord—who had interrogated (or, from a certain point of view, "interviewed") many of Japan's surviving naval officers—was struggling to turn a series of non-job-related interviews into his first book: *A Night to Remember*.[1]

The book itself was defeating Walter. Although he now had enough material for a second book (fated to become the basis for a film titled *Tora! Tora! Tora!*), he feared that neither would ever be published. Walter had not yet found "the music of the words," had not yet found his voice.[2]

About the spring of that same year, he came across a novel by another struggling writer, named Morgan Robertson, who in 1898 had published a science fiction story about a futuristic luxury Atlantic steamship—the largest floating object ever built by human hands, destined to make its acquaintance with hubris and an iceberg on a cold April night.[3]

The novel was an obscure "penny dreadful," which, commercially, had failed miserably.[4] It was regarded in its day as a storyline so improbable and so contrived that no reader could be expected to suspend disbelief. As it turned out, scientific and historical reality eventually caught up with and exceeded science fiction.

On a cold April night in 1912, the Royal Mail Steamship *Titanic* struck an iceberg four hundred miles from Newfoundland, just like Morgan Robertson's fictional ship. It foundered more quickly than anyone believed feasible, and before escape became possible for most, much as Robertson's ship did. It was filled with some of the world's richest and most famous people, just like Robertson's ship. Both ships (as attested to in letters to Walter from real-life witness Charles Victor Groves, and as foreshadowed by Robertson's fiction) left behind the controversy of whether survivors had been mistaken (through binoculars) for fur seals or other wildlife and were, in real life as in fiction, adrift on floating debris or sheets of pack ice.[5]

The science fiction ship was 800 feet long; Walter's real-life *Titanic* was 882.5 feet long. Both ships were nearly 70,000 tons displacement, with three large and remarkably powerful propellers, capable of accelerating each vessel above twenty-two knots. The crews of both ships were complacent about racing ahead at nearly full speed into the night toward an ice field that they'd been warned lay directly ahead—because each ship was believed "unsinkable."

And stranger still, Walter Lord thought, that Morgan Robertson had named his fictional ship the *Titan*. In a spin-off tale (also predating the *Titanic*), Robertson's *Titan* had a sister ship, named *Gigantic*. This time around, called "practically unsinkable," the fictional *Gigantic* was sunk in bright daylight, during a war that was believed terrible enough to end all wars. The real-life *Titanic* also had sister ships—two, in fact. Completed in 1915, one sister was sunk during the First World War, on a bright sunny day, by a naval mine in the Mediterranean. Still under construction when the *Titanic* sank, the real ship's name had been changed to *Britannic*. She was originally named *Gigantic*.[6]

And it happened again.

Decades later, after interviewing Walter about the Japanese experience of World War II, a colleague stumbled upon another strange science fiction novel—a multivolume mash-up of chapters and scattered short stories, published (mostly) in 1908.

Framed around a story titled "Beyond the Spectrum," the tale read as if someone had thrown open a window, showcasing technology that did not exist in 1908. In that year, the most advanced airplanes in the world were "spit-and-glue flimsies"—barely more than glorified kites with motors—and yet the author wrote of a great human change arising from a global war fought in the air, on the high seas, and deep under them. The skies became filled with flying fortresses and gleaming metal fighter planes. At the war's start, Japanese Americans were herded out of US cities, under a gross excess of "jingoism." They were mobbed and driven like cattle into exile that seemed to foreshadow America's real-life internment camps. In the fictional "Beyond the Spectrum" war, America's entry into the conflict began when naval forces from the Empire of Japan attacked American ships at Manila and Hawaii.

The fictional war, as it evolved into a stimulus for technological advance, led up to split seconds that ended up mirroring, as if by prophetic warning, key aspects of the moment when our species entered its nuclear adolescence.

The "Beyond the Spectrum" war opened with America and Japan in a race to develop and mass-manufacture a weapon that blazed forth with a fearful light, in some ways like H. G. Wells's Martian death ray,[7] unleashing the power of the sun. The flash was accompanied by "invisible radiation"—wavelengths beyond what the human eye can normally see—much like the rays that fell on Hiroshima and Nagasaki in 1945. The 1908 novel described smoldering ships limping into port, driven by stokers or anyone else who happened to be located belowdecks, because the rays were so intense that they burned or blinded officers and crew who had been on the bridge or anywhere else topside.

And how strange to think that the author of "Beyond the Spectrum" died in frustration and obscurity, in much the same way that Robertson's 1898 novel about "the wreck of the *Titan*" went out of print almost as soon as it hit the bookshelves: a tale too fantastical to seem believable, even by the likes of H. G. Wells. "And strangest of all," Walter remarked, "to see, on the cover of 'Beyond the Spectrum,' Morgan Robertson's name—again."[8]

Robertson's fictional weapon was called "radiation,"[9] and it marked the moment at which humanity was forcefully awakened to the possibility that civilization would die of civilization.

The real weapon was called "atomic," and it ushered in the beginning of a challenging new phase for civilization, filled with peril but also with a certain amount of promise. This is a phase of high-tech acceleration through which we seem on the verge (if we are wise and pay attention). of being able to sustain the kind of civilization that can actually thrive on Earth. And afterward, as H. G. Wells envisioned and as Walter Lord hoped, we may stand up as a child stands on a footstool, and reach out among the planets and beyond.

Thus begins an inevitable stage in the life of any electronic civilization's history—a phase that (succeed or fail) must be so brief and so rare as to now be happening only once among all the stars in our galaxy. (If other civilizations have evolved, they long ago succeeded or failed.) With such grace do we move forward as probably the newest, brightest, and most interesting creatures around.

This is the story of a human awakening, of a clock that started ticking at 8:15 a.m., August 6, 1945—toward what end, no one knows. Truly no one. And when the countdown started, deep within a nuclear core that awoke (initially) no wider than a wedding band, the human species (the whole species) was conscripted to an odyssey—everyone, young or old or yet to be born, within that first one-hundred-millionth of a second above Japan.

I remember the very strong scent of cherry-wood sap. I remember the cherry blossoms in spring. On August 6, I saw the orchards of Hiroshima aflame. It smelled like cherry pie.

—Memories of a young girl,
Case 2016B (1985),
Messages from Hibakusha

CHAPTER 1:
SUNRISE

It was the day Mrs. Aoyama's blood burst into vapor and carbon steel. It was the day a third part of her flesh—a billion sparks of carbon—ascended higher than Mount Fuji, like a snowstorm of micro diamonds. It was the day *Homo sapiens* became adult, and it began with unsettling calm and beauty.

As dawn approached, only gentle breezes stirred. Even the usual buzz of cicada song seemed oddly subdued. Southward, the sea sparkled like a field of polished beads, brass-bright against the universe. On a lake, the air was still, with the reflection of a castle reproduced in such exquisite detail that if koi were not occasionally gulping at the water's surface, the lake would have been indistinguishable from a carefully polished mirror.

Near the lake's shore, during that first chip of time, turtles were raising their golden eyes above the koi—each turtle head a set of twin periscopes gazing in opposite directions. Even reptilian brains would have registered almost immediately that something had gone terribly wrong with the sunrise—the second dawn of the day. Faster than nerves could respond, faster than water could begin to ripple, the turtles were blind and the tops of their shells were bleached. The mirror-lake reflected cicadas in flight, and dragonflies, and birds, all blazing forth like dazzling diamonds. One whole side of Hiroshima Castle also flared in eerie, stunning silence.

From young Toshihiko Matsuda's perspective, more than fifteen city blocks south of the castle, the sun was shining from the north, so brightly that the Matsuda boy was about to leave his shadow on a wall in his mother's garden. He appeared to be bending down to reach for his jacks and marbles or to pull out a weed. During the next few milliseconds, the wall behind the boy was flash-printed with his shadow and also with ghost images of the plants that surrounded him. The leaves, though barely more than paper-thin, were providing his skin with some small measure of protection from the searing white glare. On the wall print behind him, marking the moment of the sun's awakening, could be seen the shadow of a leaf that had just detached from its vine and, though falling, would never reach the ground. Nearby lay five glass marbles. They would be found days later, melted and resolidified into green blobs.[1]

Deep within the Matsuda boy's radius from the "sun's" core (its "hypocenter"), young Nenkai Aoyama's mother must have been outdoors and already at work on the same patch of ground she had been working every other morning by 8:15. She tended a temple garden with a half dozen monks. The vegetable patch was adjacent to an eerily shock-cocooned landmark, the Industrial Hall, that history would one day name "A-Bomb Dome." On this particular day, Mrs. Aoyama had saved her son's life by having suddenly, as if in a panic, rushed him out of their home and away to his school's work detail nearly an hour early. Nenkai's last memory of his mother was her inexplicable command, "You must hurry."

"Maybe she had a premonition," Nenkai would reflect, years later. "I just don't know."[2] At Moment Zero and nearly a mile behind the boy, ash and blood-derived steam exploded away from the place where his mother had been standing, and from anyone else working in the garden. The jets of carbon and steam erupted at more than five times the boiling point of water. Atoms of iron separated from blood. Bones became incandescent. And a moment later, Mrs. Aoyama was not. And the monks were not. And during the last third of a second before a wave of plasma and compressed air reached the ground, save for shadows of newly forged carbon steel boiling like coffee on the pavement, save for flaring ash, the people walking nearby were not. And as the blast wave plowed roof tiles into the river, and the water flash-froze many thousands of tile surfaces turning suddenly to lava, the tiles themselves recorded for futurity the thermal shock that melted their outermost layers within only one small part of a second. And within that same tiny chip of time, the outline of someone sitting on the steps of an office building was traced on the stone surface lying outside the person's shadow—traced by a hundred thousand steam-catapulted granite flakes that sprang from the rock like kernels of popcorn, almost directly beneath the false sunrise. The effects on slabs of stone and tile revealed much about what happened to people near the heart of the detonation.[3]

Only a short walk from the garden where Mrs. Aoyama and the monks became a vapor in the heavens, in a house where no one and nothing should ordinarily have survived, Shigeyoshi Morimoto received a quick and intensive education in the strange physics of shock cocoons. Morimoto was one of Japan's four champion kite makers, which was why he and the three other "kite men" had been drafted and transported to Hiroshima to design high-altitude observation platforms for ship convoys. At a quarter past eight on the morning of August 6, 1945, Morimoto was so close to the bomb that had he been located outdoors and unshielded, the gamma rays and the neutrons that fell on him would have killed him even without a flash (from the ordinary, visible spectrum of light) violent enough to shine through his skull as if through glass, violent enough to blast his brain like an array of high-tension laser beams and burn a shadow of him into the earth. The multitiered, heavily tiled mansion in which Mr. Morimoto was standing shook and compressed around him and the two cousins he had been visiting; but the combination of roof tiles and three layers of thick wooden beams overhead attenuated the gamma-ray bursts by a factor of about seven, and possibly as high as ten. Rooms filled floor to ceiling with shelves of books further attenuated the rays and the blast of compressed air that quickly followed. In a sense, the cousins were being safeguarded by their thousands upon thousands of books. They were safeguarded by culture. The compression of the upper three floors occurred as though the building had been designed with lifesaving crumple zones of wood and shelves (or protective shells) of thick paper in mind, simultaneously absorbing and deflecting the force of the uranium fist and cocooning the Morimoto family so gently that they survived near the center of Hiroshima with only a few minor bruises—even as the uppermost story of their mansion converted mostly to ashes and vapor.[4]

Another Morimoto relative, thirteen-year-old Tomiko, had left her mother's one-story house in a hurry that morning after exchanging some harsh words and slamming the door behind her. At Moment Zero, Tomiko was at a school factory-work assignment 1.2 miles away from the detonation point and preparing to go indoors. She heard a plane's engines growing suddenly very loud, and when a silent flash enveloped the world, her entire body was shielded in shadow. To her, the flash was red—"like morning sun reflecting off the ocean." Her school training, though intended for protecting oneself from a much smaller conventional bomb falling much nearer, acted in conjunction with a shadow thrown propitiously over her body. She dropped immediately to the ground, opening her mouth to let the blast from any sort of bomb press the air out of her lungs without rupturing them. Tomiko simultaneously closed her eyes as tightly as possible, pushing her eyelids against cupped hands. When she looked up again, the factory was gone—not just hidden behind a sudden storm of smoke and black dust, but simply gone. The building had nonetheless served a purpose in shielding her.

Within this very same neighborhood, Tomiko Morimoto's house was also gone, and her mother with it. She remembered how even in these days of strict rationing to the point of a hunger that never went away, her mother had managed to hoard a small amount of rice and serve her a breakfast of miso soup and seaweed. She would only realize much later that her mother, while claiming each morning not to be hungry, must have been giving Tomiko almost all the food she had saved.

The bombs of August 1945 had an unanticipated side effect that frightened the scientists and engineers who first entered the two cities—and which summarized the dawn of atomic death in a lesson they and the world should never forget. During that first split second of an atomic bomb's awakening, people, animals, plants, and inanimate objects left shadows on flash-burned surfaces. Although a boy named Toshihiko Matsuda survived for many hours after being flash-burned on one side of his body and irradiated by neutron spray and gamma rays, his shadow continued to speak for him on a garden wall, seven city blocks from the Hiroshima bomb's point of detonation.

("*I'm not hungry*, Mother had said, sending me away to school with what must have been the only lie she ever told me.")

And while putting on her shoulder bag for the school work detail: "I'm so sorry," Tomiko would lament decades later, "I was only thirteen and, as many at that age, often in a bratty mood. I had unkind words. And, oh—I never wanted to tell this: All my life, I have been sorry that the last she saw of me, putting on my shoulder bag, I was angry and slamming the door. That's why I want to say to everyone, when you walk out that door, please, *please*, leave only with a hug, or some word of love. I had no idea, but you do not want to be like me. I always, always feel remorse."[5]

The false sunrise did not only smash factories and crack concrete in Hiroshima. It sometimes left a crevice in one's soul.

Those witnesses nearest the hypocenter, like the Morimoto girl who would forever regret her last words to her mother, seemed never to have heard the blast. The kite maker, the elder Morimoto, was among those who insisted that the shock wave, when it crushed the mansion, arrived as a disconcertingly silent explosion.

Another to whom the false sunrise came in silence was seventeen-year-old Kimiko Kuwabara. She happened to be no more than a fifteen-minute walk from the Morimoto mansion, at the city's Central Broadcast Center. Much military-related information was passing through the center, including coordinates for sightings of B-29s, often referred to as "B-sans." The structure was therefore "bunkered up," or hardened against attack, and all the glass was bulletproof.

Kimiko had been made late for work by a series of B-29 air-raid alerts—not her fault, but she had been reprimanded anyway. In this particular station, men operated all the electronic equipment, and the young female conscripts from local schools were obliged to clean the offices, polish the glass, and trim the many rapidly growing bushes that were trying to obscure the view outside. On this morning, Kimiko would ordinarily have been outdoors by 8:15, working on the shrubs and exposed to the full fury of the rays and the surge of superheated air; but earlier flyovers by B-29s, surveying and radioing out weather conditions over the target, had done more than leave Kimiko quietly seething over a humiliating and undeserved scolding. The planes had altered her schedule and put another person outside in her place. And thus was Kimiko tidying the station manager's office when she heard a voice call excitedly from the courtyard: "It's a B-29 flying up there!"

A woman went to the window and saw a commotion in the sky that apparently frightened her. She managed to blurt out fragments of sentences—about seeing something like a long, silvery light bulb gleaming in the sunlight and falling fast, falling *really* fast, somewhere in the direction of the Dome—before she ducked from the window and dived toward the floor, shouting to everyone, "Get down!"

A plane's engines were droning out there—droning loud, as if it might crash. Kimiko dismissed the *Get down* order as just another of many false alarms she had heard lately, so in the final countdown to Moment Zero, she simply wanted to see the plane that had been causing all the commotion—becoming more distant, less noisy, and doubtless less easy to see with each passing second. A siren started to wail and went dead.

She never reached the window.

"The flash was red," Kimiko would record, "the same light that occurs the moment you strike a match, but far more intense." In immediate obedience to her air-raid training, she covered her eyes and ears and squatted down on the floor. The transition from flash to smoky darkness seemed to have occurred within the same instant, accompanied by the strangest of sensations: "In the darkness, I felt as if in a state of weightlessness, with a crackling feeling spreading throughout my body. Not that it was painful, but it was such a bizarre sensation that I thought I must be dying."

During these seconds, Kimiko did not notice the bulletproof glass coming apart or that it had, itself, been transformed into uncountable thousands of little bullets. At least three of the speed-slung fragments cut through her left cheek, but people in front of, behind, and beside her were shot dead.

When she climbed out to the other side of a broken steel door, there were huge clouds where, minutes before, the city had stood beneath a clear blue sky. And the lighting! The clouds, and the colors, belonged to another planet. And then, as if to emphasize the point, part of a wagon, still attached to the hindquarters of a horse, crashed to the earth like a meteor. Other meteors followed: the lid of a grand piano . . . the roof of a streetcar . . . A tennis ball bounced down from above . . . A roasted turtle pounded down, along with dozens of other objects that had no business being in the sky. They rained across more than half the city, rained down everywhere beneath the colorful new clouds.

All this, Kimiko was certain, had begun in silence. She was located just within a mile radius from the hypocenter.

"I'm certain," she would tell history. "It began with no sound of an explosion. No sound at all."[6]

With increasing distance, the noise did grow perceptible, then bone-rattling. Almost two miles away from the hypocenter (almost a mile past Tomiko Morimoto and Kimiko's radius), sixteen-year-old Haruno Horimoto had been an engineering student at the railway's streetcar division, where young women were treated with much more respect than at Kimiko's location. At Moment Zero, Haruno was taking a quick breakfast break in the girls' dormitory when a blast that she thought might deafen her nearly ripped the roof off the building. Outside, a cloud in the shape of some hellishly deformed flower was thundering six miles high and still rising—and below it, in the direction of home, the center of the city was swirling and boiling, and sending up, here and there, whirlwinds of flame. Perplexed, and with her ears still ringing, Haruno knew only two facts. First: "People are injured and dying everywhere and will need help." Second: "My mother is directly beneath that cloud."[7]

Two miles away, on the southwest side of the mushroom's stem (at Haruno's same radius from the detonation point), a young ship designer named Tsutomu Yamaguchi was permanently deafened in one ear by the blast wave.

He had been living in the city for only a few weeks, and during each of those weeks, a foreboding grew within him: *Hiroshima will be destroyed today*. It seemed to be the last thought he had before falling asleep, and the first thought that came to him when awakened by uneasy dreams. In those dreams, the emperor was the harbinger of death. It was madness. Incongruous. Madness. Yamaguchi's parents, like the parents of everyone else he knew—and like most everyone in his own generation—had worshipped photos of the emperor and his family, in much the same way that ancient Romans worshipped their emperors as living gods before their empire fell in flames and ruin and disease. He could not understand why, during an earthquake or an air raid, each family grabbed and protected its photo or painting of the emperor before grabbing its own lifesaving evacuation rucksack. He could not fathom how people worshipped a man and his children as descendants of the sun itself, based on the mere luck of family rank.

Yamaguchi kept his failure to comprehend to himself, naturally. Here in Hiroshima, based merely on rumors that he once questioned the wisdom of war, the artist Harumi Nakazawa had been abducted by the police for many months of foot-breaking and finger-breaking torture. The artist's whole family was cut off from food rations and shunned. Possibly because his paintings were once hung in the great Industrial Hall (the same building whose iconic dome still stood defiantly beneath the detonation), Nakazawa's family was among the lucky ones. Elsewhere throughout the city, other families, having been pointed at and judged guilty by accusation alone, simply disappeared.[8]

Yamaguchi too was among the lucky ones. Now nearing the end of his twenties, his scoring on IQ tests and his talent for drawing, combined with his ability to work out the physics that simplified hull structures even before he sat down to "show the math," had compelled one commander or another to keep him out of the military reserves, assigning him instead to design ships at various naval yards south of Hiroshima. From his many work stations, Yamaguchi concluded, based on the increasingly primitive materials from which he was being asked to contrive designs, that Japan had been running out of everything for more than two years and would soon be down to wooden hulls and oars—while

America, with its industry revved all the way up, must be sending out new aircraft carriers and planes at a frightening rate.

And I'm a lucky elite, he thought acidly at least once each day.

Two very long years ago, his infant son had died from a common cold that degenerated into bacterial pneumonia, which could easily have been treated if not for a lack of medicine even for the families of "elites."

When the government controls the food and finances and health of everyone, it quickly runs out of everyone else's money and food and medicine. This thought, too, Yamaguchi kept to himself, and for all the correct reasons. When the government sent him and two fellow engineers north to the shipyards of Hiroshima, perplexingly, almost no one else aboard the train had been motivated to question the never-ending propaganda explaining how suffering was only temporary because Japan was winning the war—notwithstanding certain disturbing revelations. From time to time, the train's windows became a gallery of charred landscapes.

Yamaguchi and his two colleagues, Sato and Akira, saw clearly that America's futuristic "B-sans" owned the air, and industrial centers were being firebombed out of existence at the mere will of someone who by now must be saying, "Just pick a target." During the train ride, they had expected to find most of Hiroshima already firebombed—and yet, they arrived at "a glimmering oasis of life in a vast national desert of destruction."[9]

Up to this moment, what had troubled Yamaguchi most about Hiroshima, compared to what he knew was happening to other cities, was precisely the glimmering beauty of the rivers and the undisturbed greenery that surrounded them. Add to this the *quiet*—"a quiet that could be felt." It was the quiet one knows if imagining a panther stalking its prey, padding about in the forest, waiting for the perfect moment to pounce.

What the young engineer had dreaded even more than the dark gallery was how the train to Hiroshima took him away from his wife and from his new son—who, this time and at least in this little corner of history, were both staying alive and in good health.

After many a phone call to upper management at Mitsubishi Corp., Yamaguchi and his two friends had convinced at least one sufficiently high-ranking commander that there was little to be accomplished in supply-poor Hiroshima and their skills could be better applied closer to home, on the better-equipped southern island. This morning, final clearance for the trip homeward was in hand.

At breakfast, during this last morning of the old world, Yamaguchi's friend Akira had asked, "Should we buy our train tickets now, or just show up at the station?"

Yamaguchi thought about it for a moment. As a general rule, the trains were no longer accessible to civilians. Service was restricted almost exclusively to those traveling on official government business. "I doubt it will be busy," he replied, "so we can just get out of here and show up at the station and . . . Oh, *no*. My name stamp!"

Trying to plan anything during a period of such escalating, universal chaos was an effort so fraught with stress and distraction that mistakes were bound to be made. The stamp was still in a desk at one of the Mitsubishi dormitory buildings, and Yamaguchi would need it when he reached the south office.

"Don't worry. I'll be back within a half hour," he said, and rushed out.

"Hope the next train isn't leaving too soon," Sato had called after him. "We don't want to be waiting all day."

"I'll be quick, believe it!"

He had thought of adding, *We've plenty of time*, but thought better against saying it, because he really did not believe it. Few people wanted to get away from this city more quickly than Tsutomu Yamaguchi. After running a sixth of a mile along the main road, he decided to take a shortcut through a potato field and was approaching a woman dressed in a black *monpe*, when three parachutes suddenly bloomed overhead and something like the power of a thousand flood lamps flashed before his eyes. Responding instantly with his navy air-raid training, Mr. Yamaguchi dove to the ground and rolled into the nearest irrigation ditch, simultaneously protecting his head with his hands. A mile farther from the detonation point than the Morimoto mansion, and even with his ears covered, the sound that came to him was earth-shattering. His eyes were closed and buried in mud, but he could see and feel the glare of the fireball as if the light were shining through the back of his skull and striking his retinas—which, in fact, it was. He would report later that it seemed as though the sun had fallen to Earth, and that even the mountains let out a scream.[10]

The ground roared and quivered, snapped and leaped, tossing Yamaguchi out of the ditch and some four or five feet into the air. In later years, he would be unable to tell for certain whether it was the ground shock or the air blast or some convergence of both that had coughed him out of the ditch and made him airborne. His world became confusion and tumult filled with rushing dust and occasional clearings in the storm, through which he viewed . . . "*things*—irrational things."[11] At the very moment he seemed on the verge of falling back again onto the potato field, the fireball imploded over the city and rose at stupendous speed, creating a vacuum effect that, for a second or two, appeared truly determined to draw the engineer farther from the face of the Earth and toward the center of the city; but instead the implosion merely levitated him for what would be recalled as an impossibly long time on a cushion of air and thick dust, and he guessed that at no point was he any more than six feet above the ground. Through one of the clear-air openings in the sea of dust—even as he still drifted over the field—Yamaguchi glimpsed distant rows of houses warping out of shape and flying toward him in pieces. He felt like a mere leaf, tossed on a lake of rushing black fog. Then, abruptly, he and all the larger pieces of the houses (including whole rooms full of furniture in mid-flight) dropped to the ground. Smaller pieces continued flying toward the city center without him—and, miraculously, without ever having struck him along the way.

After Yamaguchi regained his composure, he realized he had been dropped into a new ditch, some unknown number of paces from the one into which he had dived. Sitting up and looking around while checking for fractured bones, he beheld a blizzard of burning paper and shreds of smoldering clothing falling out of the sky, flickering like thousands of tiny lanterns and incense burners in the limbs of knocked-down trees and on the leaves of potato plants. It appeared to him that the contents of an entire office building had been hoisted into the heavens, then ripped up, blown apart, scorched, and strewn about. He could not find the sun—or, at least, not the real sun he had known. The blue sky appeared to have been erased, and darkness prevailed, making Yamaguchi feel as if he were in the depths of the ocean. Pieces of buildings were still in flight. "I could hear the sound of flying roof tiles shattering in the air," he would write later—"objects falling, and the noise of all manner of destruction. It was impossible to identify each noise or its cause."[12]

Sitting in a mud pool, Yamaguchi became suddenly aware that one whole side of his body was intensely hot. The exposed skin on his left arm had been literally roasted brownish black, like the skin of an overcooked chicken. Even then, before he knew anything about atomic bombs, the engineer began to suspect he had just survived a heat ray of some sort; and he realized that his white shirt and his light-colored pants had reflected the rays and spared him much. He had last seen the woman in the black *monpe* running in fright from the parachutes, running toward the center of the field. Running upright, she had exposed her entire body to the full fury of the flash, while clothed in the all-absorbing equivalent of India ink. Yamaguchi glanced around in every direction, but he never did see a trace of her again.

When the noise and the black dust subsided and Mr. Yamaguchi looked up again, he saw a pillar of fire and ash reaching into the stratosphere. Only much later would he find a way to describe it: "Like a giant tornado enclosed within a volcanic plume, but the base of it did not move. Only the top of the monster seemed active, growing higher and wider."[13]

When this cloud falls to the earth, Yamaguchi told himself, *every living thing will die.* He realized that even if he survived the cloud, which soon splashed him with oily yellow mist, the B-29s might return. Suddenly, all the burning of his body went away, to be replaced at once by the image of his young wife and child alone at home. He contrived a plan then to find a train or an automobile that was still working, or a horse that was still alive, and by any means necessary find a way out of Hiroshima and toward home.[14]

Home was Nagasaki.

The flash. The blast. The radiation. Instantly, the house collapsed. A cow landed on top of the debris that landed on top of me. My legs were being crushed. Grandmother pulled me out from under the cow. She had been outside, flash-burned. The skin on her back was peeled away and hung down from her body in long strips. She died. My aunt took me in. She was uninjured, but in October her hair began to fall out and purple spots appeared on her skin. She died one day while she was eating. We had a lot of rain, that autumn. Everywhere the layer of ash was washed away, and thereafter a large number of skeletons became exposed to the open air.

—Echiyo Fukagata (age 11),
Messages from Hibakusha

After Pearl Harbor, they came for my family. There were the internment camps for Japanese Americans. Some of us were deported [after] war's end, deported and told never to return. "Back where you came from!" But we were born here. I was born here—in the prison camp. We were Americans, patriotic second- and third-generation Americans, deported "back to Japan." That is how my family came to be in [fallout-contaminated] Hiroshima.

—Tak Furumoto,
Case 2016A

There are punishments and curses given to us in life for nothing we personally did wrong, and occasionally for things we did right. What we do with such blessings—that is the true measure of the human being.

—Victor Chan and J. R. Finch,
personal communication (2010)

CHAPTER 2:
BUTTERFLY, BUTTERFLY

1

"Certainly it seems now that nothing could have been more obvious to the people of the earlier twentieth century than the rapidity with which war was becoming impossible. And as certainly they did not see it. They did not see it until the atomic bombs burst in their fumbling hands."[1]

With such grace did H. G. Wells imagine and write a living example of chaos theory in 1914, decades before mathematician Edward Lorenz proposed that under precise (albeit improbable) conditions, even some of the smallest events—perhaps even a butterfly flapping its wings in London—could initiate currents that escalated, step by sequential step, to a surprisingly dramatic effect. Under the rules of Lorenz's butterfly effect, it became possible to believe that given enough time, given enough throws of the natural and historical dice, wing flaps in London or New York could trigger a typhoon over the Pacific.[2]

The first flap of the butterfly's wings was H. G. Wells's science fiction novel *The World Set Free*. In 1914 it received universally bad reviews because, much as in Morgan Robertson's "Beyond the Spectrum" mythos, every character in it seemed developed with less attention to depth than the cardboard-and-canvas covers in which the author's pages were bound. By 1932, almost everyone except physicist Leo Szilard had forgotten about Wells's failed novel; but Szilard was enough. In his fictional world, Wells had described several ways of creating a nuclear chain reaction in a bomb, one of them involving a spherical core fashioned from an element that did not exist until humans created it—which Wells named after one of his mistresses: Carolinum. In the real world, Szilard was led by a Wellsian thought experiment toward uranium and other naturally occurring neutron-emitting metals, from which a newly created element could be manufactured and fashioned into a spherical bomb core—which the scientists named after a Roman deity of death: plutonium.[3]

When Szilard first read Wells's novel, he and Albert Einstein were developing a relatively obscure patent for a refrigerator with no moving parts. Years later, Einstein would lament that had he known about the world to come from *The World Set Free*, he'd have confined the remainder of his life's work to such trivialities as designing better refrigerators and wristwatches and playing the violin.

The second flutter of wings was provoked by Szilard's draft proposal for US Patent 2,708,656 with Enrico Fermi; and by 1938, both scientists had moved to Columbia University in New York.[4] Together they discovered that Otto Hahn and their other counterparts in Germany were, for the moment, failing to initiate or sustain nuclear fission because of a flawed design. Szilard and Fermi designed a more simplified experiment, and Szilard recorded: "We turned the switch on and saw the flashes. We watched them for a little while and then we switched everything off and went home. That night, there was very little doubt in my mind that the world was headed for grief."[5]

Within a year, the series of experiments set in motion by *The World Set Free* was gestating into a perfect storm of butterflies. In August 1939, Szilard and Einstein cowrote a letter to President Roosevelt, warning that atomic bombs could indeed become a reality and that German scientists were not developing nuclear power merely to satisfy their intellectual curiosity.[6]

In almost no time at all, the storm intensified into a swarm of tornadoes. Szilard, inspired by Wells, had initiated the Manhattan Project.[7]

2

Scattered in random fashion throughout a city of a quarter-million people—a city in which survival appeared to be governed by sheer chance—any two random survivors were all but guaranteed to be strangers. But despite an arithmetic that should have rendered the survivors strangers, their lives tended to defy probability, becoming oddly connected.

The Sasaki family was an example of this. During the first minute after the detonation, two-year-old Sadako was sitting on a crate that had been suctioned with her through the side of the family home. Trying to settle into a more comfortable position on her seat of broken wood, she looked around in seeming wonder (and simultaneous fear) at all the bright new colors in the sky. Yet Sadako was already on a road converging toward a child who had only recently been born almost half a world away, in one of FDR's Japanese American internment camps. Both families were locked on a path that would never allow them to step out of history's way. So too was the Covell family interlocked, in spite of the reality that only one person, the youngest daughter, still survived after a sudden frenzy of beatings and mass beheadings by Japanese soldiers.

In that moment, no one could have anticipated that the Hiroshima hypocenter was simultaneously the epicenter for a ripple effect that would create uncounted billions of paper cranes. This ripple effect, strange to relate, would cross into the twenty-first century and to the children of every continent, spreading the image of the paper crane across the high seas and, carried aboard Russian submersibles, down to the beds of the oceans. This ripple would somehow manage to travel around the world, under it, and out of it, from the International Space Station to an engraving in a computer chip outward bound for Mars. A few of the origami birds eventually carried the plea, "Come back to Hiroshima." All of them would symbolize one word: *Omoiyari*.

In the beginning, the word seemed fated to come out of Hiroshima—fated to rise like *inori*, like a Buddhist prayer. The word was still a long way from evolving its many meanings, from "never again the A-bomb" to ways of perhaps making it so; from "always think of the other person first" to "just send forth random acts of human kindness" and "pay it forward."[8]

On the morning of August 6, 1945, nothing could have been further from the mind of seventeen-year-old Saito Michiko than some stupid prayer word. She was located just beyond ten city blocks from the hypocenter, down on the second level of a mostly underground communications and command bunker. Here, unlike in other offices around the city, the men had realized that there was a certain efficiency in pulling the mobilized female students away from cleaning and groundskeeping chores and instead training them to maintain and help operate the electronic equipment. Saito's steel-and-concrete-reinforced compartment had been designed, so she was told and so she believed, to withstand a half-ton bomb pounding down and detonating only twenty feet over her head.

When the clock on the compartment wall cracked open at a quarter past eight, all those standing outside the building either died instantly or were alive-seeming only to themselves, for a little while. Saito should have been among them. She was supposed to have been released from her midnight-to-eight-a.m. shift fifteen minutes before Moment Zero; but an air-raid alert, triggered by one of the "sightseeing" planes that seemed to be constantly flying over the city, delayed the morning relief crew's arrival.

Then three new planes approached. One of them dropped ray-and-blast monitors attached to radio transmitters and rip cords. Large parachutes bloomed over the city, and the planes reportedly peeled away from their path and were suddenly flying away like bats out of hell—*definitely trying to get away from something.*

A man shouted for Saito to press the warning switch and send out a new air-raid alert. Mere seconds later, as a siren began to rev up and as Saito tapped out words on a telegraph, there had erupted, through the tiny slit of a bulletproof observation window, "the light of a thousand flashes of magnesium and phosphorus igniting at once."

The saber of wood-searing light, lancing deep into the room, did not touch Saito; but the blast did. Pounding up through the concrete flooring itself, the concussion felt like a triple crack of thunder and a roar, with the floor breaking like eggshells and shooting fragments into the air. "And this was accompanied by a wind blowing like a tornado."

Just like Kimiko at the Central Broadcast Center and Yamaguchi in the potato field, Saito had a sense of being hoisted off the ground. And her world faded to black—*flashed* to black, *snapped* to black. Her period of unconsciousness must have been very brief, or history would never have recorded what Saito did during the first three minutes. She sat up and looked around in utter confusion. Everyone was gone, or buried and unmoving under a thick layer of dust and concrete.

This building absolutely does not stand up so well against a direct hit from a half-ton bomb, as advertised, she told herself. But when she stepped outside, Saito knew at once that something much more wide-ranging than a direct hit had occurred. The sun was gone. Cicada song—in August, normally loud and shrieking from every direction—silenced. No insects. No birds. No blade of grass. All the buildings nearby were gone or going—going down in ashes and flames, sinking into the earth. The people were gone. The main headquarters building was gone with them.

"*Defend your position to the death!*" she had been taught. *Even if you are the last Japanese on Earth,* she supposed, *the call to duty must hold.*

The war, it seemed, had finally reached a stage at which someone invented a weapon that made everyone disappear, perhaps all over the world—every living creature except herself lost, the moment someone tried to test the damnable thing.

Saito did not stay on the surface for very long. When she climbed down again into the pit, the last girl on Earth heard a telephone ringing.

Another young woman was at the other end of the line, trying to relay a message from Tokyo to anyone in or near the main headquarters building. "It seems Hiroshima has been hit," the caller said. "What is the situation?"

"I have no idea what has happened," Saito replied. "But the whole city is destroyed." She spoke these words into what was, by most accounts, the only phone line still functioning in all Hiroshima.

An officer took the phone away from the woman on the other end. "Repeat . . ." Static cut into his words. "Give time . . . the sound . . . the status of the city is . . ."

She tried to explain that there was only one drawn-out series of sounds—only one weapon, in one moment: "I do not know exactly what time it was, but the clock is stopped at 8:16. There was only one—*one long thundering and shaking*. Only one sound, one bomb blast. And the whole city appears destroyed."

"Only one blast? And . . . city appears destroyed?" the officer shouted. "What kind of ridiculous story is that?"

Saito thought of something cleverly sarcastic to say but kept it to herself. She was trying to present a calm, logical response when either the man on the other end of the line hung up or the line simply went dead.

For many long seconds, she held the silent phone, wondering what to do next, until a moderately dangerous avalanche of loose rubble slid into the compartment, and a rescue worker called out from above, "Anyone here? Anyone need help down there?"

"I'm fine," Saito called back.

"Not for very long," the man said. "Hurry with me and get out of there. A fire is coming."

Not for very long, indeed. Actual tornadoes of flame were emerging like dragons awakened—dragons of a particularly evil kind.

Incomprehensible. More and more of them awoke, like summoned spirits. As she and the rescuer fled north, flames erupted as if from nowhere and spread everywhere. Upright tree trunks and leaning telephone poles were spontaneously smoldering and setting themselves afire.

"This can't be," said the young woman who had just transmitted the first on-site, immediate description of central Hiroshima dying.

"No, this can't be," her rescuer agreed. The city was smashed like a cup, and a hellish irrationality held dominion over all the land.

In the exact antithesis of what Saito's own change of schedule had produced, her mother had volunteered the night before to take the place of a neighbor on a work detail. This swerve of history placed her very near Mrs. Aoyama and the Hiroshima Dome when the sky opened up. Later in life, Saito would derive some small comfort from the realization that Mother had died so immediately that the nerves in her body did not last long enough to begin transmitting even hints of pain. *But truly*, as even a quick look around the bunker had already taught her, *the line between life and death is as thin as a knife's edge.*[9]

3

Nearly fifteen hundred miles away in the Philippines, Peggy Covell knew that she should not be alive. From the age of fifteen, she and her parents, along with many of their American and Philippine neighbors, had been hiding safely in the mountains of North Luzon. Life away from the conveniences of electricity and telephones, streetcars, and the corner grocery store had been a sparse but generally pleasant existence. Peggy liked planting seeds throughout the woods, cutting up sweet durian fruit, and seeking out the kinds of fallen logs that were just right for cultivating tons of mushrooms in the caves.

Then, almost ten months ahead of Hiroshima, General MacArthur's soldiers came ashore in the Philippines, sending a wave of chaos fleeing before them. The wave of former Japanese occupiers was forced up into the mountains. It swept over the hidden civilian retreat. Only Peggy Covell escaped, and now she lived with a perplexing guilt over having done so while, behind her, everyone she loved had died.

Now that the criminals were either killed in action or imprisoned, she learned how her parents, who were Christian missionaries, had been summarily executed, ostensibly for being spies. One of the Japanese soldiers confessed that after her family's crime was fabricated and the verdict read, the captives requested, and were granted by the commandant, a half hour to open their Bibles and pray before being made to kneel beneath swords.

Peggy's tears of grief and bitter indignation evolved quickly into "a terrible hatred for the Japanese." She cursed the emperor and his ancestors, cursed the executioners all the way back to their remotest ancestors—and also their *descendants*, if any, for centuries into futurity. This was her state of mind when she approached one of the prisoner-of-war camps for Japanese captives and volunteered to "help" the injured. Among the first prisoners she encountered, during the weeks before Hiroshima's Moment Zero, was a young flight engineer named Kazuo Kanegasaki. He was a close friend of the man who had led the raid on Pearl Harbor. His hands had actually maintained and prepared the planes that made her whole world turn turtle and that led to the massacre of her family.

In the end, Kazuo came to be under Peggy's thumb—"in her clutches," in a manner of speaking. En route to that first meeting, among the biblical passages that flitted through Peggy's mind, Deuteronomy cried out for justice: "For near is a day of their calamity . . . Mine are vengeance and recompense" (32:35, paraphrased).[10]

4

Kazuo's close friend and mentor, Mitsuo Fuchida, had been following the long, strange path of an improbable historical presence, and improbable survival, even before Hiroshima. Raised on what he called the "catechism of war," Fuchida was only three years old when Russia conceded defeat to a Japanese emperor and began making economy-busting payments to victorious Japan. Reflecting on his childhood, he would record later that this victory, and the increased wealth having made possible the buildup of naval armament, "played its part in the increasing military madness of my country."

At age eighteen, in Japan's naval academy, he saw as early as 1921 how the winds of war were gathering and veering toward America. All naval practice maneuvers began to point in the direction of American sea power and against the "white apes" as the future enemy, "and every effort was made to influence the nation against them." Simultaneously, the hatred was inflamed against other "inferior races"—the Koreans and the Chinese.

Now, with the Americans and the British and soon even the Russians and the Chinese closing in, there was barely time to reflect. Soon enough, the OSS interrogator-turning-historian Walter Lord would be asking Fuchida, "Back in '41 and '42, with the invasion of the US and Indochina, and bombings against even the British in Australia, what were your warlords thinking in the emperor's palace?"

Fuchida already possessed the grim truth: "Only a fool fights a war on two fronts. Only the heir to the throne of the emperor of fools opens a war on three and four fronts."

I should not be alive, Fuchida reminded himself at least several times each day. Even at Pearl Harbor, he had survived more than twenty antiaircraft piercings of his plane, and afterward he had walked away from three plane crashes and the sinking of an entire carrier force.

In 1929, en route between Formosa and China at an altitude of just over a mile and a half, a plane had literally died in his hands. With no land in sight and a glide radius of only seven miles, he aimed toward a lone Chinese junk, off toward the horizon, and managed to maneuver his aircraft into a wing-breaking skid almost beside the vessel. Fuchida would describe, for Lord and others, how his plane nosed over to one side and began to sink, but the captain of the fishing boat rescued him.

Ordinarily, a Chinese captain should have wanted nothing more than to have a Japanese pilot fall out of the sky for him to kill, but this "inferior" had shown uncharacteristic humanity toward his enemy.

Months later, Fuchida came to the aid of a sinking boat, from which he rescued none other than that same Chinese captain. "Don't mistake coincidence for fate," the OSS man would tell him upon hearing of this. "Don't make the mistake the other way around, either," became Fuchida's stock reply.[11]

As if to support his stock answer, an unexpected change of schedule had saved him at the Battle of Midway, where Japan lost a huge fraction of its most skilled pilots. Fuchida was stricken from flight duty that day. An emergency appendectomy confined him to a hammock, in the sick bay of the same ship from which he had begun the war with the code words "*Tora! Tora! Tora!*" Two American bombs struck the aircraft carrier *Akagi*'s flight deck. Another caused the hull outside the infirmary to twist open and fall away, during an instant in which Fuchida and most of his surrounding deck space were spilled into the ocean. Despite both legs fracturing above his ankles, Fuchida managed to keep himself afloat until the crew of a small destroyer pulled up alongside and hoisted him aboard. Nearly twenty minutes had passed since the spill-out, and the carrier was listing heavily to one side. Once the gaping hole in the ship's hospital deck slid down level with the sea, the *Akagi* began slipping away even faster, toward an inevitable capsize. Inside, live ammunition casings must have begun falling against one another in great, shifting mounds, with bombs and torpedoes and bullets throwing off sparks. Part of the carrier blew completely away, and the Pacific gulped down what remained of her. More close calls were to follow Fuchida—naturally. And so it came to pass that on August 5, 1945, a day before Moment Zero, he had been attending a conference in Hiroshima's headquarters building, and he should still have been there if not for a sudden reassignment. Instead of being inside the very same building that Saito witnessed collapsing into dust and flame, Fuchida was in Tokyo when the young woman's phone message arrived: "One bomb blast. And the whole city appears destroyed."[12]

Within minutes of receiving this news, Dr. Yoshio Nishina knew that Saito's interrupted description—combined, only a little while earlier, with the split-second cessation of all other phone contact and radio broadcasts from Hiroshima—was consistent with the effects of the uranium bomb he had designed. Nishina's bomb lacked only a sufficiently pure amount of the precious uranium-235 isotope, but its geometry was actually in some ways more efficient than the weapon that had just detonated above Hiroshima. On one wall of Nishina's office hung a painting of a submarine-launched version of his bomb detonating in San Francisco Bay, shredding the Golden Gate Bridge. The nuclear physicist knew exactly what an atom bomb could do, but he was having a terrible time convincing War Minister Anami of what had just occurred.

"We must send a scientific team to Hiroshima at once," Nishina insisted. Anami did not quite believe in the atomic bomb, and he believed even less in sending one of Japan's top scientists, by plane, into skies that were already dominated by American B-29s and, maybe soon, by the deathly Hellcat fighters. But if it was necessary to know whether Nishina's "fantasy" was real, the lives of the most valuable scientists could not be risked in the learning without their having the best chance possible, under escort with the best surviving pilots.[13]

Fuchida's name came quickly to mind. Earlier this day, he had volunteered to lead a squad of the newest and most technologically advanced man-guided bombs the empire could provide, on a one-way assault mission against approaching American ships.

Now yet another reassignment would divert Fuchida from a prior path, this time sending him back again to Hiroshima. The OSS man and others like him had already observed that while we humans have no choice but to live forward through time, we can understand life only by tracing the chain of cause and effect backward. Only when he looked back could Mitsuo Fuchida understand how, in a manner that no observer of history could have foreseen, the dawn of atomic death was saving his life.[14]

5

A mile and a half northeast of the hypocenter, eight-year-old Keiko Ogura opened her eyes. She was not aware, yet, how a change in the daily routine had saved her. She was also unaware that her recollection of a strangely silhouetted hill nearby—its edges flaring out suddenly like the brilliant white corona that silhouettes the moon during a total eclipse of the sun—went back only minutes earlier, and not hours. Keiko thought she must have been unconscious from morning through dusk, because the soot and debris in the air made it appear to her that the bright and cloudless morning had become night. Not even the scientists understood, quite yet, how being located within the shadow of a hill could shield a person. Though she was thrown to the ground by surges and reversals of air pressure, Keiko's clothes were neither singed nor torn.

On the other side of the hill, each of the city-facing houses had been kicked apart, and many were starting to send up plumes of smoke and fire. In the center, in the direction of the Dome and the T-shaped Aioi Bridge, a tower of black smoke was rising like the trunk of a monstrous tree, or the neck of a dragon, to join a giant cloud that appeared to be shedding streamers of black rain. The child's school was directly under the roots of that cloud.

Keiko realized then, *I'm alive only because Father changed the plan for the day.* Home for what was to have been a brief visit, away from his usual wartime duties, Father had awakened this morning in a sudden panic, saying, "Today you shouldn't go to school. Something might happen."

I'm here, she told herself, *because he had a kind of premonition.*[15]

This was far, far from being the only such claim. Nineteen-year-old Toshimune Sanae recalled, "My mother told me later that my brother had said—*quite unusual for him*—'I don't feel well today. I don't want to go to school.' He went anyway. My father found the buckle from his belt, and his partly melted glasses. Maybe it was a premonition. I heard many stories like this about people who died."[16]

Southward of Keiko Ogura's location and much nearer the hypocenter, at only seven-tenths of a mile—only fourteen city blocks from the artificial sunrise—Takashi Tanemori's second-grade teacher had decided to give the seven-year-olds a few minutes of extra playtime outdoors, to burn off a little energy and settle them down for lessons from the local governor's office about sacrifices to come. At Moment Zero, the most important thing in the world for little Tanemori was a game of hide-and-seek that brought him indoors while his friends scurried after hiding places among the bushes and trees outside.

And when all the birds in flight, all the mosquitoes and cicadas, became uncounted thousands of dazzling fireflies, Tanemori's classroom vanished in the purest white he had ever seen. Even with both hands closing reflexively over his eyes, he saw the bones of his fingers shining through shut eyelids, just like an X-ray photograph. And in that same moment, seemingly soundless as the light, he was cocooned in a tiny cave of wood and stone that formed around him near the outermost wall of a three-story schoolhouse compressed down like a big cardboard box to barely one story tall. Outside, his friends appeared to have been spirited away, leaving behind, here and there near leaf-stripped bushes, little piles of smoldering rags.[17]

Inside the school, history would record only one other child who lived. Her name was Mizuha Takama Kikuzaki, and she was almost twelve years old on the day of the bomb. Mizuha's neighborhood friend, her future love, her future husband, should have been walking toward the school to receive his daily "war effort assignment." Instead, just like Sanae's brother, he awoke feeling ill; but this time, the kid stayed at home. The boy with whom he normally walked to school was outside and alone when the sky opened up and burned him to death. Friends and parents could never recognize his face. At this distance from the hypocenter, only the boy's watch could identify him—welded

A Crevice in Time: (1) During the first millionth of a second, not even light from the bomb-flash reaches Hiroshima's A-Bomb Dome—which stands 1,800 feet, almost directly below the point of detonation. (2) After one-five-hundredth of a second, the outer layers of the building's decorative granite fly apart like popcorn, the tops of roof tiles liquefy, wood and leaves and clothing and skin flash to vapor, and reflection effects at ground level render the air itself hotter than a solar flare. (3) During the first one-tenth of a second, the lower hemisphere of the bomb's shock bubble (a shell of superheated plasma and compressed air) touches the earth—and throughout the first two-hundredths of a second of shock bubble contact, the building offers just enough resistance to shunt some of the force away (much as the prow of a ship shunts water off to either side)—a moment in which the building becomes mysteriously shock-cocooned.

(4) After two-tenths of a second, the nuclear shock bubble begins to collapse. As the bubble implodes and becomes a rising fireball, it vacuums irradiated debris—dust of the crow's feathers, dust of the vagrant's rags, dust of the monk's robes, dust of Mrs. Aoyama's femur, hoisted into the stem of the mushroom cloud. Beyond the hypocenter, the leading edge of a blast ring punches out horizontally over the land, flattening the rest of the city. (5) The eerily preserved Dome and tree remnants around it so haunt those who arrive afterward that the Dome becomes an international monument. (6) Unlike the aftereffects of a full-scale nuclear war, outside rescuers and rebuilders and re-planters return to Ground Zero.

to flash-desiccated flesh and a skeletonized wrist. Its dials had stopped at a quarter past eight.

Mizuha began to wonder how she came to be in this strange manifestation of hell.

The answer was all so painfully simple.

Defiance got me here.

In March 1945, firebombing raids throughout the country were intensifying. A third part of Tokyo and a hundred thousand families—what was left of them after the years of conscription—were gone.

In Hiroshima, the governor ordered group evacuations of elementary schoolchildren. No one really believed that the fleets of B-29s, the storms of napalm and phosphorus, would allow the city to remain white in winter and pink with springtime cherry blossoms for very much longer.

Mizuha had prayed many a night not to be sent away to one of those distant farm towns, surrounded by temples and mountains. But in this home, there were more than the silvery new B-29s to fear. Her family, though politically well-connected and descended from wealth, was learning that such strength was no guarantee against suspicion and persecution by the increasingly empowered secret police. When empowerment came into the equation, with the empoweree's fringe benefit of confiscating any treasures the accused might own, the danger doubled and doubled again. No one could hope to remain immune.

Mizuha's father, Takama, was himself a government official who operated two factories vital to the palace warlords. One factory produced antibiotics and other pharmaceuticals; the other produced military supplies for the ever-shrinking front lines, retreating mile by mile homeward, toward mainland Japan.

The behavior of warlords and their minions reminded Mizuha's family of certain hornets that, in the autumn of their lives, from the moment high-altitude snowlines start advancing down mountainsides, turn murderous and sting everything and everyone in sight.

This was no time to be a scholarly, artistic, multilingual family.

Mother Tadako, fluent in English and German, had worked as a translator during the war's birth stages. She had worked at this throughout the years in which Japan spread out to and claimed much of the Pacific world, ranging from Manchuria and Korea through the Philippines and to the bombing of Darwin, Australia—then from Micronesia across Midway to the bombing of Hawaii.

About the time future manga artist Keiji "Barefoot Gen" Nakazawa saw his father returned home by the secret police with his feet beaten and degraded to puzzles of dislocated joints, Mizuha's mother was accused of spying for the Americans, though the only foreign language she allowed herself to speak (and only as part of her assigned work) involved translation of letters and papers left behind by Japan's fallen German allies. In these "vengeful hornet" times, coworkers and neighbors were rewarded with extra rations if they ratted out their friends or neighbors as subversives.

During July 1945, American reconnaissance planes had photographed fishing fleets that no longer left the harbors of Hiroshima, because naval blockades and firebombings had denied most of them their fuel. Even the most civilized neighbor or friend, after only a week of hunger, could be pushed beyond civilization and into lying for a tiny bag of white rice and the head of a fish.

Targeted by anonymous accusers, Mother was charged and abducted by empowered uniformed cowards and fools who could not tell the difference between German and English. The men beat her, they concussed her, and they assured her of execution if she did not confess to spying for the Americans, the Brits, and the Scots.

Evidently (though Mizuha would never know for sure), Mother defied her abusers.

During the "investigation," Mizuha's unborn brother was beaten prematurely out of Mother's womb and died in her arms later that day.

They returned her to the house in a condition that, to an outside observer, would have made her seem a lucky *Kempeitai* survivor: bruised and exhausted but mostly unharmed physically. But even young Mizuha could sense immediately that her mother would never be right again.

Defiance got me here.
And, humanity, you are despicable.

And so Mother and Father realized that when the call came for the youngest schoolgirls to be loaded onto buses and transported for safekeeping to camps in the countryside and away from Hiroshima's secret police, this was a chance to keep at least one of their children alive.

Mizuha missed her family; and she had found cruelty rising in too many of the other children. Most of them did not enjoy the new girl's widely gossiped-about blessing of a father kept back and pressed into service as an elite source of medicines and factory-made guns.

These were days of such material shortages that Hiroshima's new guns had declined to tin cartridges for hardwood splinter-shooters. This was what it came to when lunacy was empowered: famine, wooden bullets, and a hungered people shambling toward such rebellion that a city physician would soon fall into "irrational" anger toward a soldier, carrying with himself a harmless-appearing shovel. Stepping outside his Buddhist upbringing, the doctor became mission focused on sending a warlord's food-looting servant to a shallow grave with his head caved in. Only the rational certainty that the other soldiers would likely stop him and kill him by dragging could turn him away from the deed.

In the "summer camp" beyond Hiroshima, most of Mizuha's fellow campers no longer had fathers, because they were taken away to the Pacific War. For two years and more, many of those fathers had ceased sending letters home and were listed as "missing." The children hated being taken away from their mothers, and they'd been more than merely turning cruel; they were being groomed specifically for savagery.

Girls as young as nine and ten practiced with sharpened bamboo spears—practiced at blocking and stabbing maneuvers until those actions became muscle memory, using the only weapons that would be made available to the campers. Soldiers told children that they must prepare for a fight to the death because the American apes, if they broke through and captured them, would dissect ten- and twelve-year-old girls like animals, and rape them, and eat them, in almost that order. (Almost.)

At night, the children were instructed to write letters home to their mothers in Hiroshima. Mizuha understood without being told that their letters would be read and "fact-checked" by the new "teachers." Punishment would be swift and brutal if a soldier read anything indicating "bad thinking." Mizuha had no doubt of this.

"Dear Mother, I am enjoying life with my new friends and teachers," she lied. "It's a nice place. Please don't worry, because I'll study hard."

She and her friend Yasuko, observing and judging what was turning during each passing hour into the lies of an "honorable" Children's Crusade, would write the truth later: "War plays unfair tricks with fate; it cheapens human life to the level of a worm."

Infested with the camp's fleas and lice, hungry and surrounded by lies, Mizuha made a prison break toward home. If anyone thought to recapture her, there must have been too few people to spare for the chase. And so, with her mother's blessed Lady of Mercy in mind, Mizuha reached home in two days, bowed, and prayed her thanks: "Thank you, Mary, that I'm in Hiroshima."

And they saw it from the camp, at Moment Zero: a stupendous lightning flash in the distant blue sky, and then "far between the mountains, what appeared to be a small round cloud." The spear-trained child Yasuko Kimura would write, "The little round cloud rose bigger and bigger, finally taking the shape of a mushroom. The mushroom—very strange—grew just like a slow-motion movie."

Yasuko and the girls standing with her were now orphaned, most of them before the noise of the airburst arrived, lagging behind the deaths of their mothers at only the speed of sound—loud enough to leave a permanent, maddening ringing in their ears.

Mizuha had returned to her old school and was permitted to rejoin her class on the day of the cloud and the orphanings. She was deep within the building when it compressed. Huge wooden beams crisscrossed and interlocked overhead in so unlikely a geometry that they formed a protective tent around her while all but one other child was lost.

The combination of thick wood and bricks and the rest of the rubble kept most of the bomb's rays from penetrating through to her. For anyone standing outside at this distance, unshielded and in direct line of sight with the flash, even the visible spectrum of green and yellow light had the power to penetrate and instantly parboil internal organs down to a depth of five inches. The light vaporized skin down to bare muscle, and the rising cloud hoisted the vapor into the heavens, where some of it condensed as water droplets behind the rising fireball—condensed and soaked up flecks of radioactive dust.

The tent of wood and rubble shielded Mizuha during the critical first thirty seconds of quantum machine-gun fire—shielded her from gamma rays and volleys of neutron spray and even DNA-scrambling nuclei of iron and tungsten and fractured bits of uranium from the bomb itself, propelled to substantially destructive fractions of light speed by the most powerful ball of magnetic field lines on Earth—which, during a tiny chip of time in which the magnetic cannon formed, lived as an atomic accelerator aimed at people and crows and every other living thing.

Had Mizuha been outside among the second graders, playing hide-and-seek with Tanemori's friends, the particle beams and neutron spray and gamma-ray exposure alone would have penetrated her with the 1945 nomenclature of almost three hundred rads—a dose that (when received within the span of only a few seconds) was going to kill about half the people it poisoned. But the water droplets condensing in and around the rising cloud were swirling with newly created atomic nuclei that were vanishing in such explosions of exotic energy as would have filled the bomb's creators with terror. And the radiating droplets returned to the streets and the ruins as black rain, falling most heavily as horizontal gusts across Mizuha's neighborhood and inflicting upward of two hundred rads in secondary radiation exposure (inflicting at least one-third of a lethal dose) even if two stories of overlying rubble had protected her from 90 percent of the weapon's prompt radiation effects.

Mizuha burrowed and squeezed her way to the surface about the same time a similarly protected girl (a fourteen-year-old named Takiko) came running into the area in search of siblings. She saw only students on the ground who could not lift themselves. Some, burned and pressed into the turf, were difficult to discern as human shapes, save for their shreds of carbonized clothing. And to the Tanemori boy, a few appeared still to be engaged in their game of hide-and-seek, as if simultaneously ashed and frozen in the positions of hiding.

As the downpour diminished to an inky drizzle, the game had been going on for a very long time.

Other child corpses, engaged in another outdoor game at Moment Zero, overlapped one another in a pile, as though in a final embrace. A baby was crawling on top of the pile.[18]

6

Southwest of the unknown baby and Tanemori and Mizuha and a school where the new weapon converted Hiroshima's rain to radioactive ink and drenched all who still moved and breathed there—southwest along exactly the opposite side of the bomb's hypocenter, and just beyond a mile and a half (or a twenty-five-minute walk) away from the zero point—Tsutomu Yamaguchi, the shipbuilder who had survived in a potato field, was still trying to plan a way home to Nagasaki. The engineer's plan was threatened by his exposure to the effects of the bomb, within the fringe of Ground Zero. But it could have been much worse. Except for a couple of pebbles embedded in his skin, flying debris had missed him. All that had been necessary to protect him from DNA-scrambling gamma rays, X-rays, and a spray of neutrons was the mile and a half of sea-level air that separated him from the detonation point. Within that volume of air, combined with the season's high humidity, the atmosphere alone was the equivalent of ten or eleven feet of water, and a ten-foot-thick shield of air and water was the best radiation protection of all. Nonetheless, the visible rays of light—the bright flash—had burned straight through the atmosphere and seared his arms. And then came the bad water, a whirlwind of brownish-yellow mist that descended suddenly from a great height and enveloped him. The mist was surprisingly cold, like frost, but it radiated an imperceptible heat, born of leaking neutrons and flickering helium nuclei, along with a whole gyrating menagerie of heretofore unknown particles. No one in Hiroshima understood what was happening. Not even Leo Szilard had anticipated it.

The yellow mist (and at this location, it was far more dilute than the black rain that slicked Mizuha's skin like oil) passed quickly, and rays of sunlight actually began slanting down across southern Hiroshima, irritating Yamaguchi's flash-burned skin. Most of the atomic cloud cover was drifting northwest, where more of the bad water—great shifting blankets of it—drew a dark curtain across the heavens, blocking out the view so utterly that it was impossible for Yamaguchi to tell if anyone or anything still existed in the north.

Near the Misasa Bridge, behind sheets of black rain nearly three miles north of Yamaguchi's position, two-year-old Sadako Sasaki came to be sitting in a half-sunk fishing boat while her mother and the other adults tried to bail water out. Sadako's brother Masahiro, only four years old, tried to help. More than a dozen people, most of them showing signs of flash burns, were trying to climb into the boat. Masahiro reached out and pulled as hard as he could at a man's hand; but a commanding voice at the tiller ordered him to stop. "You'll swamp us if you bring any more people aboard. This is not a time for compassion. It will only get us all killed." The boy retreated from the gunwale and sat down hard against pieces of blast-damaged wood.

South of the bridge, barely visible through here again, gone again, and here again gusts of black rain, a whirlwind of fire rose higher than the city's tallest department store—twenty, maybe thirty stories. Another of the fiery serpents was struggling to be born along the near shore. And another appeared alongside it. And another. And another. From both sides of the river, Masahiro's world was a gallery of impossible images. A two-story house with one side torn away had all its furnishings on display. Table settings were perfectly in place despite being completely aflame, and everything stayed intact until the entire structure leaned forward and tumbled into the water. Even when sheets of dark rain provided occasional shielding from the glare of the fires, the air remained astonishingly hot. Driven by thirst, Masahiro and his sister licked the filthy black rainwater from their lips. Its taste and smell were metallic. Yet no one aboard could have imagined that the rain was dangerous. It seemed a wonder enough that they had survived the past twenty-five minutes at all.

From afar, the engineer in the potato field watched the rise of the city's fire serpents and saw clouds filled with colors he was certain human eyes had never before witnessed, and for which no names existed.

Where the hell am I? Yamaguchi wondered.

Where no one has ever been, he replied to himself.[19]

7

What human beings had experienced within the very first split second of the bomb's awakening was unprecedented. Trapped at the bottom of that tiny crevice in time, Setsuko Hirata was almost twenty years old and a bride of only ten days. From a certain quantum point of view, there really existed no "here" and "then" and "now." Setsuko lived in human time frames, in the realm of days and hours. The process that killed her was born in the realm of jiffy time: the travel time of light across the diameter of a proton. The universe smaller than the jiffy and the proton acted by its own rules and never failed to confound whenever observers from the universe of the very large were permitted to get into the act—which meant quite a lot when the confounded included Szilard, Fermi, and Einstein.

At Moment Zero, Setsuko was seated in her living room, slightly south of the detonation point. Deep within the bomb, from a volume of maximum fission no wider than a wedding band or a child's marble, sprayed the ghostliest particles in the known universe, called neutrinos. A trillion of them passed easily through Setsuko's body, tracing a straight line between the bomb core and her heart, at the speed of light, without "noticing" that they had passed through anything at all. The very same neutrinos that passed through Setsuko's heart continued traveling along that same diagonal line (with the same quantum indifference) down through the Earth itself. They shot through five thousand miles of rock and magma and up through the floor of the southern Indian Ocean toward interstellar space. Setsuko's neutrino stream would still be lancing out beyond the stars at light speed, beyond the far rim of the galaxy itself—still telling their story (as it were), a million years after the last stone blocks of the Great Pyramid were eroded down to lime, and the OSS man's beloved *Titanic* was reduced to an iron-oxide fossil bed sandwiched between layers of siltstone.

When Setsuko's neutrino stream erupted unseen near the French islands of Amsterdam and Saint-Paul, not quite one-tenth of a second after detonation, she was still alive. Ceramic roof tiles ten feet above her head were just then beginning to catch the infrared maximum from the flash—which peaked just shy of two-tenths of a second after the first atoms of uranium-235 began to surge apart. The earthen tiles threw a small fraction of the rays back into the sky, but in the end, they provided Setsuko with barely more protection than the silk nightgown her beloved Kenshi had bought her only a few days earlier during their honeymoon at the Gardens of Miyajima.

Overhead, the instantaneous transformation of matter into energy had produced a light so intense that if Setsuko were looking straight up, she would have seen a nuclear shock bubble's lower hemisphere shining through the single layer of roof tiles and wooden planks as if it were an electric torch shining through a hand and revealing the bones of her fingers in a darkened room. And within those first two-tenths of a second, she might have had time enough to become aware of an electronic buzzing in her ears, and a tingling sensation throughout her bones, and a feeling that she was being lifted out of her chair, or pressed into it more firmly, or both at the same instant. And the growing sphere in the sky . . . She might even have had time enough to perceive, if not actually watch, its expanding dimensions before its shock wave pressed down against the roof.

Setsuko's husband, Kenshi, was located at the Mitsubishi weapons plant two and a half miles away. He was a soldier who came back from the Pacific islands with permanently damaged legs and who afterward was reassigned to the "dishonorable, behind-the-lines work" of being an accountant. He exercised every day to strengthen the muscles around his broken and diseased bones so he might return to "the business of men" and better serve his emperor. In the office that morning, his limp was finally well concealed. He was able to begin grasping at hope when, through a window, came the most beautiful golden lightning flash he had ever seen or imagined he would ever see. Simultaneously, there arose a strange buzzing in his ears, a sizzling sound, and a woman's voice crying out in his brain. He would be sure, days later, that it was Setsuko's spirit.

The voice cried, "Get under cover!"

With all the speed of instinctive reflex, he dropped the papers he was carrying, dived to the floor, and buried his face in his arms. But three long seconds later when the expected shock wave had not arrived, he was left in adrenalized overdrive—with time to pray and wonder.

Outside, in utter silence, a giant red flower had billowed over the city, rising on a stem of yellow-white dust.

Kenshi knew immediately that this was not a normal bombing. He had seen the effects of bright incendiary weapons bursting at close range on the battlefield and in the cities of Kobe and Osaka—and always an explosion immediately followed the flash. This was more like a distant and very strange lightning strike: Nearly five full seconds followed the flash, during which the light itself began gradually to fade without a hint of concussion—at least, not until the first shock wave came up through the floor and uprooted the building's entire foundation and bucked Kenshi two feet into the air. Trailing only slightly behind the ground shock, the airburst hurled the windows indoors as thousands of shattered pieces, each traveling at half the speed of sound. One of Kenshi's coworkers had stepped up to the windows, evidently curious to learn why the light was fading without sending forth a blast. Her face and chest were pierced by at least a half pound of speed-slung glass before the wind lifted her toward the opposite side of the room.

Kenshi landed on his back, and when he stood up, he discovered to his relief that he was completely unharmed, then discovered, to his horror, that he was the only one so spared. Some of his fellow workers had fallen and did not move. Among those who still moved, he could tell from his prior observation of battlefield injuries that none would continue doing so for very long.

Even after making this assessment, Kenshi did not realize the full magnitude of the attack until he stepped outside. In the distance, toward home, the head of the flower was no longer silent. It had been rumbling up there in the heavens for more than a minute, at least seven miles high, and it had dulled from brilliant red to dirty brown, almost to black. As he watched, the flower broke free from its stem, and a smaller black bud bloomed in its place. It was, a fellow survivor would recall, like a decapitated dragon growing a new head.

A whisper escaped Kenshi's lips: "Setsuko . . ."

He ran toward her. As fast as his legs could move him, he ran. The main street leading toward home seemed more like a field than a road. Twenty minutes after leaving the accounting office, in the middle of the field, Kenshi found two blackened streetcars. Their ceilings and windows had vanished, and they were filled with lumps of charcoal that turned out to be passengers carbonized in their seats. A great fire had apparently risen here, and it either whirlwinded away or quickly ran out of fuel. It left behind corpses that could sometimes be deceiving at first glance, not cremated all the way through, but more the substance of logs burned to the point of resembling alligator skin, blackened, with grayish-pink matter trying to leak out between the scales. One of the trolleys appeared to have stopped to pick up more passengers when the flash froze it in time. Pavement had discolored and granulated under the flash, and the vehicle's shadow was permanently imprinted within the granulation. Two people were about to ascend its steps when the heat descended, and caught them, and converted them into bales of coal with shirt buttons and lunch boxes. In every direction, Kenshi saw people and horses and oxen looking like charcoal.

"Setsuko," he whispered again. "Setsuko . . ."[20]

8

All these horrors, from a reaction zone initially occupying a volume no greater than Setsuko Hirata's fingertip.

This was as H. G. Wells said it would be from the moment he penned his 1914 description of an atomic bomb: When matter is burned, as when gasoline is burned in a car engine, a little bit of its mass disappears from our universe. It gets converted into energy. In the case of a gasoline engine, the amount of matter that disappears and re-emerges into our universe as energy is only a few parts per several billion. During Hiroshima's Moment Zero, crew members aboard the atomic strike plane felt their mouths vibrating. Exotic particles far less ghostly than neutrinos, tunneling through metal, partly melted the fillings in their teeth. What the crewmen felt was the by-product of a more efficient conversion called fission: up to parts per several thousand (instead of many billions), with all its energy released during a chip of time immeasurably small yet far more devastating compared to the slow burn of a forest fire.

The act of gathering rare metals that knocked down a city and instantly vibrated fillings in teeth more than a dozen miles away had traveled a strange, winding road from the Belgian Congo, through the cattle yards and slaughterhouses of Manhattan's Hell's Kitchen, to Hiroshima.

In June 1942, three years after Szilard and Einstein alerted President Roosevelt that America might be in a race with Germany and Japan to develop an atomic bomb, Germany's attempt to sustain fission in an experimental reactor depended on the designs of Werner Heisenberg. As the originator of quantum mechanics' uncertainty principle, Heisenberg worked above and beyond sheer brilliance in everything he set out to do—except for this one project, for which it would seem, from a certain point of view, that suddenly he turned massively moronic. Heisenberg's nuclear program required many tons of "heavy water"—which, in its own turn, required the output of an entire hydroelectric dam to separate the desired element from normal water and which, in addition, produced a difficult-to-obtain resource that needed to be transported on ferryboats and trains. If the dams and production facilities themselves were not blown up by the Allies (they were), the boats and trains were easily targeted. Heisenberg never did mention to his colleagues that ordinary pencil graphite, instead of heavy water, would have enabled a reactor to be efficiently built and operated. All that was really necessary was to obtain supplies from a sufficiently large pencil factory. Heisenberg also presented (faulty) equations showing that a uranium-235 bomb need only be refined to a quarter the purity of the Hiroshima device. He further advised that to create a nuclear explosion, nearly every neutron emitted by the (diluted) metal had to be captured and used in the spontaneous cancelation of the "strong" force (which normally kept protons from repelling one another and causing their atomic nuclei to split and radiate). His equations produced an impossible geometry: a bomb far too large and heavy to be carried by a plane, and quite unpleasant (deadly, in fact) for anyone gullible enough to assemble the damned thing. When American occupation forces captured Dr. Heisenberg a few months ahead of humanity's Moment Zero in Hiroshima, the army's embedded scientists—who had feared that a German atomic bomb might be imminent—sent a message back to the White House: "Baby not born. Mother not even pregnant."

In December 1942 (about the time Heisenberg began leading Germany's nuclear goals along roads that dead-ended), Enrico Fermi and Leo Szilard's team, working in secret beneath an abandoned football field in Chicago, succeeded in building and operating the first controllable uranium reactor design (aided, of course, by supplies from a pencil factory). Aroused by the implications of this success, President Roosevelt released two billion dollars in government funds for the refining and production of fissionable metals.

A year after this, another swerve of history directed the road to Hiroshima from Los Alamos Laboratory through Columbia University, to Hell's Kitchen. Lieutenant Colonel Kenneth Nichols, dressed in ordinary civilian clothes, was advised by Harold Urey at Columbia to visit the office of an immigrant mine operator named Edgar Sengier.

As Sengier records history, "The colonel confirmed his credentials and asked me if I could help the United States to get some uranium ore from the Belgium Congo. All he would reveal was that it was crucial to the Allied cause. I asked him when he would like to have the shipment and he told me, 'Right now . . . But, of course, we'd settle for a few months from now.'"

"How much do you need?" Sengier asked.

"Oh, about a hundred tons—*to begin*, if you can acquire it."

"Well, I just happen to have that much stored right here in New York City."

According to Sengier, the colonel thought he was joking. Chemist Harold Urey had suggested that a few cubic yards might be in Sengier's possession, but a hundred tons? *Impossible*.

After a ride to a row of ramshackle warehouses in one of the city's roughest neighborhoods, the lieutenant colonel became a believer. The wood-and-tin structures were piled almost floor to ceiling with rock-loaded oil drums.

"Two hundred tons, right here and in the barn next door," the miner announced. "And there's more on Staten Island."

"*More?*"

"Another thousand tons of it, total." Sengier nodded indulgently, then added, "You know, I was waiting for your visit." He then turned the entire stockpile over to the United States government and received in return one of America's most significant bills of sale since a handful of men from the Canarsie tribe sold the Manhattan people's island to Peter Minuit, then loaded their bounty into canoes and rowed home to Brooklyn.

Edgar Sengier was by all accounts a tough, adventurous rock hound who had lived in the Belgian Congo. In 1939, an anti-Nazi acquaintance of Enrico Fermi visited Sengier in Africa and warned him that Hitler's scientists were experimenting with uranium fission, with a view toward building a nuclear weapon. Fearing a German invasion of the Congo, Sengier stripped from the jungle's soil and bedrock every ounce of uranium-rich pitchblende he could find. A year later, he had loaded the pitchblende onto a couple of ships and accompanied the cargo to New York. Then Sengier contacted Harold Urey at Columbia University and informed him that he had hidden a large quantity of high-grade uranium ore from the Nazis. Neither the lieutenant colonel nor the scientist (who ended up working directly on the chemical separation of uranium-235 from U-238) ever imagined that more than a thousand tons of high-grade uranium ore—an amount sufficient to destroy several cities—already happened to be sitting in steel drums, some of them on the floors of a Hell's Kitchen cattle yard's straw-and-manure-slicked barns. This became the secret source of almost all the Manhattan Project uranium that went into the Hiroshima bomb. Much of the remainder went into the nuclear reactor system that generated the Nagasaki bomb's plutonium.[21]

Beyond Hiroshima, the postwar A-bomb tests and strontium-90 blanketed the world . . . And should people remain ignorant? Should we just be bystanders? Who are nuclear weapons [made] for? [We must] take the first step and get people to sit down at the discussion table.

>—Hideaki Ito
>(director of *Silent Fallout*),
>to the UN in October 2024

Whatever we believe about how we got to be the extraordinary people we are today is far less important than bringing our intellect to bear on how we get together around the world and get out of this mess we've made. That's the key thing now. Never mind how we got to be who we are.

>—Jane Goodall

When he was asked what weapons will be used in World War III, he [Albert Einstein] said, "Well I don't know, but I can tell you what weapons will be used in World War IV . . . Stones."

>—Peter Lax
>(Manhattan Project
>mathematician), on Trinity

CHAPTER 3:
PROFILES OF THE FUTURE

1

Throw the dice of history long enough, and any improbable event becomes possible, no matter how impossible it might seem. Not very far from where Leo Szilard and Albert Einstein set in motion the key events that started the Manhattan Project, a major avenue was named after a man who had died exploring the limits of probability and possibility, in a corollary of the butterfly effect. On May 9, 1864, Union General John Sedgwick was admonishing his troops for their fear of Confederate sharpshooters at the Battle of Spotsylvania. The snipers' rifles were of inferior quality and more than five hundred yards away. The notoriously lacking quality control of rifle manufacturers on the opposing side made Sedgwick stand braver and taller. "I'm ashamed of you dodging that way!" he shouted to his men, followed shortly by his last words: "They couldn't hit an elephant at this dist—"

Under the bombs of August 1945, Kenshi Hirata was also pushing against probability curves, though he had no more premonition than General Sedgwick that he was walking through one of the truly rare pivot points in history, toward the seemingly impossible. As Kenshi made his way toward the center of the city in search of his wife, the streets and fields sprouted what at first sight resembled thousands of tiny flickering lamps. He could not determine what the lamps might actually be. Neither could any of the scientists who would hear of this later.

Each jet of flame was about the size and shape of a doughnut. Kenshi knew that he could easily have extinguished any "ground candles" in his path merely by stepping on them, but he was "spooked" by an instinctive sense that it might somehow be dangerous to touch the fiery doughnuts, so he stepped around them instead. He looked toward the city center and thought of his wife, Setsuko. The path homeward required him to circumnavigate a giant column of flame in which steel beams could be seen glowing bright orange. They sagged, and the building's entire framework appeared to be sinking into the ground like a wounded ship slipping beneath the sea. He thought of Setsuko. Nearer the hypocenter, not very far from the city's municipal office, he passed over warm road surfaces where great fires must have risen, then inexplicably died. All the people simply disappeared here, and all the wooden houses, on either side of the road, were reduced to grayish-white ash and terra-cotta roof tiles. He thought only of Setsuko.

Home was near the center, where towers of flame had flared, billowed into the heavens, then vanished. The roof tiles had boiled on one side, and most were cracked into thousands of tiny chips. Evidently, the entire structure was simultaneously roasted and pounded nearly two feet into the earth.

And yet, amid all this havoc, although dry-roasted and stripped of their leaves, trees were still standing upright and unbroken in a four-hundred-foot-wide area within his immediate neighborhood.

Kenshi could easily have walked away from the city with no radiation injury at all had he not gone into the center of the blast area searching for Setsuko. Once he breathed the dry dust, then cleared the dust from his throat by drinking brownish-black water from a broken pipe, his cells were absorbing strange new variations on some very common elements. These new manifestations, or isotopes, tended to be so unstable that by nightfall, many of them would no longer exist. Like little energized batteries, they were giving up their power. Unfortunately, they were discharging that power directly into Kenshi's skin and the lining of his stomach, into his lungs and blood. The quirk that spared him a lethal dose was the initial collapse of the shock bubble and the rise of the hot cloud. A substantial volume of pulverized and irradiated debris had been hoisted up into the cloud, and most of the poisons had already drifted miles away, passing over Mizuha and the Sasaki children, coming to them as black rain. Much of the rain was the ash and water vapor of leaves, animals, and people located between the Hiroshima Dome and a radius that extended out to Kenshi Hirata's home. Even beyond the Hirata radius, steam that had risen briefly from Tsutomu Yamaguchi's flash-roasted arm (and from the potato plants around him) was suctioned toward the hypocenter. Leaves, animals, and people were in the rain—thousands and thousands of people.

By sunset of that first day, Kenshi had begun excavating his home, searching for Setsuko. Beneath tiles and wood that had been converted to embers, he unearthed kitchen utensils—which, though deformed by heat and blast, looked all too painfully familiar. They were wedding gifts from Setsuko's parents.

In this very same neighborhood, where a memorial park would one day rise, had lived the older sister of Keiko Ogura, the eight-year-old whose father, on account of a "premonition," kept her away from a school that became the skeleton of steel beams Kenshi had seen melting. Keiko's sister, like Setsuko, was missing in or around a rectilinear depression in the ground that used to be a house. The missing sister's husband had also come into the central blast zone, searching. Kenshi saw him not very far away, doing exactly the same thing: kneeling in the dust, sifting gingerly through it. The other man was never to find any trace of the woman he sought; and as Keiko eventually recorded it, her brother-in-law would continue coming to this place, kicking at the soil with his feet and wading into the river even as a museum and memorial statues and tall buildings went up—"sixty years, searching for signs of her."

Like the other man, Kenshi was down on all fours, digging and scraping. All the while, his subconscious seemed to be screaming out a warning. He had an odd, instinctive, and impossible-to-ignore sense that the ground itself might be dangerous and that he should leave the city immediately. The thought that stopped him was Setsuko: *If she is dead, her spirit may feel lonely under the ashes, in the dark, all by herself. So I will sleep with her overnight, in our home.*

Around midnight, he was awakened by enemy planes sweeping low, surveying the damage. The sky, in a wide, horizon-spanning arc from north to east, glowed crimson, with low-hanging decks of smoke reflecting fires on the ground. Though there was little left to burn in what American fliers were already calling Ground Zero, flames grew all around the fringes of the bomb zone, creeping outward and outward.

The planes circled and left. Kenshi put his head down again, on the ashes of his home, and lay in the otherworldly desolation of the city center. The silence of Hiroshima was broken intermittently by more planes and by explosions near the horizon in the direction of the waterfront and the synfuel gasworks. As the ring of fire expanded to the gas tanks, there were no working fire hydrants or fleets of fire trucks, and only a handful of firefighters were left alive to prevent the tanks from igniting. Kenshi heard huge metal hulls rocketing into the air on jets of flame, crashing back to the earth one by one, and sometimes shooting up again. But Ground Zero itself was deceptively peaceful, and the noises that reached Kenshi from the outside world did not trouble him. He was too exhausted and too filled with worry about Setsuko's fate. If anything, the distant crackle of flames—even the occasional pops and bangs—lulled him into a deep slumber.[1]

2

North of Kenshi, the Sasaki children and their mother had been safely landed ashore by the crew of the foundering "lifeboat." They now tried to hunker down in an open field away from the fires and away from increasingly hungry, ill, and desperate crowds. Sadako and her brother watched enormous pillars of smoke drifting up against the sky and blotting out the stars. Only at their bases did the pillars dance with reflected light from the flames. Higher up, they ceased to reflect anything at all; rather, they absorbed the light as if someone had spilled ink across the heavens.

Seventeen-year-old Kimiko, who had been saved by a reprimand that put her inside the Central Broadcast Center while everyone outside perished, arrived with her mother in the same open field. Mother seemed to possess a similar kind of survivor's luck. At Moment Zero, the whole house flew apart around her, except for the small corner bathroom where she happened to be standing, having just closed the door behind her. Kimiko, meanwhile—within only a few short minutes of climbing out of the compound and witnessing everything from wagon wheels to horse heads falling out of the sky—noticed other signs that the world was in for a change. As Kimiko and a few other survivors from the Broadcast Center explored outward, it became possible to take this entire region of the city and wrap it up in a single word: *flat*.

An isolated exception to the "rule of flat" seemed to be a tall pine that stood intact until, still during those first few minutes, whirlwinds of fire slithered up from behind and the tree burst into flames with a terrific roar. The glowing tornadoes had the ability to snuff out life long before they actually reached a tree or a person, because some of the monsters were being orbited by sheets of corrugated tin roofing and other metallic debris, "in a landscape more terrifying than any painting of hell." Each roofing sheet was a missile, fast enough to cut a man in two.

After seeing this and escaping it, Kimiko had lost track of time, had walked around in what she now supposed must have been something like a dream state, until a coworker took her by the hand. He led her past the city's dead and still-moving dead to a rescue boat sent by the military, with orders to retrieve surviving communications and electronics workers. Kimiko's rescuer introduced her to the soldiers as a communications expert and thus managed to hold open a space in the boat. But Kimiko struggled away, insisting that she be allowed to leave and find her mother.

The young man called out, "It's too dangerous there. Fire."

"Yes, I will have to go around flames to get to her."

"Don't be ridiculous."

"I'm sorry, but I have to try," Kimiko said, and ran away from her guaranteed safety. Following a set of train tracks toward home, she stepped over flash-burned wooden railroad ties that were smoldering and still near kindling temperature. One in particular gave her pause, putting forth a jet of smoke that morphed into flame. There, she came across two railmen. The three of them seemed to be the only uninjured creatures in the area. The railmen reluctantly agreed to let her follow them toward the neighborhood of the Misasa Bridge but warned, "Walk exactly where we walk, *when* we walk."

The tracks and the cleared land around them were, in their own way, a long and generally life-preserving firebreak. Still, there were dangerous places where they had to stand off and watch from afar while the flames either died down or moved on. Only after it had consumed everything did one of the largest and stubbornest firestorms eventually move away. Finally, about midnight, Kimiko found her mother standing in an open field.

Mother had been praying "for whatever gods may be willing" to return one of her two daughters alive.

One was saved.

The other was missing.[2]

3

Another who had gone off in search of a parent was sixteen-year-old Haruno, the apprentice streetcar engineer who was safely sheltered in a workshop cafeteria two miles from the bomb's hypocenter. While assisting coworkers in tending to strange wounds—glass piercings and occasionally burns caused by patterns in clothing, whereby the darker cloth had absorbed the flash and branded skin with stripes and flower patterns—Haruno began to feel physically ill. It was not the wounds or the disaster itself that made her sick, so much as worry that the effects of the explosion must have been so much worse where she knew her mother to be: near the place where she saw the tree-shaped volcanic cloud rising from its roots.

A sympathetic boss advised her not to go there, in the direction of the Dome; but before sunset he had given her a small provision of rice and bowed deeply, hoping to see her again.

Another apprentice, her own age, said, "You know we will need you here. The tracks are still good and tomorrow we'll have two streetcars running again. We'll need to run them as ambulances."

"Just a few hours," Haruno promised. "That's all I need, and I won't even sleep before we begin work tomorrow."

The path toward the Dome required her to detour around at least two great firestorms that seemed determined never to give up. The new path crossed through land slicked by black rain. The puddles and the pavement glistened strangely. After nightfall, some of the mud pools seemed actually to glow. At two a.m., a shroud of smoke still hung over the city, and the shroud's reflected firelight from multiple directions was bright enough to read by. Home was near the city center's landmark T-Bridge and the Industrial Hall. Haruno believed she might have found the right foundation, but no one and nothing stirred here, and there was not even a remnant of a familiar dish by which the family home could be identified.

There seemed little left to accomplish, and it was time to head back toward the shop. But her head hurt and she was not feeling at all well, and despite being exhausted to a point at which she should have been famished, Haruno had lost her appetite for the last of her rice ration.

She sat down hard in the soot and ruin of the house.

Perhaps, if I close my eyes and rest here for just a minute or two . . . just for a little while . . .[3]

4

The first soldiers to reach the hypocenter came only an hour ahead of sunrise. The War Ministry had sent them in with stretchers—for what purpose, they could not understand. "There was not a living thing in sight," one of them would later recall. "It was as if the people who lived in this uncanny city had been reduced to ashes with their houses."[4]

And yet there were statues. A man had emerged from a shelter into a hellscape where not a single brick lay on another brick. Somehow, on a piece of land where everything else had been thrown down, the flames converted this man into a pillar of charcoal and left the pillar itself undisturbed, standing with its arms thrust toward the sky. In the direction of the Dome and the T-Bridge, another statue man, similarly fossilized, and covered in a light snowfall of ashes, was still pulling a large two-wheeled cart in which two charcoal children sat holding their knees.

"The dead-alive effect"—that's what scientists decades later would call the almost identical phenomenon when they discovered it in Pompeii's sister city of Herculaneum. Parents were conversing and sharing food at Herculaneum's marina when, in one small part of a second, they were flash-fossilized in mid-word and mid-swallow. And somehow, just as mysteriously as in Hiroshima, while buildings around the Roman families were torn from their foundations, cast out to sea, and dissected in mid-flight, a strange shock-cocoon phenomenon that accompanies most every explosive event left Herculaneans still sitting in a circle, around their sleeping children, in the midst of an eruptive force a thousand times more powerful than Hiroshima.[5]

Most of Hiroshima's statue people were considerably less intact than the man with the cart and two children. Outside the cart's shock cocoon, others must have died standing, and perhaps many dived to the ground as the nuclear flash and superheated air transformed their tissues into structures barely more resilient than carbonized paper, then scattered them like burned leaves, in blast waves and whirlwinds of flame. Broken statue hands and shadowy images were disturbingly common.

The most complete carbon fossils were sometimes the most distressing of all. The searchers found a statue that appeared to have spent the last moment of its life trying to curl up into a fetal position. One of the soldiers probed it with a rod, brushing a veneer of ashes away and expecting the fossil beneath to crumble apart. Instead, it opened its eyes.

The soldier flinched and asked, "How do you feel?" There seemed to be nothing else to say.

Instead of saying what he felt like saying—*How do you think I feel, you idiot?*—the man replied that he was uninjured and explained, "When I came home from my job, I found that everything was gone, as you see here now." The man insisted he needed no aid in leaving, nor did he wish to leave.

"This is the site of my house," he said. "My name is Kenshi."[6]

5

Sunrise now brought only the briefest respite for Kenshi Hirata's Mitsubishi colleague, Tsutomu Yamaguchi. He had managed a couple of fitful naps in a half-sunk fishing boat. The ration of two biscuits he carried for emergencies remained uneaten because he was having trouble keeping down even a few sips of water. Appetite had failed him hours earlier.

During the night, a soldier told Yamaguchi that the local Mitsubishi plants appeared to be permanently out of action and that any surviving engineering personnel should return to headquarters in Nagasaki. Yamaguchi had assumed that the rail services were every bit as dead as the Mitsubishi shipyard, but the soldier informed him that there were plans to send a train out of Koi Station to Nagasaki in the late afternoon.

After a few hours of mostly unsuccessful attempts to sleep in the ruins of the boat, Yamaguchi was nonetheless determined to set out for Koi. Normally, he could make the trip in forty-five minutes. *But now?* he thought. *Who knows if I will ever reach the station, much less Nagasaki?*

The soldier had assured Yamaguchi that as a high-ranking naval engineer, he would get a priority seat. The shipbuilder had long ago ceased really caring about military priorities or the war effort. All he wanted was to get home to his wife and his infant son.

With nothing else in mind, he was able (with varying degrees of success) to harden his heart against all that the grim sunrise revealed: a mother singing a lullaby to her dead child, a horse's head burning like an oil lamp, with bluish-green flames jetting from the eye sockets of its skull.

The ship designer had to cross two rivers on his way to the station. The narrower of them no longer had a bridge, but in the shallows nearby, islands of floating bodies were piling up against rocks and concrete supports like a natural dam that could now be crossed like a bridge. Even when he tried to keep his mind focused on nothing except the recollected faces of his wife and child, crossing that dam—over spillways lined with shirts and shoes—pained him severely. From deep within, a poem began to form in Yamaguchi's mind:

And the river flowed as a raft of corpses . . .[7]

6

From the moment Kenshi realized that the cloud had risen directly over his home, he prayed and held out hope that Setsuko might somehow have escaped harm. When he left the dockyard, he had packed a few extra biscuits for her. Now, a day later, he dug on all fours into the compressed ashes of his kitchen, descending nearly two feet deep. Whenever he paused to eat a biscuit or to sip water from a broken pipe, he sprinkled a share of the food and water ceremonially onto the ground—an offering to Setsuko.

As the August sun climbed higher and a fresh snowfall of gray and black ashes blew through, the pipe stopped dripping. Kenshi was soon out of water as well as running low on biscuits, but he continued digging, hoping against knowledge that his failure to find any trace of her meant that Setsuko might not have been home when the flash came.

As exhaustion, thirst, and now hunger began to compete with the first mild signs of radiation sickness, he completed his excavation of the entire kitchen. Three of his neighbors came into the ruins from the outer fringes of the city, also searching for loved ones.

"She is not here," Kenshi announced to the women. The oldest of them, seeing him in such poor condition and hearing his pleas for anyone who might have encountered Setsuko, gave him her water and went away seeking help for him.

Like an archaeologist probing ahead with a cross-sectional trial trench from a kitchen straight into the living room of an ancient Pompeiian house, he excavated forward. When the dust of the trench had produced not the slightest trace of her, Kenshi began to grasp again, ever so slightly, at hope. He was soon joined by a small crew of men who worked in the city's sawmill and who knew the couple well and had heard from a surviving neighbor of Kenshi's distress.

Together they moved from the trial trench to the rest of the living room, excavating almost knee-deep. Not a single hint of Setsuko was found.

"She is still alive somewhere," Kenshi said.

"To make sure, we must dig a little deeper," the mill owner replied.

Minutes later, hope died. One of the lumbermen unearthed what seemed to Kenshi to be only a bit of seashell.

"We both love conches and giant clam shells," Kenshi insisted. "Setsuko uses them as table decorations!"

But already he knew in his heart that it was not a seashell. The men quietly stepped back. Suppressing an uneasy feeling, Kenshi excavated gently with his fingertips, slowly widening and then deepening the area from which the "shell" had come. He touched a shadowy figure in the ashes and was able to see a pattern that indicated to him her final moment. She had been sitting when it happened.

Returning to the kitchen, he excavated a metal bowl, singed but otherwise completely undamaged. Kenshi recognized it as the very same bowl he and Setsuko had brought with them from her parents' home on the train to Hiroshima, only ten days before.

Ten days, he lamented, *and this poor girl's [ashes are] to be put in this basin that she had brought with her from her native place.*

He was thirsty under the broiling sun of midsummer. Sweat had formed long streamers down his back, and his trousers were soaked. He felt faint. His friend, the mill owner, offered him a canteen and he drank, then sprinkled some of the water over the basin—in the sense of giving his wife "the last water to the end of her short life."

The mill owner invited Kenshi home for a late but hearty lunch and offered a place to stay until he decided where to go next.

Kenshi had already decided. As a surviving member of Mitsubishi management, he would be able to claim priority seating on any trains still running. "If I can get to Koi or even all the way out to Kaitaichi Station," he said, cradling the bowl of ashes and bone close to his chest, "then I will be able to find a way to bring Setsuko home to her parents."

"Then, all the more reason for you to have a good meal before you leave," his friend insisted. "The lumber mill is gone and there is no guessing what will become of us now." He then called Kenshi aside and explained very quietly, almost conspiratorially, that he and his wife had been hoarding a small ration of fine white rice and dried fish, just in case the gradually worsening conditions came down to what Westerners called "a rainy day."

"Well, it's rained fire and black hail and I've even seen horse guts falling out of the sky," the mill owner said. "So, this must be the day."[8]

7

Haruno's intended few minutes of just closing her eyes had turned into hours of fitful sleep, during which she felt as if something in the air and the ground were literally drinking the strength out of her. Nevertheless, she excavated trenches through what, to an almost absolute certainty, was home, yet no familiar furnishings had survived. She wandered down to a wind-blasted and partly uplifted steel-and-concrete bridge, where people seemed to have been seeking shade beneath a ledge. All of them were horribly burned and disfigured, and dying. Those who could speak murmured for "Water . . . water . . . water . . ." When she shared with them what little clean and saltless water remained in her own canteen, a strange peace seemed to pass through them, and their "spirit-lives" drifted away like smoke leaving a snuffed-out candle.

Haruno found some small mercy in being certain that her mother was not among this burned and suffering group. If the weapon that summoned fiery dragons out of the Earth had killed Mother during the very first instant, Haruno supposed that even if spontaneous painless death was but a very small consolation, she would take it.

The student engineer returned to the streetcar repair shelter filthy, feverish, thirsty, and barely able to stand up. Others were showing similar symptoms of fatigue, fever, and intestinal upset—and especially those who had likewise journeyed toward the city center, seeking out relatives and survivors who might be helped.

As sunset approached on August 7, one of the streetcars was nearly ready to start traveling the outer fringe of Hiroshima, reconnecting family members on opposite sides of the town and ferrying burn victims to suburban medical tents. In hurried, makeshift fashion, the tent shelters were being erected by students, nurses, veterinarians, eye doctors, dentists, and a handful of local farmers.

Haruno and her friend Aiko wanted to get to work by nightfall, but their boss was concerned that they were showing symptoms of what was already being spoken about, in hushed tones, as the rapid onset of something called "disease X."

"You are not well enough," her boss said. "Neither of you is ready to fix or drive a tram."

A man from the Transportation Ministry gave them each two pills. Haruno recognized them as "the famous heart medicine, Kyushin," an odd herbal remedy often laced with toad venom. The effect on Haruno was rapid reenergization. There was no question in her mind that by sunrise she would be on her feet and able to set out on the work of reuniting and rescuing people. Aiko, however, fell rapidly more ill, having developed strangely beautiful purplish-and-yellow spots all over her skin. For what seemed a very long time, she spoke only about rising from her cot.

"We've got a job to do," she insisted. Young Aiko died singing a song, "The Ocean," over and over.

Haruno would remember her as the bravest person she had ever met.[9]

8

More than five miles from the streetcar maintenance shelter, on the opposite side of the detonation point, fifteen-year-old Kinuyo Fukui was now part of the rescue operation.

At Moment Zero, she had been living with her little brother in a house only slightly more than a mile from the hypocenter. She was born in the south, where her parents were divorced when she and her brother were very young. But two or three relentless hags from the local gossip committee stood with an old tradition that any child without a father could never be anything of worth, and they all but physically branded the children. The hags were politically well-connected, and nothing could be done to stop them, so the mother had sent both children north to Hiroshima, and they missed her terribly. On the morning of August 6, Kinuyo was taking care of her little brother, trying to make sure twelve-year-old Kuniyoshi got away to school's work detail on time. But that day, he resisted. The result, when she looked back upon it, was a possibly lifesaving growling session between siblings.

Kinuyo gave up on "the little brat" and set about her morning chores. At the moment of the flash, she was running laundry out on a clothesline, and immediately the house collapsed. The flash's visible spectrum of light, alone, was enough to cause permanent blindness and instantly broil skin. And yet, at a radius of one mile, thin white bedsheets and a precious gauze dress she'd made from her father's clothing were all that became necessary to reflect the rays and cast a shadow over exposed flesh, and shield Kinuyo from burns. Not many people would appreciate, in years to come, that America's "silly" *Duck and Cover* film—which would draw decades of mockery by suggesting that one could be protected by ducking beneath a white picnic sheet during the critical first second of a nuclear flash—was scientifically correct, derived from the actual experiences of atomic-bomb survivors.

When Kinuyo was thrown indoors and the house collapsed—from a height of two stories down to the height of a man's shoulders—its tables, wooden support beams, and other large pieces of debris combined to form a protective tent around her, just like the one that was, at that same moment, forming around the homesick escape artist Mizuha, forming against odds of one chance in many hundreds. The blast and collapse knocked Kinuyo unconscious, but there was not a burn anywhere on her body, and long before the city's whirlwinds of fire began to hatch out of the ruins, she was discovered and pulled from the "tent" by her brother.

On August 7, and apparently on account of their uncle's connections to strong bureaucratic friends, both brother and sister were evacuated on a military boat to the former quarantine hospital island of Ninoshima. There, it was determined that Kinuyo had lost her hearing in one ear. As in the curious case of Tsutomu Yamaguchi, one side of her head must have been facing the hypocenter when the shock wave struck. There was also a steel nail in her leg, embedded so deeply in a bone that the technology to safely remove it was decades away.

Like Haruno, in spite of her distress, and now even in spite of injuries, she began applying her field-medicine training (a part of every young adult's schooling ever since the March 1945 incendiary bombings of whole cities began). Now and again, her consciousness tried to block out the things she saw and smelled and the soft wet things upon which she slipped and fell. But what Kinuyo could never forget was being unable to give a patient rice water to drink, because it was impossible to identify the person's mouth. By the afternoon of August 7, it was widely known that the kids' entire ward of homes had been swept away. Out of many hundreds in the second ward, only the two siblings and four other people survived. A sympathetic soldier acquired train tickets for Kinuyo and her brother. He advised that they should return to their mother in Nagasaki.[10]

9

North of Kinuyo and her brother, deep within Ground Zero, Kenshi Hirata was sweating more profusely despite cooling breezes that no longer carried smoke. He and the friend from the lumber mill had just walked across a part of the city that looked to one survivor "like a huge lake, and beneath its waves, it was possible to detect tiled roofs and the outlines of much else."

The Mitsubishi accountant arrived at the mill owner's house, rather amazed to see that it had survived behind a hill, with only a few roof tiles dislodged. Nausea came and went, which made it easier for Kenshi to eat slowly and to keep his portions small. He did not want to take too much of the last good meal in town for himself, and away from his friend's family. All the while, the silvery wedding bowl lay at his side. From the ashes of his wife, isotopes of potassium and iodine were being liberated. They settled on Kenshi's trousers and on his skin and in his lungs.

As they ate, a young soldier came to the door with news that Hiroshima Station might never run again and all the high-priority seats at Koi Station were already taken for the evening of August 7. No trains were running out of Kaitaichi, owing to what the sixteen-year-old message-runner called "the most amazing train wreck ever!"

He explained excitedly how a train leaving Hiroshima during the flash had been fried so severely that even its dead man's switches must have failed: "The thing shot right through Kaitaichi and just kept on flying. They say it was doing at least a hundred and fifty K—and completely on fire—when it finally hit a truck in a crossing and went off the rails!"

Kenshi merely thanked the boy for his report and asked him if any trains would be leaving Koi tomorrow.

"Yes," he said. "There's one leaving at three p.m., and you have provisional seating—which means you're on it, as long as you can get there."

Kenshi decided to make an early start. Many roads and bridges had ceased to exist, and how long the walk to Koi would take was anybody's guess. He filled his canteen and put two biscuits and a few grains of rice in his pants pocket, then cut some strings and wrapped a cloth tightly over the top of the basin so that Setsuko's ashes would not spill if he tripped on the debris that filled the streets.

Before he left, Kenshi asked his friend for permission to pick a flower from his garden. Then, saying his thank-yous and goodbyes, he went down to the river, where he threw offerings of a flower and rice grains into the water and bowed three times, in accordance with a Buddhist tradition that acknowledges a place of the dead.

Bodies were now being pulled from both sides of the river, and on the road ahead, mass cremations had already begun.

How, Kenshi wondered, was he going to tell Setsuko's parents what

happened to her? He could think of nothing else. He did not know yet that he would soon have much else to think about. It might even be said that his rendezvous with history these past two days had been merely the twilight before the dawn. Kenshi Hirata would reach Koi Station with time to spare, and at three o'clock in the afternoon of August 8, he would set out to bring Setsuko home to her parents, aboard the last Nagasaki-bound train to depart Hiroshima.[11]

10

"Hell ship" was, by comparison with reality, an almost polite name given to refitted and often very poorly ventilated cargo ships. In each vessel, at least one cargo hold was usually crammed with five hundred Allied prisoners of war or slave laborers, who were intended to serve double duty as human shields. Twenty-three-year-old John Baxter started out of a Southeast Asia prison camp, months ahead of Moment Zero, aboard the *Ussuri Maru*. Most of the cargo compartments were filled with bauxite—a mined, dusty mineral that coated the POWs' skin and hair, then infiltrated their eyelids, nostrils, and lungs. Baxter lived on two half-cup rations per day of boiled rice with a minute portion of dried fish or radish—and only one pint of water, per slave, per day. The men discovered that it was possible to extend the water ration by drinking their own urine. Each learned that he could easily endure three recyclings before the urine became too salty to be safe. From the moment of this discovery onward, it was all a matter of carefully spacing out the recyclings. The urine itself was germ-free, so long as one drank while it was still fresh and warm.

For a while, Baxter found refuge from heat and dehydration in one of the cattle pens on the forward well deck. Beyond the pens, every square foot of deck space was piled with explosives and captured antiaircraft guns, bound for Japan. Evidently, someone had decided these weapons would soon be needed more on the home front than in occupied Java.

By early 1944, it was widely known even to slaves that the Japanese had been losing naval control of the sea and were becoming desperate, afraid, and therefore more dangerous. The prisoners already understood their dual role. They already guessed that word had been leaked as a deterrent to Allied submarine commanders, warning that if they sank ships in an imperial convoy, they must be prepared to gamble against how many of those ships might be carrying their own people.

Baxter appreciated the strategic significance of the warning. He also knew that it probably would not work, could not be *allowed* to work. And so, one day, from a vantage point near the cattle pens, Baxter had watched a torpedo scarcely miss the *Ussuri Maru* and strike the next ship behind instead. He saw the other ship's forward cannon fly nearly two hundred feet into the air, along with several flailing human shapes. An even larger detonation—likely stowed ammunition and fuel—swiftly followed, and the entire bow section simply broke away and disappeared while the engines in the stern continued plowing forward for too many seconds at full speed, driving the remaining two-thirds of the vessel below the surface like a duck diving after a fish.

The entire convoy was suddenly firing into the air, trying to create a shield of flying lead against what the Japanese must have presumed to be an air attack. Hot lead began falling everywhere, with potentially lung-piercing and skull-cracking force. Under these conditions, hiding belowdecks became the better part of valor. There, lying on the keel and its cargo, Baxter and the other prisoners could hear how quickly the convoy's commanders realized that the attack actually came from below. Depth charges sent their concussions echoing through inch-thick steel plating with enough force to give a man a strong kick in the spine if he happened to be leaning against the hull.

"Among us," Baxter had recorded in his head in preparation for a secret log, "the more experienced sailors could distinguish between the explosion of a depth charge and a torpedo hit against one of the other ships—and it became ominously evident that the convoy was suffering considerable loss."

Beneath the waterline, they were also able to hear, at a distance, the turbulence of a strengthening typhoon. At twenty knots, the captain steered directly toward the storm, and the rest of the little fleet followed, in a desperate effort to render targeting by the submarines impossible by driving straight into the storm's towering waves. Of Baxter's estimated thirty ships that started out from Java, soon only five remained, en route to what was rumored to be a work-to-death coal mine somewhere on mainland Japan. During the storm, prisoners actually heard, through the hull, ships being sunk by wind and waves and imploding before they dropped just a few hundred feet below. They heard large deck structures torn off their own ship and washed over the side. The shifting piles of caustic bauxite kicked up immense quantities of dust and threatened to suffocate them if the stench of uprooted makeshift latrines did not do so first.

Baxter tried to console his companions by remarking, "Somewhere, there is always someone worse off than ourselves."

Several of them returned him a look that said, *What planet are you really from?*

Aboard another hell ship, bound for the same slave labor mine, Alistair Urquhart could definitely say the Fates had left him worse off. He had already survived the infamous "death railway" slave camps, including a bridge over the River Kwai—which proved far worse in reality than fellow POW Pierre Boulle's novel or David Lean's movie could ever depict. Now Alistair had survived multiple torpedo hits on his hell ship. The soldier supposed he must have lived this long only on account of being a stubborn Scotsman, for it was well known among his people that the Roman emperor Septimius Severus, after strengthening Hadrian's Wall, had set out in AD 210 to make the Highlanders pay for the expense of conquest. Emperor Severus died in AD 211. The Scot was determined to see it end thus for Japan's emperor, so long as the South China Sea could be survived.

After the *Kachidoki Maru* broke apart and disappeared around Alistair Urquhart, there had been intense fighting on floating islands of debris. Even among fellow prisoners, survivors were killing survivors, piling their weight atop and overturning the largest wooden islands repeatedly. Alistair swam away from the crowds on the sea, seeking out smaller and more obscure debris. He remembered a voice yelling, clear and bright and in the King's English, "Get off, or I'll kill you!" Another seemed to reply weakly, "Daddy will be home soon."

The Scot had found a badly damaged one-man raft, but it provided at least some small measure of protection against the sharks. In this part of the sea, they tended to grow only about eighteen inches long, but they traveled in groups of two hundred to three hundred, and they came around at dusk. Predation by this species, if he fell asleep and was rolled overboard by a wave, meant being nibbled to death. During his second day adrift, while storm clouds passed in the distance, a Japanese survivor from the same ship paddled toward him in his own one-man raft and inexplicably seemed to be shouting encouragement: "You'll be picked up soon."

Alistair had no water and no food—nothing worth stealing and nothing with which to defend himself—but he took a stance that left no doubt he was prepared for a fight to the death. The other man stopped about five feet away, shouted, "Here!" as he tossed the Highlander a tin of food, then paddled away.

Tongue swollen, driven half mad with thirst, Alistair guessed that somewhere between two and five days might have passed before he heard another human voice. He remembered that the moon had been full each night and that he was roused suddenly to consciousness by shouting all around. The crew of a Japanese whaling ship had hoisted him aboard. While adrift, his body had become severely sunburned on one side and all his hair fell out. He now had little recollection of what the whalers did during the following days, only that they must have given him water and some food before docking somewhere and turning him over to the military police, who then transferred him to yet another hellbound vessel.

And already, a new crisis had arisen, but during those last months leading up to Moment Zero over Hiroshima, neither Alistair Urquhart nor John Baxter had any way of guessing what was brewing the day they were taken ashore by two of World War II's last hell ships, at the port of Nagasaki.[12]

My doctor informed me that I have stomach cancer, and in October [2010] I underwent surgery at Nagasaki University Hospital. One university professor has written that "The atomic bomb killed people three times over." I think these words truly represent the horrific nature of the three destructive forces of the atomic bomb: its heat rays, the explosion, and its radiation.

—Yoshiro Yamawaki (age 11), Nagasaki survivor

I am not a doctor, but I will answer it anyway. The radiation casualty . . . as I understand it from the doctors, they say it is a very pleasant way to die.

—General Leslie Groves (the Manhattan Project), testimony to the Special Senate Committee on Atomic Energy

CHAPTER 4:
NEUTRON STAR

1

Before he climbed aboard the Hiroshima strike plane, Jacob Beser heard Navy Captain William Parsons tell the rest of the crew, for the first time, that they would be carrying only a single bomb. No mention of atomic power was ever made. Indeed, Parsons's navigator, Theodore "Dutch" van Kirk, knew nothing more beyond his own suspicion that "*chemists*" had developed a new kind of firebomb.

Beser—an *Enola Gay*–assigned radar expert who had verified and then defended Parsons's controversial inclusion of a bomb-mounted radar sensor that would trigger one of Little Boy's fuses at a precise distance above the ground—knew a bit more than the rest of the crew but wondered how he came to be here in the first place. He had been studying mechanical engineering at Johns Hopkins University when, in December 1941, Japan, Germany, and Italy declared war on the United States. Cutting short his studies, the twenty-year-old Beser enlisted to join combat units in Europe. He was Jewish; and despite censorship of the Holocaust by *The New York Times* and most every other major media outlet, Beser knew that members of his family were being decimated under Hitler. He wanted to fight Nazis, not the Japanese, but history forged a different path for him and would have the final say. Thus was he to become the only crewman to find himself seated aboard the actual bomb-carrying strike planes during both the Hiroshima and Nagasaki missions. His educational background and his scoring on the military's standard IQ exam must have gotten him red-stamped (and, *quite against his will,* held back from combat for a role in military engineering)—held back for this particular place in history, on Day One of his entry into the army.

For reasons that seemed out of reach and perplexing to Beser, the military had decided on keeping him in the USA for an inordinately long time. Many, many weeks would pass before anyone even began to explain to him why. Theoretically, he could appeal to the adjutant general of the army and be sent to a combat unit in Europe with the rest of his classmates from Johns Hopkins.

It seemed cut-and-dried in theory, but in practice: "I don't know why," the general said, "but even I can't touch you. Your file has been flagged for some reason." Soon afterward came an order from Washington freezing all personnel in Beser's unit—"Nobody in, nobody out."

His new group commander was Paul Tibbets, who called the young engineer to his office and explained that the team he was forming would be independent, able to operate anywhere in the world. "Don't ask questions," Tibbets instructed. "You won't be told the purpose of this group for a while. But just trust me." The newly minted Lieutenant Beser noticed that one of the men with Tibbets was a physicist, well known to him. He pointed this out to Tibbets and to the officers with him, hinting at his suspicions, but all anyone seemed interested in was a deeper probe of his background, experience, and engineering skills.

Eventually, they shook his hand and said, "You've been hired."

What for? Nobody was saying. *I'm now part of the crowd,* he thought, *and I don't even know what crowd I'm part of.*

From the start, everything about the group operation was so unreal as to be laughable, so long as one did not know too many details. One evening, Beser's team was told to be on the flight line at 7:00 a.m. sharp, packed for three or four days of travel.

"Where are we going?" Beser asked. "I mean, do I take warm clothes or summer clothes, or what?"

"Take both," came the reply.

From a friend who was piloting the transport, he received a little more of an answer—which at first hearing answered nothing, but in hindsight foreshadowed everything. "All I know is that I filed clearance for the letter 'Y' and I won't know where it is until we get near."

"The letter 'Y'? Gee, I've never been *there* before."

At "Y," Tibbets and a naval officer named Ashworth escorted Beser to the office of a Szilard–Fermi colleague from Columbia University, Norman Ramsey, who explained that he headed the "fusing and firing section" of what he called "a weapon" in development.

"We want this weapon to burst over the ground at a preselected altitude, and we have been working very hard on the problem, and we aren't nearly as far along as we should be." *Of course they aren't*, Beser thought, and as was typical of his character, he did not keep the thought to himself—which was perfectly fine with Ramsey and Parsons, who did not want yes-men on their team. After Beser explained to them the various design errors that seemed to be screaming out for attention, he was flown around the continental United States from one lab and factory to another, to help solve the radar proximity fuse problem by questioning every solution.

On the morning of August 6, 1945, although most of the *Enola Gay*'s crew did not know what they were carrying, the key puzzle pieces had long ago snapped together for Beser—after only a few lunches in such places as the town called "Letter Y" (which would later become known as Los Alamos). Once people like Enrico Fermi and Niels Bohr had started showing up, "It simply added up," Beser would tell history. Then, in conversations with Ramsey, as altitude settings for detonation approached one-third of a mile for a single weapon, he got Ramsey to confirm his conclusions without ever repeating the words H. G. Wells had put to paper in 1914: "the atomic bomb." Ramsey spoke about "the fundamental forces of the universe," and Beser was able to spell it out on his own; and to him, the words spelled, "Oh, mother."

Near the end, the same thinking that would infect and threaten Project Apollo and other high-technology programs crept into the atomic bomb: "Better is the enemy of best."

After the results of the first A-bomb test on July 16, 1945, two of the Manhattan Project scientists, upon realizing the blinding power of the flash, came up with a newer and better idea: Attach two very loud air-raid sirens to the bomb's tail so that the greatest number of people for miles and miles around will be looking directly at the source of the flash and be blinded at the moment of detonation. But this would have required the addition of more machinery to a bomb that was already too heavy to guarantee that a plane could safely take off with it from the cliff at the end of Tinian Island's runway. Every ounce counted. Antiaircraft guns and ammunition were removed from the *Enola Gay*, and there had even been suggestions that the crew go on strict diets and collectively shed a hundred pounds of body weight before the mission. To Szilard, the better idea—a bomb equipped with sirens to blind more people—was inhumane. To the ounce-counters, this "better" was unwarranted complexity.

And so on.

Parsons had perfected the best design he could come up with—for a radar system that would determine the bomb's altitude by pinging the ground at the speed of light and triggering a fuse at precisely the right instant. This system was completely self-contained within the bomb; but someone had a "better" idea.

Paul Tibbets brought Beser along to one of the final technical briefings, in what seemed to be, in Tibbets's mind, more or less a courtesy invitation. Beser was a radar specialist, and even though this was a radar proximity fuse, he was to "sit and listen to the discussion." Officially, this time, he was not expected to make any remarks.

Rather than rely on a radar-based altitude sensor sealed within and dropped with the bomb (along with an air pressure sensor as backup), the presenters started talking about triggering the explosion with a ground-based radar beam, near the harbor of the targeted city.

"Sending an advance team, with heavy equipment, into enemy territory?" Beser wondered.

The idea, the presenter explained, was to select the right altitude and detonate the bomb using shipboard radar. Driving a submarine close enough to the target was not viewed as a difficulty because the "nearby" island of Okinawa was now under American control and (with whole fleets sunk and even fishing boats out of fuel and locked down) there seemed little left of the Japanese navy to offer any resistance.

"*Bullshit*," Beser whispered quite loudly.

General Leslie Groves halted the presentation and asked Beser, "Would you elaborate on that remark?"

Jacob Beser's son would report decades later that this was not the first time his father had helped Paul Tibbets "feel like the floor should swallow him up."

Where to begin? Beser thought. "Is there a way to make this project any more complicated?" He laid out the reasons why the newer, "better" idea would not work, starting with the added complexity of getting vessels deep into enemy territory at both the primary and secondary target cities, for each mission . . . letting more people know about a weapon that was supposed to remain secret . . . letting an inexperienced crew on a sub "play" with the bomb's radar frequency under conditions requiring only that someone aim in the wrong direction and bump into the wrong switch to trigger the device before it got anywhere near the target, while still in the airplane.

In the very end, "best" won (very quickly) against "better." Beser flew into history with both A-bombs, and both weapons flew with Parsons's and Ramsey's original detonation plan. (A barometer, a small clock, and two ground-impact triggers were added as backup detonators. There was no siren.)[1]

Up to the moment the planes left Tinian, Leo Szilard had hoped one of the atomic bombs could be demonstrated for Japan on an unpopulated island, and not on a city. He was overruled at every level. Kamikaze raids, intended to terrify the Americans, had done precisely that. Field Marshall Shunroku Hata and the other warlords never did give much consideration to how their enemy responded to that kind of fear, or to the dawning reality that American behavior became twitchy and utterly unpredictable once confronted by a military opponent so dedicated to a hive mentality that its pilots were willing to ride their own planes all the way into their targets.

During the months that had elapsed since February's final mopping-up and securing of Tinian Island from the last pockets of Japanese resistance, the island completed its evolution into a maze of runways that brought the emperor's homeland within range of massive B-29 raids. In the century ahead, most people would think that in the summer of 1945, Japan was more or less an untouched bastion of bustling towns, farms, and green hills. And then in one week, two atomic bombs were dropped out of the blue, and the war ended.

It wasn't that at all.

Ahead of Hiroshima, more than sixty of Japan's cities already lay in state under black shrouds of smoke and ashes. In swarms sometimes three hundred planes strong, every sort of experimental incendiary chemical, from phosphorus to napalm, began to fall night after night, after night.

Everything about the August 6 launch from Tinian Island had a surreal aspect. Paul Tibbets withdrew a box from his pocket and spoke with his crew. He explained that the flight surgeon had provided pills—one for each man—in case the planes went down in enemy territory. The surgeon knew some of the methods of torture that could be expected; and he knew that most everyone talked under torture.

"I'll give them to any one of you if you want the pill," Tibbets explained.

"Six minutes and you're gone," the flight surgeon had assured. "You won't know anything."

The men simply looked at the box—silently, except for Captain Parsons. "I'd like to have one," Beser's colleague from Los Alamos said. Tibbets understood Parsons's position. Alongside Tibbets and perhaps Jacob Beser, Parsons knew far too many technical details about how the gadget's trigger systems and central reaction zone worked, and Beser had already guessed much about how the weapon would crack open a window between the quantum world and ours.

Beser's Jewish tradition allowed him to order Tibbets to shoot him if they crashed and were about to be captured, but the same tradition damned him for all time if he took Tibbets's offer of "self-silencing." The navigators, flight engineers, and other crew had been kept in the dark about what their team was carrying, so there was probably no need to offer them pills—only dark goggles, with instructions to put them on when their captain gave the order, about three minutes out from the target. They were advised not to look at the source of light.[2]

On runway A, Paul Tibbets started the atomic strike plane *Enola Gay*'s run at 2:45 a.m. Three minutes later, Charles Sweeney flew Dr. Luis Alvarez's scientific escort plane *The Great Artiste* off runway B, and three minutes after that, George Marquardt followed in the photographic escort plane *Necessary Evil*. The three planes remained staggered at ten-mile intervals throughout the three-hour flight to their first rendezvous point. Thirteen minutes out from Tinian, while flying only at 4,600 feet, Parsons descended into the *Enola Gay*'s unpressurized bomb bay and began inserting cordite charges into the bomb, following a detailed checklist he had written during his practice sessions and keeping Tibbets informed, through an intercom link, of his progress with the arming procedure. On the deck above, as the gadget came alive, the man whose questions and "pain-in-the-ass" interventions would guarantee that the bomb's radar trigger detonated at precisely 1,850 feet kept watch for enemy radar frequencies, just in case Japan's ships were not sunk so nearly to extinction as was supposed. The last thing Beser needed was to be passing over any ship or installation—friend or foe—that happened to be sweeping anywhere near the same radio frequency as his radar proximity fuse. At the first faint whisper of such a signal, at the mere potential of an A-bomb flyswatter sweeping into their path, he would have to tell Tibbets to move the plane off course immediately; because once Parsons had awakened the bomb's sensory systems, an aberrant and sufficiently powerful radar signal at close range, and under the right improbable conditions (such as the fuse self-activating and searching for its trigger signal), could pull the trigger inside the bomb bay.

At 5:45 a.m., as the red hull of the sun was emerging on the horizon, all three planes banked to one side over the rendezvous point of Iwo Jima, then set course for mainland Japan.

Two hours later, Claude Eatherly's advance scout plane, *Straight Flush*, triggered a brief air-raid alert throughout Hiroshima while conducting weather reconnaissance. This was the same alert that made Kimiko late for work and was about to produce a severe reprimand that would place her, like the Morimoto cousins and young Mizuha (Takama) Kikuzaki, within one of Ground Zero's rare and lifesaving shock-cocoon events.

Straight Flush sent out a coded message: "C-1," which translated as "Clear weather, primary target." The time was almost 7:45 a.m. Beser was crossing over from the ocean to the mainland of Japan while ascending to a bombing altitude of 5.6 miles. Parsons was by then out of the freezing bomb bay, with the cabin's pressurized hatch sealed behind him, and the device below now fully operational. Everything was proceeding as Tibbets promised: The mission for which they had been training was going to be completely different. Firebombers usually cruised at only one-fifth this altitude.

Three minutes from the T-shaped Aioi Bridge, the commanders of the *Enola Gay* and its two escort planes ordered their crews to put on the black goggles. Beser could not wear his goggles, could not let his world go dark. He had too many instruments to monitor. There was a timing fuse monitor—a backup to his radar-triggered altitude fuse, along with his ever-vigilant search for any radio frequency that had even a one-in-a-thousand chance (given a minimum 30,000-foot distance between the plane and the ground) of surging strongly enough to set the bomb off prematurely. Though Japan's radar beacons were relatively weak, they were still among the loudest radio signals on Earth. The newest American and British systems would eventually be detectable from interstellar space, making the

Earth, from World War II onward, steadily outshine even the sun at certain radio frequencies. *But so far, so good,* Beser told himself. Fortunately, no one was sending up flak bursts. Nor, it seemed, were enemy planes being scrambled to intercept Tibbets's three "strays"—for, by now, the Japanese had been intentionally lulled into complacency about groups of two and three planes that flew over like sightseers and dropped no bombs. However, even as Beser's electronic countermeasures seemed (so far) unnecessary, all three aircraft were moving into a realm of total uncertainty. No one had ever tried flying away from a nuclear blast before, and the risk of being blown out of the sky by their own weapon was quite real. Yet if unprecedented risk was the price of throwing open the doors to a nuclear frontier, then the planes and their crews would be expendable.

Planning for the worst and hoping for the best, Beser was placing his bets on what history would later call "the Tibbets maneuver," and what one critic, on first hearing of it, had already labeled "the bonehead maneuver." It required a reversal of course and a crash-dive acceleration—at one point straight toward the ground—during a time frame in which the bomb itself was also falling earthward.

The genesis of the maneuver was a question of simple spatial geometry. During the forty-three seconds between the release of the bomb and detonation, how much space could a B-29 put between itself and the bomb so that the B-29 would still be?

Tibbets's maneuver was a variation on an ancient geometric formula he had learned in junior high school—"a gift from the Babylonians and Egyptians," he said, "with which we can calculate the distance from a point on a tangent to a semicircle." If the plane was traveling at a ground speed of 450 miles per hour at an altitude of 30,000 feet, then on release the bomb would start out with the same forward momentum as the plane, falling on trajectory toward its target. The last thing in the world any pilot still taking in air and in his right mind wanted to do was what bomber pilots had been trained to do: stay in a tight formation into and away from the target—which amounted to flying in formation with their bombs.

Under the old rules, the Hiroshima formation would have traveled almost 5.5 miles by the time the bomb detonated below them, and barely more than a mile behind—in which case, few pieces of airplane larger than dinner platters would ever be seen again. Tibbets saw immediately that if the planes simply shot off perpendicular to the line of trajectory, the bomb's forward momentum would carry it almost four miles downrange during the critical forty-three seconds; and if, instead of fleeing sideways at a mere ninety-degree angle, he dived at the ground for a few seconds and used gravity to accelerate a little bit beyond his fastest cruising speed, while turning in a direction exactly opposite the bomb's trajectory, he could take the plane more than nine slant miles away from the blast.

The tactic was totally unheard of, and totally brilliant. Aboard the *Enola Gay*, at 8:14 a.m., Tibbets radioed a high-pitched warning signal to his two escort planes. Thirty seconds later, at precisely 8:15:15, the signal stopped and four objects dropped simultaneously: one from *Enola Gay*, and three monitoring canisters from *The Great Artiste*—the very same parachute-equipped instrument packages that Tsutomu Yamaguchi observed just ahead of the flash.

The peel-away part of the maneuver squeezed Jacob Beser into his seat. Behind him, and behind the tail gunner's windows, Hiroshima still lay in brilliant sunlight within the braided outlines of its seven rivers, awaiting the day's second sunrise. Beser did not see this. He saw the fuse indicator come alive with radioed telemetry after the bomb separated from the plane. He kept count of the timer. His equipment recorded the radar altitude fuse blinking once, and within that first tiny sliver of time, faster than human reflexes could begin to record the event, the bomb's outgoing telemetry disappeared from Beser's screens. The entire interior of the plane blazed out pallid white, as if the damned thing had gone off right next to him instead of almost ten miles behind.

At the helm, Paul Tibbets had become aware of a strange taste. As the flash blazed forth, he heard and felt a crackling in his jaw, and simultaneously came the unpleasant stench and flavor, "like an out-flowing of lead." Pieces of the bomb (quantum artifacts) had passed through hull and flesh and crashed inside his fillings. The pilot would recall later that the light from the bomb seemed to have substance—a light that could be felt and even tasted.

Jacob Beser's monitoring station had no window nearby, and yet he was still temporarily flash-blinded. He did not know that Kenshi Hirata's "dragon-headed" cap of the mushroom cloud was already rising higher than the plane, higher than Mount Everest. Over his headphones, he had heard copilot Robert Lewis remark, sometime during the first minute after Moment Zero, "My God, look at that son of a bitch go!"

About three minutes after Moment Zero, the plane circled back to survey the target. Beser, the one man aboard the *Enola Gay* who had not worn his eye-protecting goggles during the flash, could finally see clearly again. He climbed aft, gazed up through a window, and saw that the cloud was eight miles high or more, roiling and changing colors as he watched. Looking down, he could scarcely believe what had happened. He could not see the city at all. The movement on the ground reminded him of what sand at the beach looked like if one stood in two feet of water and vigorously stirred up the sand until it billowed. "Well," he would record later, "[those billows]—it was as if the whole goddamned ground was doing it. And I could see new fires breaking out on the periphery all the time."

The image of roiling sand in water stayed with him. Beser loved the sea, and though nothing would ever keep him away from sailing on deep water, he could never again go to the beach and wade into the surf after Hiroshima.

Robert Lewis, after an initial moment of amazement—"My God, look at that son of a bitch go!"—had gone completely silent. The copilot watched the billows, then wrote in his log, *"My God, what have we done?"* [3]

Down there in the swirls of fire and debris, many survivors, among them Tsutomu Yamaguchi and the Sasaki children, were embarking on another of those most improbable journeys that had already begun to surround the atomic missions.

Like Jacob Beser, Setsuko Thurlow had been diverted along a different historical path by an IQ test. During the spring of 1945, as other students were receiving summer assignments to help the army build firebreaks, a young officer separated Thurlow from the other thirteen-year-olds and brought her to army intelligence headquarters. On the test, she and about thirty other kids her age had demonstrated a special skill for recognizing patterns quickly and for decoding. Major Yanai, who was now part of the smoke—"billowing like sand," somewhere south of army HQ—had said of the long and difficult work hours the girls faced, "This is the time to prove your patriotism and your loyalty to the emperor."

"Yes sir, we will do our best!" Thurlow had immediately said with all the others. However, to herself, she had quietly longed to be with her friends instead, working outside in the fresh air and not inside a dark and windowless room near the city's Communications Hospital.

She did not know yet that within the first three seconds, all of her friends' skin and muscle had flashed to carbon and reddish iron mist along one whole side of their bodies, or that the same fate had come to Major Yanai.

Even in a windowless room, the light entered dazzlingly, through hallways: Thurlow had very much the same experience as Saito and others who survived at this same radius of nearly one mile. "A beautiful blue flash. There was no noise. Then my body began floating in the air. Then everything caved in." While the planes circled in for a closer look, Thurlow heard another girl utter her last words: "Where is my mother?" A hand reached out through the rubble, grabbed Thurlow's shoulder, and saved her.

"We must hurry. *You* must hurry," a soldier said. From the sound of it, something above and behind them was burning, working its way nearer. They dug toward the surface—or, rather, burrowed like a pair of frantic moles. Only two other girls made it with them to the top of the rubble pile. Nearby, the roofs of the Communications Hospital and another still-upright building were in flames.

Mizuha Takama Kikuzaki was one of only two children who survived in her school, two-thirds of a mile from the Hiroshima hypocenter. Her father, who was far enough away to survive without injury or radiation exposure, immediately joined a rescue brigade, and along the way found his daughter Mizuha alive. During the week after Moment Zero, he continued the rescue effort and received high doses of radiation in regions of intense fallout contamination. Mizuha, who had survived in the zone of dense and deadly black rain, would in future years be advised by doctors (fearful of a "mutant" or "handicapped" child) to abort her daughter Shiho. Only one doctor would dissent, saying to Mizuha in 1973: "I see you . . . I see your kind heart. And I know that even if the child is handicapped, you will care for it." In 1985, filmmaker Tengo Yamada would notice that teenager Shiho looked just like her mother in 1945; and so he'd cast her *as* her own mother in his classic film *White City Hiroshima*. This illustration captures a moment from the film, and from real life, in which Mizuha finds her father. The portrait is based on a photo of young Mizuha. The plate she holds did not survive the blast. Wrote Shiho (on Oct. 3, 2024): "The character on the plate reads, *kotobuki*—meaning, 'congratulations' and 'long life' (which feels somewhat ironic)."

It struck Thurlow as odd that whatever the flash was, it seemed to have set the roofs of buildings afire first. Smoke, black and full of thick soot, came blowing through the apparently deserted streets. The soot carried a stench like scorched squid. It did not occur to her yet that she might be inhaling people. After a minute passed, and then another, Thurlow began to see shapes moving within the twilight—"human beings, but they didn't exactly look like humans anymore. They looked like ghosts. Nobody was yelling. Nobody was running. Even their steps were silent, like the steps of cats—so ghostly."

Engine noise managed now and again to penetrate the black fog. "B-sans" were still circling—*their crews gloating*, Thurlow guessed. To her, Hiroshima was a city of mostly wives whose husbands and seventeen-year-old sons were away at war and lost. This world was madness. The ghosts in the fog were mostly schoolchildren, and men too old to fight. Humans (all human beings) were becoming scary to her—scarier still when they went mad. Scariest of all when they went mad together, by the multiple millions and all across the world.

More than three miles away from Thurlow, a tall hill had diverted the blast wave around a small farmhouse the way the prow of a ship shunts water off to either side. The same hill had absorbed the rays, throwing a shadow over the farmhouse like a protective eclipse. The vegetable gardens and the houses of neighbors outside the shadow did not fare as well. Nonetheless, Asajiro and Yuku of the Furumoto family stepped out into open air, shaken but otherwise completely unscathed. Even the smoke and black rain were traveling in a direction completely away from their house—which stood in sunlight, with only a few roof tiles knocked out of place. The husband and wife understood immediately that the cause of it all was something new and particularly vengeful, developed by the Americans. There was much to worry about regarding how far humans might carry their vengeance. According to the latest warnings circulated by the government, American soldiers advancing toward the homeland had degenerated to the lowest possible level of subhuman: cannibals.[4]

The Furumotos could not let themselves believe it. For if true, the possibilities were too horrible to bear. They had family members they hoped were still alive in the United States. No one could be sure. Years had passed since any letters came out of California, where a new grandson now lived, born in the Tule Lake prison camp for Japanese Americans.

Hiroko Tasaka was among the few who would be able to speak of actually having watched a B-29 that appeared to be leading two others on a beeline toward the center of the city when it veered suddenly off its path and dived toward the ground. The speed of sound was, from a vantage point of nearly two miles, downright sluggish compared to the speed of reflected sunlight, so the noise of the straining engines seemed to be coming from a spot somewhere behind Beser's retreating plane, making the B-san itself difficult for her friends to spot. Hiroko was pointing the *Enola Gay* out to another eighth grader at Moment Zero. The bomb happened to be falling miles behind the plane and over to one side of the girls' vantage point, but not far enough over to one side, or far enough away. A hat, and her own outstretched arm, protected Hiroko's eyes with their shadows; but her arm was so severely flash-burned that she would not be able to use it properly during most of the next decade. Two fingers melted together. Her lower lip melted. The earth itself seemed to melt. She heard no sound, and only vaguely remembered seeing the flash. Wandering away in a daze, Hiroko in fact became one of the silent, shadowy "ghosts" that Setsuko Thurlow witnessed.[5]

The atomic strike plane circled close one last time, but Hiroko walked in a mercifully painless dream state and could no longer hear it. And yet, by an improbable historical quirk, as way was to lead onto way, her family would become bound by marriage to one of the crewmen who had just dropped the weapon on her.

Aboard the *Enola Gay*, minds were trying to find a way of surrounding what had just happened. In what at first might have seemed counterintuitive, the atomic bomb was more personal than a conventional carpet-bombing with torpex and napalm. During a three-hundred-B-29 raid on Tokyo, it was easy for the men of any plane to convince themselves that the neighborhoods burning below were hit by all the other planes. Several crewmen said they had to think that way—*had to*, because at low altitudes they could smell what was happening to the people below. Above the nuclear fires, the mathematics of death came back to only one plane. And aboard that plane, the numbers came back to one series of trigger mechanisms, which a single crewman had monitored and safeguarded all the way down through its forty-three-second fall.

One day, Jacob Beser would refer to Hiroshima and Nagasaki as "the most bizarre and spectacular two events in the history of man's inhumanity to man." However, four minutes after Moment Zero, Beser was considering another grim mathematics: how, from island to island, the enemy had successfully inflicted a logarithmically increasing loss of life the closer his fellow combatants came to Japan. In that moment, he was content to look down and tell himself, "There are fewer of them."[6]

2

On the evening of August 7, as Kenshi Hirata tossed a flower into a Hiroshima river and prepared to carry his wife home to Nagasaki, Tsutomu Yamaguchi boarded the second-to-last train to the same city. He had developed a high fever and was suffering continually from dry heaves. By now he had discovered, to his growing horror, that he could not keep down even small sips of water. Thirst was tearing at his throat.[7]

During the day after their return to the Tinian Island airfields, none of the atomic strike crew (or anyone else) had any way of even suspecting that a revolt was brewing in Tokyo. Nor could they know how the emperor, who concluded that the widespread firebombings alone would very soon bring the entire empire to irreparable ruin, was about to be imprisoned in his own palace, by his own warlords, as he considered and then spoke of surrender.

It seemed inexplicable to Beser and the rest of the crew that in response to nearly sixty cities already massively firebombed (including more than a third of Tokyo)—and with the city of Hiroshima having all but vanished in a split second—there came only a desert of silence from Japan.

As dusk reached Hiroshima and Tinian, Curtis LeMay ordered 152 B-29s aloft to inflict conventional firebombings on several towns. They were running out of cities and were down to towns.

The night of August 7 came and went, and still no response came from Tokyo.

As the dawn of August 8 approached Tinian, Jacob Beser was assigned to *Bockscar*, the aircraft that—if Tokyo's silence persisted—would lead the second atomic mission. The weapons plants at Kokura would be the next designated hypocenter. Beser's twenty-five-year-old pilot, Charles Sweeney, hoped it would be so, because if he failed to hit Kokura, the secondary target was Nagasaki, which had too large a civilian population for his tastes. The targeting map showed far too many children's schools, and a school for the deaf, and a school for the blind. There was even a huge Catholic cathedral, with hospitals off to one side, bracketed by nurses' dormitories. Comforting himself with a prayer, Sweeney resolved then to put his personal best into avoiding Nagasaki and hitting the more heavily defended, more strictly military target. There was, of course, a greater chance of being shot down and losing the bomb during an overly stubborn attack on Kokura. But, as Sweeney would tell it later, a part of him just did not believe in dropping an atom bomb on a target that really could not fight back. This thought would eventually bring accusations of incompetence and even treason from his commander, Paul Tibbets. The same thought also meant that Jacob Beser was in for the ride of his life.[8]

3

After the sun rose on August 8, fires were still burning here and there around a city center so efficiently flattened that its most distinctive features were the geography of rivers and hills, appearing much as they had more than two thousand years ago. On the second day, a substantial proportion of the fires were funeral pyres. When Mitsuo Fuchida brought his small passenger plane down to two thousand feet and turned its nose toward an airstrip in the south, the rising plumes buffeted him with turbulence.

"I don't understand," someone behind him said. "Where is Hiroshima?"

"Sir," Fuchida replied, "this *is* Hiroshima."

As soon as they were on the ground, Dr. Nishina was out the side of the plane and examining grass and potato plants nearby, all singed and turning reddish brown on one side—the side facing some of the few things left standing near city central. These included the Hiroshima Dome and the vertical walls of a bank, and tree trunks, and telephone poles. The sticklike remnants pointed straight up at Jacob Beser's 1,850-foot-high detonation point—like Hiroko's outstretched arm, like accusing fingers.

Nishina withdrew a pair of vials from a pocket, sampled grass and soil, scribbled some notes, wrapped the vials in paper, and then ran off toward the Dome and its charcoal-encrusted trees. Others ran after him, and Fuchida followed for Nishina's safety.

Near the T-Bridge, the scientist pointed out how even people's skulls and femurs seemed to have been reduced instantly to a kind of carbonaceous gravel. He guessed that the "instantaneous nonexistence effect" extended to about four hundred feet or more in every direction beneath the exact hypocenter.

"Five, ten . . . twenty times the boiling point of water," he said. "Here and there, maybe hot as the surface of the sun. And that involves reflection effects right above the ground, in the air that moved immediately around the people."

Nearby, a trolley car and anyone standing near the crosswalks had essentially vanished. Only the streetcar's iron wheels remained, and teeth—hundreds and hundreds of teeth. Dr. Nishina remarked absently, as if it were a distracting marvel to him, how our teeth, "which decay so easily (and painfully) during life," are always the most resilient part of us after we are dead and no longer need them. It seemed a strange joke of nature that humanity's remote forebears were sometimes known only by fossil teeth evolving into new kinds of fossil teeth. The same cruel joke seemed to hold just as true for the physics of an A-bomb as for archaeology and paleoanthropology.

Dr. Nishina quickly collected and labeled more samples. When he brought a handful of blackened molars and canines close to his Geiger counter, the mysterious clicks told everyone present what he already knew.

"So that's it?" General Seizo Arisue said. "Just those few clicks tell it all?"

"That's it," Nishina said. "Just those few clicks . . . We must make War Minister Anami understand. There is no defense against this kind of power."[9]

4

Haruno, the sixteen-year-old streetcar engineer who had been sickened by hypocenter dust, looked across the desert of black, gray, and occasionally reddish-yellow ashes and saw few signs of life. There was the occasional survivor seeking the foundations of home. There was a group of men who had trekked to the center of the blast zone and, if one watched closely, could now be seen running away toward their two planes in the south much faster than they had come running in.

The pills given to Haruno by the man from the Transportation Ministry really had energized her. During the night, the dormitory and its cafeteria were designated, by a handful of mechanics and their students, as a staging area for medical treatment. Distressingly, the rescuers were all on their own. No one from the government, not even a single army truck with medical supplies, had come near, despite a Red Cross flag raised prominently over the station. The apprentice engineer felt like a nurse making rounds in Dante's hell. She had nothing except carefully torn sheets for bandages, machine oil for the treatment of burns, and a single bottle of Mercurochrome for so many incoming wounded that they were quickly filling up floor space.

By the time the planes in the south took wing and headed back toward Tokyo, she longed to venture again into the ruins. With a father lost at sea and her mother missing somewhere in the desert, Haruno was not yet prepared for the idea that she was an orphan.

Her teacher provided a merciful distraction: "Trams are to resume operations in the city today, so someone needs to serve as a crew member."

One hundred eight of the rail company's 123 trolleys were destroyed or inoperable. Haruno was assigned to bring out one of the first two surviving cars. The tracks were workable only beyond the blast zone's fringe. She could drive as far south as a major railroad station, said still to be functioning, and she could circle back along any route that worked for her. "Of course, there can be no fixed schedule," the teacher instructed. "And you don't have to collect bus fares from people with no money."

Some of her passengers expressed great surprise that the company was providing services. Many were very quiet. Some, like Aiko, had colorful stars spreading across their skin. The tram was crowded, and as the teacher anticipated, most of those still physically fit enough to carry the injured aboard had lost everything and could not pay fares.

A few of the passengers expressed wishes to make their way toward the center of the desert, in search of relatives, just as Haruno had done the day before. She let them off as they wished, but not before advising that it was probably dangerous to go in there—"and besides, nothing has survived."

One or two changed their minds and continued north with her.

A sense of purpose in running the tram and helping families decided Haruno against ignoring what she already knew, and prevented her from returning to the hot zone. Only later would she learn why people who initially appeared uninjured and healthy were "growing the stars" and suddenly dying one by one, by one. She did not understand yet that a sense of mission among the trolley workers kept her driving outside the radioactivity of the city center and probably saved her life.[10]

5

In waste fields strung with cobwebs of downed electrical and phone lines, where the roads became sheets of shifting black sand, young Mizuha, the girl who had fled to Hiroshima from an evacuation camp just in time to be buried under a flattened school building, recognized her father in the ruins. She ran toward him with such joy that her campmate, Yasuko, would one day include the event in a novel-turned-film, in which Mizuha's own daughter (still many years from being born) would reenact this rare and fleeting moment of light in darkness.

Father, who had survived in a factory outside Ground Zero, beyond the fires and the fallout, should have received no radiation injury at all had he not come into the zone of the black rains in search of his family and anyone else who might still be alive—no injury at all had he not joined the machinists at the trolley garage and disembarked as a wandering rescuer into the regions of deepest and still lethally young radioactive debris—again, again, again.

There could never be a proper assessment of how many different species of chromosome-shredding isotopes he inhaled, ingested, or adsorbed onto and via the pores of his skin. One might just as well ask how many angels could dance on the head of a pin.

In the waste fields, the bomb found a new way of killing, this time aimed at rescuer Hidemitsu Takama through his sense of duty to the injured and the newly destitute. With each trip into the hot zone, the phenomenon of radiation poisoning was targeting Mizuha's father, slaying him with his kindness, with his humanity.

Each evening, Father arrived home to a strip of land from which the expected physics and the laws of Newton himself gave the illusion of having retreated. Along the roads where he lived, even the bridges were broken and the only buildings standing nearby were the two large houses on his property—rendered windowless but otherwise having ridden through the shock waves and the firestorm completely undamaged. Mizuha was every bit as mystified as her father to see all two stories of the main structure standing like a sentinel in the wilderness. She would never cease trying to puzzle out how the house survived, or how main interlocking supports had probably been so subtly microcracked, and wood grain delaminated in just enough (probably hundreds or thousands of) little invisible places, that it became possible, decades later, for a simple typhoon gust to bring the whole thing crashing down.

At the time, Mizuha figured that a massive stone wall around the front of the property, as the shock wave bashed the stones apart, had somehow (despite being a rampart not quite one story tall) managed to deflect much of the force upward and over the roof, allowing the mansion and even the trees of the garden—once meticulously tended by servants—to stand seemingly with no permanent wounds at all. Later, she figured, "Maybe sometimes strange things happen, just because."

And even during those first days after the bomb, Father began to weaken, with the purple stars of Hiroshima's "death sand" appearing on his skin.

After the initial joy of finding Mizuha walking away alive from a school where only she and the hide-and-seeker Tanemori had survived, the deteriorating health of other family members began to draw Father emotionally as well as physically into the domain of terrors. Mother Tadako seemed not to be healing from scratches and punctures delivered by flying mini daggers of glass. Even without an immune system weakened by radiation, even had an X-ray machine survived (and a source of electricity with it), even had not every X-ray plate in the city been penetrated and bleached by gamma rays, little blades of glass were, by a factor of hundreds, more difficult to sleuth out than the usual kinds of shrapnel.

Their younger daughter, Futaba, suffered no immediate injuries but was near an outer, hypocenter-facing room of the mansion at Moment Zero and so, in addition to receiving fallout dosing, was not nearly so shielded from the initial rays as Mizuha at the school, or anyone located deeper within their home. Because the two sisters were children still growing fast enough to feel the usual pains of lengthening and readjusting bones, damage to the cellular software of protein production and bone growth was already resounding through organ systems faster than most children's chromosomal watchdogs could identify precancerous mutations and call in repairs. Worse, the body easily confused strontium-90 and other radioactive elements with bone-building calcium, and the new toxins accumulated quickly in growing children.

At age fifteen, Mizuha's brother Kunihiro had entered Moment Zero essentially fully grown, and his bones would have been relatively safe from strontium-90 if they had not been fractured and forced to begin a process of healing and regrowth. At the factory to which his school had assigned him, the blast had caused a swelling of his spine that could not be reduced or prevented from starving off and crushing the nerves leading down to his legs. He could not be treated medically. The use of his legs was impossible to preserve in a city without medicine, where few physicians were left alive. And at another factory assignment, younger brother Gyoji was severely flash-burned along one side of his face. His bones and the marrow within, and additionally the cells of his liver, were already laced with gamma ray–emitting and positron-emitting poisons. Gyoji's and Futaba's tissues were irreversibly on a path to early-onset cancer.

In this manner, the atomic bomb began to reveal itself, more specifically and on a grander scale than any weapon heretofore fashioned by human hands, as a child-killer.[11]

6

Hundreds of miles north of Mizuha and her weakening family, Mitsuo Fuchida had already delivered Dr. Nishina and General Arisue to the palace with their firsthand eyewitness confirmation that the device used against Hiroshima was indeed atomic. Fuchida was instructed to go away and assist engineers in their designs for one-way bomber missions against the American fleet.

The pilot departed the palace grounds with no suspicions about warlord Arisue's treachery and the emperor's looming imprisonment, or any inkling that he was leaving the compound just barely in time. A friend of his (Kazuo, who had fallen under control of the Philippine orphan Peggy Covell) once summed up the history of Fuchida's life as "fool's luck." Kazuo had this idea of some mad deity hurling lightning bolts directly down at his friend, with terrible marksmanship, hitting everyone else instead.

And thus, no one who knew Fuchida seemed surprised that he should survive the war, all the way from Pearl Harbor through Hiroshima and the Palace Revolt, into the occupation force's interrogation period:

"I need to know how it all began," insisted the OSS man, Walter Lord.

For a long time, Fuchida would sit silent, looking past his interviewer and regarding him with contemptuous indifference.

"We all know that your battle plan for Pearl Harbor was crazy—maybe even just crazy enough to be brilliant. Except for one flaw, of course."

As intended, mention of the flaw grabbed the pilot's attention. By the time the interrogations began, Walter knew from the existing record that Fuchida claimed to have raised his voice to superiors aboard the aircraft carrier *Akagi*, demanding that he be given permission to return with a third wave of planes to make sure all the fuel storage tanks of Pearl Harbor were eliminated. Fuchida's insistence that he saw from the start how to more completely strand the American fleet was being disputed by a handful of angry Japanese veterans ever since the *Akagi* sank beneath Fuchida at Midway. To even suggest the controversy was to strike at a very raw nerve.

"I *did* see that the tanks were still there. I *did* tell them!"

"I understand," said Walter in his most sympathetic and gentlemanly manner. "I believe you did see it, and told it so. The question which divides us goes back a little earlier: What were those guys in the palace thinking? *What?* 'Oh, we'll just bomb Pearl Harbor and sink their ships and we'll never hear from them again'?"

"That's exactly what they were thinking!" said Fuchida.

"You're joking, right?"

"Not at all," he would emphasize repeatedly. Fuchida asked Walter if he remembered the USS *Panay*, and the OSS man nodded. Exactly four years ahead of Pearl Harbor, while America's workforce began pulling the nation, one slow step at a time, out of the Great Depression and Dust Bowl era, imperial warlords were already drawing their plans against

Pearl Harbor and against the entire Pacific region. During their 1937 invasion of China, Japan targeted the USS *Panay* while her crew led a convoy of refugees away from the port of Nanking. Along the Yangtze River, the entire convoy was sunk. Most who survived the sinkings perished when Japanese planes returned and strafed the lifeboats. A few of the lifeboats were intentionally left unharmed so that someone would remain to tell what had happened, and so that the Japanese could scrutinize the response of the officially neutral United States—scrutinize America, as a behavioral psychologist might assess the responses of a rat during an experiment involving electric shocks and rewards.

The sinking of the USS *Panay* on December 12, 1937, was only a probe—the mere thunder of an approaching storm. The lightning was yet to come.

Fuchida, the former commander of the squadron that bombed Pearl Harbor, explained how, as was anticipated, an America still weary from the lessons of World War I did nothing more than protest loudly about the *Panay*, then accepted merely symbolic reparations of cash for lost property and personnel. A British ship was also sunk with the *Panay*, and the probe had produced the same mealymouthed response. The warlords saw a weakness and an unwillingness of Americans and British to fight back. In fact, it seemed for a while that Americans were willing to make "gift offerings" to Japan in hopes that the warlords, during their expansion beyond Korea, across Thailand and southern China, could simply be appeased into staying away from the Philippines, Hawaii, and other American interests. To Fuchida, America's continuation of business as usual with Japan, and the attempted bribes, should have been laughable were the attempts not so pathetic. All the way into the cusp of 1941 (until punitive embargoes were finally imposed for the "Manchuria incidents" and other aggressions), America continued to sell its Texas and California oil to Japan at a price barely above its spot value. And as Manhattan's subway system expanded to become one of human civilization's great engineering marvels, the city's elevated railways were dismantled, and much of their steel was shipped to Japan at bargain-basement prices. "The better to build more planes, torpedoes, and aircraft carriers," Fuchida understood.

Other officers confirmed Fuchida's belief. Without exception, they all were taken by surprise when America finally fought back.

To this, Walter Lord added one more observation: "They bombed Pearl Harbor with the Ninth Avenue el."[12]

Only a half block west of the el, at a firehouse on Thirty-Eighth Street, a radioactive trace of Mr. Sengier's barrels of uranium ore would still be detectable more than a half century later, marking the time and place that gave the Manhattan Project its name. Making a pilgrimage to Thirty-Eighth and Ninth, Walter marveled at how it was possible to walk south from his home and stand on a perfectly ordinary street corner that was actually a fantastically improbable pivot point in history, from which sprang both the beginning and the end of the Second World War.

7

In the aftermath of 1941's Day of Infamy, when confronted with the hard fact that there was no evidence of sabotage or espionage by people of Japanese ancestry along America's West Coast, California's attorney general, Earl Warren, had replied that the very absence of sabotage was "the most ominous sign in our whole situation."[13]

With words such as this, the path of Tak Furumoto's life was set even before he was born: a path that was going to lead from California to Hiroshima, toward the CIA in Cambodia, through three poisonings, and even to Donald Trump.

In time, he would come to say of nearly "*too* interesting" a life, "I would not trade it, even though it was rough." The defining moment was Executive Order 9066. It took his family's successful produce business away forever. It took their home. It took their dignity. Tak's parents were given just ten days' notice to sell, give away, or lose all furnishings and belongings. They were permitted to bring with them only what could be crammed inside a single suitcase, to a patch of desert habitat with overcrowded military-style barracks ringed by barbed wire, guard towers, and searchlights. As in any prison, there was no such thing as privacy. Worse yet, medical supplies were substandard or nonexistent. Although several world-renowned Japanese American doctors were incarcerated with their neighbors, they were allowed few surgical instruments or medicines. Some believed the injustice would have to hit bottom and, sooner or later, get better; but there was no way these American-citizens-turned-prisoners-of-war could predict how deep the bottom might go. There were even a handful of Native Americans and Chinese in the camps, and a few who appeared to be thoroughly Caucasian, because under the new order, if an ancestral intermarriage had produced a person with as little as one-sixteenth Japanese blood (as alleged by the US Census Bureau), this was enough of a crime to warrant summary judgment. To compare, even a defendant in the Salem witch trials had the right to know the accusation and to at least see the face of an accuser.

Among the small handful of people who seemed to have no business being locked up in camps for Asian Americans, some claimed to be political prisoners who had written or spoken "bad thoughts." As more journalistic prisoners came in, there also came rumors of mass executions in Europe's "ghetto camps." No one wanted to believe it, but they all feared it.

The worst of the internment centers was California's Tule Lake Segregation Camp—the so-called No-no Camp. Tak's family was sent there because of what they recalled as "a very unfair question, *a loaded question*, whereby the government asked: 'Regarding your loyalty to the Japanese emperor, would you disavow the emperor?'"

Tak's parents already knew that in Japan, people were being taken away and tortured or killed if they or a relative said, or were rumored to have said, anything questioning the emperor or his warlords. "*And this unfair piece of paper was to become a public renouncing of the emperor.*" Fearing for relatives who were living in Japan, Mr. Furumoto had answered no. Concerns about what might happen to his wife and young children if the ongoing mistreatment worsened and he should not be near them and able to help dissuaded Mr. Furumoto from saying yes to a request that he join an American combat unit. And if his persecutors were ever to make good on their frequent threat of deporting families back to Japan, a yes answer to either question could turn the old home country deadly for his wife and children. All Mr. Furumoto had to do was look around. Of nearly 5,500 men sent to the Tule Lake maximum security center, 1,300 had already been marked for eventual deportation to Japan. (All that remained to be worked out were the logistics.)

By August 1945, Mr. and Mrs. Furumoto had been added to the deportation list.

Tak was born only ten months earlier.

There were actually pictures of the child in the camp. The single great luxury his father had managed to sneak in and preserve was a functioning camera. Equipment for a darkroom was scrounged, along with the necessary chemicals. The prisoners dug basements under the barracks, to play cards underground in the cool earth after curfew and to assemble at least one photo lab. Father was risking punishment should he be caught with a camera and film. "But what more can FDR and his attack dogs do to me than they have done already?" he said. Mrs. Furumoto was growing prematurely old, year by year, before his eyes. Depression had a hold on her. The photos told it so.

And so the Furumoto family would leave the camps with a very rare photo album of life behind guard towers (from which an elderly civilian who lost his way one night had been shot dead). Other photos also went out into the world beyond. Imprisoned journalist Toyo Mitatake built his own camera, mostly out of scrap wood, with which he was able to expose the film he had sneaked into California's Manzanar camp. His 1944 photo of three boys behind barbed wire, showing beautiful snowcapped mountains on the horizon but a machine-gun tower nearby, eventually got out of the camp. It was developed and published and became the internment camp era's most iconic example of photojournalism.

Among the few luxuries actually allowed in the camps were radio receivers. This is how the Furumoto family learned that something terrible might have happened to grandparents in Hiroshima. News traveled slowly in the 1940s. There were no satellites, not even a working trans-Pacific phone service. They could only make vague guesses based on the strange words that came over the radio during the days following Moment Zero.[14]

"The first atomic bomb," President Truman had said. "It is an awful responsibility that has come to us. We thank God that it has come to us instead of to our enemies. And we pray that He may guide us to use it in His ways and for His purposes."

"*How?*" a friend of the family said later. "How can anyone expect God's guidance in the actual *use* of atomic bombs?"[15]

Those who were able walked silently toward the hills, their spirits broken, their initiative gone. When asked whence they had come, they pointed toward the city and said, "That way." When asked where they were going, they pointed away from the city and said, "This way." They were so broken and confused that they—[we]—moved and behaved like automatons. Our reactions [would] astonish outsiders who reported with amazement the spectacle of long lines of people holding stolidly to a narrow, rough path [over hills of jagged debris] when close by there was a smooth, easy road [to travel], going in the same direction. The outsiders could not grasp that they were witnessing the exodus of a people who walked in the realm of dreams.

—Dr. Michihiko Hachiya
("ant-trail walker"),
Hiroshima Diary

I cannot believe they actually used that awful thing on people.
—General Dwight D. Eisenhower

CHAPTER 5:
SURFING THE IMPROBABILITY CURVE

1

When Tsutomu Yamaguchi's train arrived at Nagasaki Station on August 8, his burned arm and face were swelling, stinging, and itching mercilessly. The pressure from ballooning muscle tissue was tearing open new wounds in his skin, and the wounds leaked foul-smelling signs of infection. During his walk home from the station, he met an old school friend who had become an eye doctor. The friend repaired and disinfected the wounds, then wrapped both arms and one side of Yamaguchi's face in fresh white bandages—which explained why his mother let out a shriek after he entered the house. She called him "Ghost!"

In Japanese mythology, ghosts did not have feet. And word was already spreading about something monstrous in Hiroshima that had killed almost everyone.

"Have you got feet?" his mother asked timidly.

Yamaguchi showed Mother his feet and reassured her that he was not the ghost of her son. His wife, Hisako, came running into the house and took him by his one good hand, and kissed him as if nothing at all had happened to his face. Such displays of affection before other family members were unusual for a Japanese woman, but these were unusual times.

Yamaguchi forgot his pain and tried to reassure Hisako that he was fine despite all the bandages. Seeing that his son was peacefully asleep in the sling on her back, "I just stroked his head gently," Yamaguchi would write later, "for I did not want to surprise him with my bandaged appearance."

Hisako announced that they now had a new house of their own, which she had bought with some of their savings and which he had not yet seen. The little frame house was more than a half hour's walk from his parents' home, but he was sustained by the thought that once the three of them were home alone, they would be able to rest quietly. He made the forty-five-minute trek falteringly but happily.

The place was small but beautifully crafted from hardwood. There was even a balcony built for two, from which Yamaguchi and his wife could look across the river in the direction of the Maria Cathedral and the heavily forested hills beyond. But the peaceful family evening Yamaguchi had been hoping for was not to be. As with most Mitsubishi families, they had been required to choose living quarters located adjacent to the shipyard and its offices. Everyone knew that this put them at increased risk of being killed if the B-29s came.

Only a week earlier, a study of maps by several priests had revealed that almost every city of any importance was already wiped away under nightly firebomb raids. In Tokyo, the Americans had preserved only the quadrant where the Imperial Palace stood. Beyond Tokyo, at the time of the mapping, there was the Kokura industrial center still standing, and Kyoto, Nagasaki, and Hiroshima. Now there were only Kokura, Kyoto, Nagasaki, and a wide perimeter around Tokyo's palace grounds. Those who were aware of the situation—including the Yamaguchis and their neighbors—expected that the B-29 raiders would leave the palace and its emperor unharmed because therein lay the only hope of extracting a surrender from Japan. This meant a one-in-three chance that Nagasaki would be next.

Almost from the moment Yamaguchi and his wife arrived home with their child, neighbors started showing up at the door, wanting to know what Mr. Yamaguchi had seen in Hiroshima. He was nauseated and fatigued, and his fever felt as if it was still climbing, but he decided to answer every question and offer advice: "Wear white clothes, which will reflect the heat ray. Black clothes tend to catch fire easily. Keep all the windows open because, if glass shards are stuck in the body, treatment is very difficult. And if you see the *flash*, you must at that very moment hide yourself behind a sturdy object."

He hoped that his advice to his neighbors was unnecessary. He prayed that the white flash and the multicolored cloud would not follow him to Nagasaki. He hoped so, but he really did not believe so.[1]

Advancing slowly toward Yamaguchi from the north and gaining steam, the last train from the Hiroshima suburbs to Nagasaki had just departed its station. Master kite maker Morimoto and three of his helpers—Doi, Shinji, and Masao—were traveling together in the same car. All four of them had survived Hiroshima without any visible injuries, but Morimoto was trying to fend off a persistent nausea, and Doi was drenched in perspiration—yet at the same time, he complained about intermittent chills.

They did not know yet that behind them in central Hiroshima, nearly three thousand Japanese Americans who were trapped after their citizenship was revoked in 1941, having endured years of being ostracized and barely surviving, were now among the atomic bomb's dead and dying.[2]

The Samejima family was also aboard the last train out of the city. Mrs. Samejima was traveling with two young sons and four-year-old Mami.

"My father went to war on the morning of the day I turned ninety days old," Mami would later record. He died during the battle of Iwo Jima, and though the government notified the family of where he had died, someone in command had evidently decided that families should not learn that no Japanese defenders remained to recover the bodies of the lost. So boxes containing anonymous cremated defenders of other islands were sent with name labels. Mami's mother and siblings were given "let's pretend" remains of a loved one. In the summer of 1945 they were living in the countryside near Tokyo, and Mrs. Samejima had managed (through the proper political connections) to obtain tickets for what was to be a two-day train ride, through Hiroshima and onward to Nagasaki, where she and the children could return her husband's ashes to his parents. On August 6, the train had been passing through a tunnel when the bomb exploded. The tunnel behaved so like a protective cocoon that the train was still operable. Not even the windows broke. But once wreckage on the tracks stopped them, once they emerged into the blackened desert, once they breathed the soot, and once Mother collected drinking water from a ruptured pipe, they became *hibakusha*—the exposed. The detonation had, for an instant, created uncounted varieties of every element that ever had or ever would exist during the entire history of the universe. And now the residua of creation were beginning to threaten overthrow of each person's immune defenses. After two days in Hiroshima, waiting to continue the journey home, no one was feeling quite well. And yet, here and there within the night train, voices could be heard murmuring, "Almost safe now," or "Thank goodness we're finally off to Nagasaki."

Mami's mother agreed.[3]

In another car, Kenshi Hirata nearly dozed off, but a sudden bump in the railroad tracks and several bright flashes outside his window snapped him to full alertness. Off to one side, an orange glow began blooming against the sky, spreading there, brightening. The town of Yahata was dying under what he guessed to be at least a fifty-strong B-29 raid.

He thought of Setsuko.

Kenshi's intestines still did not feel at all well, and he noticed bleeding under the skin of his fingers—and though he felt weak and achy, he was afraid that if he dozed off, he would drop the bowl of precious bone chips and ashes lying on his lap.

Additional swarms of night raiders helped him keep sleep at bay. En route to Nagasaki, the young widower witnessed the firebombings of two more towns: Tobata and Yawata. It was difficult for him to believe that the situation had deteriorated to such an extent that B-29s were being sent far afield of the cities, to target even the small towns. The bombing of Yawata introduced a new FUBAR factor into the probability curve and the flutter of butterfly wings, guaranteeing that tomorrow, the lives of Kenshi Hirata and Jacob Beser would converge a second time.[4]

2

At two a.m., Jacob Beser and the rest of *Bockscar*'s atomic strike crew had taken positions at their individual corners of the plane and begun running through their preflight systems checks. Pilot Charles Sweeney was about to start the engines when the flight engineer leaned forward and said, "We have a problem. The fuel in our reserve supply in the rear bomb-bay bladder isn't pumping. We've got six hundred gallons of fuel trapped back there."

"Any idea what the problem *is*?" Sweeney asked. "Could it be instruments?" he suggested hopefully.

The engineer replied that checking and double-checking had proved his gauges to be giving accurate readings—which meant that the only means of correcting the problem involved replacing a pump. According to the rulebook, they were not allowed to proceed unless every piece of equipment, including every backup pump to every reserve fuel bladder, was fully functional at the moment of takeoff.

Beser heard Sweeney call for an "all stop," followed by the unlatching of his shoulder straps and a scramble down through the nose-wheel ladder. Paul Tibbets was already at the plane's wing when Sweeney emerged. Beser could not hear their conversation, but he knew that whatever it was, a decision needed to be made quickly. If they went by the rulebook, the mission would have to be aborted, and at the worst possible time. A weather plane had already sent a coded report from the primary target of Kokura. The forecast called for clear skies, but not for very long. A band of rain and mist was expected to move in from the Pacific and might linger for several days. Indeed, most of Japan's large south island might become clouded over for a week or more—and then the typhoon season would be in full swing.

Beser knew that whatever Sweeney and his commander were discussing out there, it had to be mathematical and immediately resolved; it had to be logical and unsympathetic. The radar expert could feel the probability of his dying at an advanced age from natural causes dropping by the minute. After what appeared to be very little discussion, the two men evidently decided, *To hell with the book*. Sweeney climbed up again through the hatch and announced, "We're going." Less than ten minutes later and only slightly behind schedule, *Bockscar* took off from the runway. The clock ticked forward to 2:56 a.m. Tinian time; 1:56 a.m. Kokura and Nagasaki time.[5]

3

Even before he arrived at Fukuoka's Prison Camp 25, Alistair, "the stubborn Scotsman," had survived the impossible. Even by the time they first placed him on a hell ship, he should not have been alive. In Thailand, a Japanese "scientist" known as Dr. Death delighted in looking for signs that a man's eyes continued to search the world in fright after a beheading if blood was forcefully bottled up around the brain for a minute or two. In his other moments of spare time, he would stand on cliffs while the prisoners worked, entertaining himself by tossing rocks and boulders down on them, laughing when he scored a hit.

Each morning, Alistair had performed an act of meditative hypnosis on himself. "To face that day alone," he would write later. "Not the next day. Just that day. The next morning was the same. I was only thinking of myself and how I could avoid dying like those around me."

At Camp 25, the Scot's mantra became "I've seen worse." Dr. Death and others with nicknames like "the Mad Mongrel" had not made the hell ship voyage (which, up until August 9, Alistair took to be his final saving grace). Camp 25 was located above a coal seam that had begun depleting years earlier and was now abandoned except in a sort of ants'-nest existence to be survived by slave laborers. Safety equipment was essentially nonexistent. Alistair's friend Dr. Matheson had kept the sick and injured alive (in a prison with no medicines) by distilling remedies from various semipoisonous weeds. Recently, a decision from the Imperial Palace stipulated that all POWs were to be executed if the Allies ever landed on Japan's shores.

The predawn hours of August 9 were, by several accounts, unusually quiet. Even the insect night shift was silent around the camp and also in the hills to the south, as if nature were holding its breath.

Nearly forty miles south along the silent hills lay the city of Nagasaki.[6]

4

At six a.m. Nagasaki time, and at ten thousand feet, *Bockscar*'s master alarm warning lights began signaling that the fail-safes, designed to prevent the bomb from detonating inside the plane, were neither unfailing nor entirely safe. Apparently, the new plutonium core was very unfriendly to electrical systems.

Lieutenant Philip Barnes looked up from his black box (the fuse-monitoring device connected to the bomb) and called out to Sweeney, "We have a master alarm."

"Repeat that," Sweeney called back, wanting to make sure he had heard correctly.

Commander Fred Ashworth confirmed Barnes's observation that the red warning light on the fuse monitor had started flashing. Jacob Beser knew all too terribly well that if this warning, like the fuel warning, was accurate, then a multikiloton nuclear weapon's firing circuits were closing and one or more detonation fuses were about to pull the trigger. Everyone who knew the fusing checklist (including Sweeney, Ashworth, and Barnes) ran it through his mind in all of about three seconds: If either of the two ground-impact fuses in the bomb's nose were self-activating, the plane would already have become a false sunrise over the Pacific, about to register on Japan's seismographs. If the barometric fuse was involved, they would be fine unless *Bockscar* descended to about two thousand feet—and the crew would remain safe next to the radar proximity fuse unless it was "deciding" to give a faulty reading to the detonator. Again, if this had happened, they would already be ions and gamma rays. Beser's equipment showed that they were not approaching any radar beams using his or any other frequency. This left the timing fuse, in which case they had considerably less than forty-three seconds remaining to solve the problem.

Phil Barnes already had the bomb's hatch open and was giving the maze of wires, circuits, and switches one of history's fastest inspections. With more than seven seconds to spare (as the timing fuse measured time), Barnes determined that the timer was not involved. A few moments later, he traced the source of the problem to a false-positive warning and corrected it.

"False alarm," Barnes called out. "None of the firing circuits were closed."

Good enough, Beser guessed, doubtless supposing that his odds of living through this war and seeing children and grandchildren had just gone infinitesimally up.[7]

5

A Camp 25 prisoner crew was still working the night shift, 1,400 feet underground in the condemned Fukuoka coal mine. The odds of survival here were tenuous on the best of days. Supplies to prop up the ceilings of the tunnels were restricted, so staying alive required such on-the-fly innovations as creating support pillars out of waste rock. The ceilings often collapsed anyway. Twenty Allied slaves had died in this manner. Even some of the Japanese overseers died.

After the spring of 1945, as the futuristic-appearing B-sans began dominating the sky, a fatal curiosity drove two British officers to attempt building a radio receiver. When caught, they were sentenced to dragging, facedown, over gravel until they implicated any prisoners who had aided in the scavenging of parts. They died without confessing, taking the names of their friends with them to their shallow graves.

"Everyone talks under torture." This widely known saying was almost always true. But not in Camp 25, not this time. [8]

John Baxter attributed his own survival to a soldier named Hyato. Baxter knew that Hyato, like the rest of the Japanese, had grown up under indoctrination by warlords who perverted the ancient Samurai codes. Except for this one man, everywhere within sight the evidence of the warlords and Japan going crazy had been horribly apparent. The whole world was going inhuman. And Baxter came independently to the same conclusion as the Thurlow girl in Hiroshima: *that we human beings can never be so frightening to history or to ourselves as when huge numbers of us all go crazy together.*

Perhaps a tad crazier than the rest, Hyato showed uncommon humanity toward Baxter and other POWs under his charge, when their treatment by his brethren was nothing but regimented cruelty. The young man risked beatings that would end in summary execution for sneaking in extra food to prisoners who were supposed to be the empire's work-and-starve-to-death slaves. Food was sometimes acquired, prepared, and packaged by Hyato's wife, who risked the same lethal retaliation if caught.

Baxter had already seen a Japanese youth from a nearby town hung upside down by his feet in a doorway. One of the guards told the prisoners that the boy was a local thief. As a punishment, every Japanese soldier passing through the doorway was obliged to punch or kick him as he hung there. Because of Hyato, Baxter survived to tell history, "Thus we discovered that the medieval practices we had thought only applied to the military and foreign nationals in the confines of our prison camp, affected [local] Japanese civilians as well."

The hell ship survivor was assigned to Hyato after an overseer/engineer observed his mechanical and electrical skills in the mines. Transferred temporarily to the camp's repair shop, there Baxter had remained since the beginning of the year—all the way up through the moment *Bockscar*'s master alarm warnings were cleared and Jacob Beser allowed himself a momentary sigh of relief.

The permanence of this ultimately lifesaving transfer owed much to the improper maintenance of mining equipment and the withholding of necessary lubricating grease by the Japanese themselves. *All the easier*, Baxter realized, *for us to camouflage sabotaging of the equipment—to further limit coal supplies for the enemy.*

The general deterioration of the country, as indicated by increasingly longer and more frequent power outages at the camp, had led to the installation of a 1910 vintage steamship boiler, dragged in from somewhere very far away so that a coal-fired turbine could guarantee around-the-clock power for the mining equipment and electricity for the officers' quarters.

There were other indicators that Japan was in a downward spiral. When Baxter's assignment to the repair shed began, work by POWs was limited to cleaning and stripping machine parts, which were then handed over to Japanese engineers, who made the actual repairs. But during the months and weeks leading up to humanity's Moment Zero, most of those engineers were taken away either to the ships and planes of the constricting front line or to an airfield nearby. At the mining camp, it had become more widely spoken even than rumors of Hitler's death that the airfield was dedicated to the final preparation of kamikaze planes, including the Ohka rocket bombs. From a hilltop at the mine, where a newly patched-together vertical drill had begun operations, it was possible to observe the horror. The war really was devolving into the eastern Children's Crusade.

"Such was the shortage of trained airmen," Baxter recorded, "that area schools were being scoured for new recruits—schoolboys were being pressed into service as suicide pilots. And we became used to the daily procession of solemn-faced youths [in] black kimonos and with sweatbands on their foreheads, preceded by a Shinto priest and an air force officer on their final journey to the waiting aircraft." Baxter estimated the boys to be about age sixteen, but some were, in fact, as young as fourteen.

The calling away of Japanese engineers so decimated the workshop staff that the shed was now almost exclusively crewed by the POWs. There were only two Japanese ex-servicemen in charge—both of them electricians who had been discharged from the army due to significant disability. One was so shell-shocked and unpredictable that he went into rages about the "dishonor" of being "shunned by suicide squads" (*whatever that adds up to, in this kind of time*, Baxter mused). The other man was Hyato, who seemed to express more interest in healing his wounded legs and secretly keeping his prisoners alive than in the efficiency of the POW work crews. Most of the machinery repaired by Baxter's team therefore had a very limited working life in the mines and was usually soon returned to the shed for further repairs. When Baxter first arrived, broken engines occupied only a tenth of the shed's floor space. With no experts able to look over the slaves' shoulders, checking their work, they became so free to make gears destroy themselves and everything around them that for more than two months, there had been no space to move under the shop's roof without bumping into broken steel. A result of this was that work shifts in the mines had to be decreased for lack of functional pumps, meaning that half-starved prisoners were able to receive rest breaks. In some cases, those breaks drew the dividing line between life and death.

Baxter prided himself in "pulling the wool over Hyato's eyes," rigging equipment to self-destruct even as the guard was smuggling food to the men. Only much later would Baxter learn, "He had an idea we were doing this, but he kept quiet." Baxter sometimes regretted that if the sabotage were discovered, Hyato would have been in almost as much trouble as the camp's prisoners. But Baxter's allegiance had to be to his fellow prisoners still down in the mine, even though he did arrive at the camp half dead himself, hosting a menagerie of tropical parasites, including an amoeba that caused dysentery. Under normal circumstances, the organism could cause dehydration. Under starvation leading to immune

Clocks in the two cities recorded the event: A quarter past eight in Hiroshima, two past eleven in Nagasaki.

system collapse, the microbe could undergo a population surge that liquefied a man's brain and spinal cord. Food sneaked in by Hyato had probably saved Baxter and others in the shop from this fate.

In August 1945, the daily ration per man was three very low-calorie meals, each with only enough cooked rice to fill a four-ounce tobacco tin. The men caught snakes and rats and shared the meat. Two feral cats wandered into the camp, evidently hunting snakes and rats. It occurred to Baxter that had the POWs not eaten so many small, prickly-boned animals, they might have lured in more cats for breakfast. "Still . . . we lost weight progressively."[9]

The morning of August 9 came on hot and sticky, as usual. The camp's commanders seemed particularly downcast about something, even downright depressed. Miles away, an air-raid siren sounded. And high above the Earth, an American weather plane glinted silver. To judge from the angle of the sun, it was almost eight o'clock.

6

At 7:45 a.m., the next weather plane reached Kokura, and *Bockscar* reached its rendezvous point thirty thousand feet above the island of Yakushima. The scientific instrument plane, *The Great Artiste*, rose a half mile away from Charles Sweeney's starboard wing, but the photographic plane, *Big Stink*, was nowhere to be seen. Fifteen minutes and 125 gallons of fuel later, the third plane still appeared to be lost. By coded signal, two distant weather planes called out "C-1" and "C-2/10-2." Though morning haze had been anticipated at both targets, the call meant that Kokura was clear, and only about two-tenths cloud cover could be expected at the secondary target.

This was the first thoroughly "no-cause-for-alarm" news that Sweeney and Beser had received during the entire mission, and it soon began to look as if it would be their last.

At 8:30, after a half hour more of circling for rendezvous—and after burning another precious 250 gallons of fuel—Sweeney scanned the empty sky one last time, then told his copilot and bombardier, "That's it. We can't wait any longer." Maintaining radio silence, he waggled *Bockscar*'s wings, signaling to *The Great Artiste* that they were to depart the rendezvous point and proceed to the primary target.

The missing photographic plane was circling almost two miles too high, and as Beser later summed it up, "He was up there tooling around but he never found us." Beser kept thinking about the six hundred gallons of fuel in the bomb bay's auxiliary bladder—and how, by the failure of a simple and laughably inexpensive pump that the designers had put in a corner of the fuselage where it could render repair or replacement almost as complex as loading the atomic bomb, they could not tap the plane's emergency fuel ration. The world's first high-altitude, pressurized-cabin bomber was impressive in its abilities and its beauty—capable of such speed that even if a Japanese Zero could reach it, there was time enough for only a single three-second pass. But it had also been designed and put into production so quickly that the pump location became just one example of a plane and a rendezvous system that had more bugs than the Smithsonian Institution's butterfly collection.[10]

7

The sound of air-raid alarms in the vicinity of Camp 25 did not reach Takato Michishita. In fact, she would remember hearing no sounds of alarm at all, except from her mother.

"Don't go to school today," Mother had said.

"Why?" Takato's older sister asked.

"Just don't," came the reply. The school was, in fact, only a few brisk steps away from the soon-to-be hypocenter.

Nearly five miles outside Nagasaki and nestled safely between hills, the world outside the small house had gone unusually quiet for a summer morning. "I have a bad feeling," Takato's mother said, and insisted that the children stay home. "And my mother single-handedly saved both me and my sister," Takato would record.[11]

8

At 9:45 a.m., the primary target, Kokura, lay directly ahead. Charles Sweeney set course for the final bomb run and was about to hand the controls over to bombardier Kermit Beahan when Beahan yelled, "I can't see it! I can't see it! There's smoke obscuring the target."

Between the moment a scout plane had radioed its last "C-1" weather report for Kokura and the moment of final approach, the wind had shifted. Below, and now directly upwind of the Kokura arsenal, the town of Yawata was still in the same condition Kenshi Hirata had observed from his train the night before—burning out of control. "The [arsenal] was all smoked and hazed in," Beser recorded.

Sweeney yelled over the intercom, "No drop. Repeat, no drop."

Beser felt the plane bank sharply to port and begin a long southward arc to a return approach, with *The Great Artiste* following close behind. That's when the first flak shells began bursting all around them.

Jacob Beser did not know yet how committed Sweeney was to hitting the more purely military target of Kokura. To him, it seemed as if Sweeney was determined to "tool around for another hour," burning another nine hundred gallons of fuel under heavy fire—and if they survived the Japanese gunners' increasingly more correct altitude settings, they would not have enough fuel to get home because of the damned design bug that left six hundred gallons of extended-range fuel locked away.

What must Sweeney be thinking? Beser wondered as an already bad situation grew progressively worse. His pilot was doing something no one in a pressurized aircraft at thirty thousand feet—vulnerable to being popped by flak shells like a rubber balloon—ever wanted to be doing. He was making second runs on a hotly defended target, giving antiaircraft gunners second chances. Beser knew that if *Bockscar* popped and if all else failed, the ground-impact fuses in Fat Man's nose would surely go nuclear during that all-important first hundred-millionth of a second. But at least it would be a fast death, and at least (so far) no one on the ground was pinging the radar fuse with a beam set just perfectly and by random chance to the worst possible frequency, just close enough and at precisely the right angle. Right now this jolly catastrophe wasn't in the equation. He had that much to be thankful for.

They overflew the target a second and a third time, and as Jacob Beser would record, "We hadn't dropped the weapon yet and the Japanese were getting curious and coming up—in Zeros—to take a look at us." By now, everyone aboard was beginning to wonder if, even with less than three seconds of firing time, perhaps this could become some Zero pilot's lucky day.

"You can relax, guys," Sweeney announced over the intercom, sounding defeated and somehow very sad. "It's time to leave all of this behind. We're going to the secondary."

Sweeney waggled his wings for *The Great Artiste* and led the way south.[12]

9

Kenshi Hirata reached his parents' home on what was to become the shadow-shield side of a tall hill at about the same time Charles Sweeney waggled *Bockscar*'s wings and turned its nose in Kenshi's direction. Seconds later, Jacob Beser learned that a ground station in their flight path had begun pinging the two planes with radar—fortunately, at a benign frequency. Less than an hour now separated them from the new hypocenter, and barely more than two miles separated Kenshi from that very same point on the Earth's surface.

As he approached the steps, Kenshi's parents came running through the door with tears in their eyes. At that same moment, an air-raid siren began to signal what was likely just another false alarm—like those that had preceded Hiroshima for days, except at the moment when the cause for alarm was real and he heard nothing. False or not, he was not taking any chances. Mindful that a second flash might appear, he told his parents to come inside with him quickly and to stay away from the windows.

Kenshi's father was shocked at the sight of him—pale, with shaking hands, and with perspiration running down his cheeks, chest, and legs. He looked like a man half starved to death.

"Have you eaten?" his mother asked.

"Not hungry," he said. "I can't seem to keep anything down." He cradled the wedding bowl to his chest and rocked it gently, and his father bowed his head.

"I knew you were alive," Mrs. Hirata said. "Even when no more word was coming out of Hiroshima, I knew you were still in this world."

"And Setsuko?" his father asked, almost at a whisper.

Kenshi lifted the bowl and bent his head toward its rim, and kissed it. "This is all that's left of her," he replied.

"We already knew this," his mother said.

"How can that be?"

"Because early this morning," she explained, "Setsuko's mother arrived at our door with the news. She knew her daughter was dead in Hiroshima because Setsuko has been visiting her in dreams."

His mother's words brought no comfort, only more agitation. He remembered how, when the flash shone down on Hiroshima, a woman's voice had cried out in his brain and had made him stay under cover while everyone else stood up and was either grievously injured or killed. He understood now that it was surely Setsuko, urging him to live.

Kenshi held back his tears, straightened his back, and said to his father, "We must go at once to Setsuko's parents with this bowl and bring her home."

When they stepped outside, though only a few minutes had passed, the day had become noticeably drearier. Thick clouds were advancing across more than half the sky.

The air-raid siren wound down and blasted the all-clear signal. *Another false alarm*, Kenshi reassured himself. The Hiroshima blast had come out of a perfectly clear blue sky. In these times, dreary days were good days. The Americans never dropped bombs if they could not see the ground. Everyone knew this and took it for a fact.

Passing a row of houses and a Buddhist shrine, Kenshi and his father heard a radio playing loudly. For some reason, everyone who possessed a functioning radio these days delighted in cranking up the decibels for the whole neighborhood to hear. Someone only a little farther down the road was also booming out the same station. Presently, an announcer broke into the music to tell his listeners that several B-29s had been deterred from their attempt on Kokura and were presumed either shot down or headed out to sea. Consequently, the air-raid warnings for Kokura and the Saga Prefecture in the north and the yellow alert for Nagasaki were being lifted.

As Kenshi walked, the cloud cover thickened quickly, and his stomach spasms abated ever so slightly. He believed that he might even be able to drink a little water now and keep it down. All he needed was a little breathing space. All he needed was for Nagasaki to be safe today.[13]

10

A fellow Hiroshima survivor, the ship designer Yamaguchi, was already at work. Although still feeling pain from his burns and barely able to drag himself out of bed even with his wife's help, he remained obedient to an order to present a full report about Hiroshima at the headquarters of the Mitsubishi industrial combine.

"Orders are orders," he had told Hisako. "And besides, if I warn them about how it happened, I may be able to save lives."

At the conference room, still bandaged and bleeding, he told the executives and engineers about the woman in the black *monpe* and how anyone wearing dark clothing near the flash zone had been simultaneously grilled and flayed. He told them how a piece of roof tile or even a harmless twig could be propelled like a bullet, with bone-piercing force.

"This piercing hazard goes doubly for flying glass," Yamaguchi warned. "If a similar device should explode here, at the instant you see the flash, you must seek any shelter available, even if all you can do is duck behind a desk or a chair." He then ordered his colleagues to slide open every window in the room, as high as it would go.

"This is beyond common sense," a section chief interrupted. "The damage to Hiroshima is nothing like this hoax you are trying to weave. How can one bomb turn out such energy to destroy an entire city? You are an engineer. Calculate it!"

"I already have," Yamaguchi said flatly, motioning with his one good hand toward his left arm and the left side of his face, covered with bandages.

"Exactly," the section chief said. "You were injured, Yamaguchi. Your brain was not working properly."

Outside the windows, a siren came suddenly to life again.[14]

11

At Prison Camp 25, about 10:30 a.m.—"Perhaps a little earlier, perhaps a little later than 10:30," John Baxter guessed—several British fighter planes came roaring in low through the mountain valleys. They were barely above treetop level, and they seemed to be trying to get away from something. The prison guards dived into shelter pits and snapped down the covers so swiftly that it looked as though the entire company were crawling into holes and trying to pull the holes in behind themselves.

The prisoners from the repair shop were obliged to stay above on the mine tailings. Overhead, a wide break in the cloud cover revealed a contrail very high up and ten miles or more to the south. Twin glints of silver could be seen at the head of the contrail—meaning not one but two B-29s, traveling nearly wing-to-wing and scratching a vapor trail across the heavens. They were pointed like an arrowhead toward Nagasaki.[15]

12

Almost as if nothing at all out of the ordinary were happening, the officer whom Ichiro Miyato was assigned to relieve stood away from the radar screen, rubbed his eyes, and offered Miyato the chair. Normally, the two techies liked to talk shop or about girls between shifts, but not this morning. Both of them had been worn down by a very difficult seventy-two hours of doubled-up schedules. Whenever relieved from their ten-hour screen watches, they were trucking new equipment to wherever it would soon be needed to put up a final resistance against the American invaders.

Miyato could easily see that all his friend wanted to do was get out of the room and go to sleep before the next truck run was scheduled. Looking at a blip coming down from the direction of Kokura, he made a try at conversation anyway.

"What have you got?" Miyato asked.

"Only another false alarm," came the reply. He scarcely bothered to look back as he put on a hat and sought the comfort of the hammock outside. Miyato supposed that the intensifying schedule and the atmosphere of defeat were enough to fray anyone's nerves, but he had expected better. At the end of the previous shift, his friend had looked so exhausted that this time Miyato decided to relieve him at 10:40 a.m., even though his own tour was scheduled to begin at eleven.

Miyato took his seat and watched the blip notch down from the northeast with the next two sweeps of the radar beam. This was nothing new to him. Surveillance planes were now joyriding all over the region, triggering at least three false alerts this very morning and generating an increasingly fatal complacency about air-raid sirens. Miyato did not want to be responsible for calling in another false yellow alert, so he made a note in the logbook, recorded the time as 10:45, and adjusted the scanning frequencies. On the next sweep, the object looked vaguely like an echo from two separate blips, but on a subsequent sweep he could not be sure. The intruder was now putting out interference—pinging back at Miyato with its own radar. Some new and powerful sort of interference, streaming out from the intruder, degraded it to a blur.

He picked up the phone to Command Headquarters.

"What do you see?" a voice on the other end said.

"Looks like a lone B-san running radar," Miyato replied. "My guess is that it's mapping. Altitude above ten thousand meters—probably above fighter range."

"Thank you," the voice said, and hung up. As in most conversations these days, the person at the other end spoke with a curious mixture of politeness, boredom, and grim resignation.

Several sweeps later, Miyato noticed that the object appeared to be holding to a straight flight path. He plotted the vector and lifted the phone again.

"What do you see?" the same voice said.

"If they stay on present heading, their course will take them straight to you. Crossing our position soon. The object should pass directly over Nagasaki in about ten minutes. You may want to take countermeasures."

Putting the phone on speaker mode to free his hands, Miyato adjusted the scan and tried to resolve the blip more clearly, but it was interfering again, using its own radar and blurring methods. He poured himself a cup of tea and waited for a response. Six sweeps, two sips, and the object was still following a straight-line heading. Miyato was expecting another polite thank-you and hang-up. He knew almost to a certainty that no interceptors would be sent. The Boeing B-29 was too high, and there simply wasn't enough reserve fuel to waste in a futile attempt to bring down a lone "stray"; and there did not even appear to be enough time. What he did not know was that Command had become acutely aware of how Hiroshima was bombed by only two or three planes flying together, as opposed to a lone "weather plane" or the typically more than fifty-strong B-29 firebomb raid.

The response Miyato received was not what he had anticipated. Several clearly agitated men were speaking in the background, and the polite voice asked, "Are you certain that you are tracking only a single plane? Is there any possibility that they are really two or three, flying in a very close formation?"

"I *did* note an anomaly about ten minutes ago. For a moment, it looked as if I might have been tracking two planes."

"Hold on!" the voice said, and cupped a hand over the phone so Miyato could not hear any of what was being said. The blip remained on its beeline to Nagasaki. The city was only sixteen miles from Miyato. Thirty seconds more passed, and the object inched closer to Command Headquarters.

The voice came back, this time more with sadness than with detached politeness: "Any change?"

"Negative. It's still on a firm heading for Nagasaki. I'm going to scan the frequencies again and see if I can get a clearer resolution of—"

"No! Keep this line open!"

"I've got you on speaker!" Miyato said, a little more sternly than was necessary. And then, more politely, he added, "I just need to keep both hands free for the radar."

"Understood," the resigned voice said, and then began to say something else but cut his words short, as if to leave unsaid, *You really don't understand.* In later years, it would occur to Miyato that what the anonymous voice actually wanted to say was, *Please, stay with me. Please.*[16]

13

Koichi Wada had been recruited from school at age seventeen to work as a repairman and driver of Nagasaki City streetcars. His first shift began each day at six a.m. Even during the morning rush hour, for lack of gasoline there were no automobiles on the roads—only horses and a few bicycles. By ten a.m., the number of people, bicycles, and horses on the streets had diminished substantially, and keeping to schedule became easier. The streetcar was no longer packed beyond capacity, with passengers hanging off the sides.

Wada was driving toward the medical school in the Urakami district when he received a radio call about a derailment ahead. The caller had instructed him to alter his route away from the college and return to the Hotarujaya Terminal, almost two miles from the coming hypocenter. He arrived shortly before the clock tower touched 11:00 a.m.

It would soon freeze forever at 11:02. Wada entered the terminal building mildly annoyed that the derailment was going to greatly extend his work schedule for the day, but this was nothing compared to the scolding that the poor driver of the derailed streetcar was receiving from three company bosses.

With all that is going wrong in the world, Wada told himself—*with rumors of fleets approaching and American B-sans openly dominating the heavens (planes that are like nothing any factory in Nagasaki can produce)—how foolish for managers to be so out of control with rage over so minor an incident.*[17]

Time was about to have its say. It always does. The inconvenient incident had diverted both Wada and the other driver from their appointed rounds. At this moment, Wada would otherwise have been near the command center, where a desperate but controlled voice was demanding that Ichiro Miyato stay with him on the phone line. As Miyato soon guessed, the man knew what was about to happen, and was afraid to die alone, without another human voice on the other end.

Miles away, in a different corner of the district, the fatherless child Mami, her mother, and her siblings were completing the same sort of journey from Hiroshima as Kenshi Hirata: returning a loved one's ashes to parents in Nagasaki. They were now traveling by rail through a complex system of hillside cliff cuts and tunnels, in suburbs northeast of the doomed city.

14

For more than three minutes, as they settled in for final approach, someone on the ground kept pinging Jacob Beser's plane—and the bomb's radar-generated altitude sensors—with a powerful radar beam. The B-29 was not the only machine in the sky with bugs in it today. The bomb itself was displaying too much vulnerability. Some sly bastard down below, using a powerful new radar sweep, kept changing his frequencies as if searching for the right one. But luckily, he did not come close—at least, never close enough to the bomb's own echo frequency to bring on a surge of adrenaline for Beser. As the plane sent out radio-wave-jamming frequencies of its own, the bomb's radar engineer could take some small comfort from his observation that the enemy's beam was not aimed in precisely the right orientation for the weapon's nose-forward sensors, nor was the fusing system getting anywhere near Parsons's previously feared self-activation point (even with the added hazard of alpha-particle heat pricklings trying to gnaw like little rats' teeth at the bomb's internal electronics). Nor was *Bockscar* ever close enough for the signal sweep from Miyato's station to be sufficiently strong, and presumably the bomb bay's doors offered enough radar-reflecting protection to keep asleep the "Fat Man," a bomb named after the unhealthy profile of Winston Churchill.

In the cockpit, Charles Sweeney never suspected Beser's realization that, were they a little closer to the source and were they flying in just the "right" direction with the bomb's sensors switched on, the overzealous frequency gyrations of a single Japanese radar engineer's hands could have killed them from the ground before anyone had even a hint that they were all about to die. Sweeney had other worries. He was too busy trying to believe what his eyes were seeing. Nagasaki was now obscured by more than 80 percent cloud cover.

On the heels of this unhappy realization, flight engineer Kuharek announced that *Bockscar* would be down to flying on vapors in little more than a half hour. Although the engineer had finally managed to coax the faulty pump into drawing little dribbles of fuel from the dead bladder, only three hundred gallons remained accessible to the engines. This meant only enough flight time for a through-and-through, single-bomb run, followed by a short dash to a ditching in friendly waters. Sweeney called Navy Commander Fred Ashworth forward. He was the weapons expert, officially in charge of the bomb itself. Officially, Sweeney was in charge of only the plane.

"Here's the story, Commander," Sweeney began, summing it up as fast as he could. "If we can't drop on the first run and if we have to circle back for a second try, we might be forced to crash-land on the ground in Japan. The rulebook calls for getting a visual fix on the target or we can't drop. If we don't get a visual on the first run and then depart, our best scenario is probably losing the bomb and the plane and the crew when we crash in the ocean—unless we try to dump the bomb at sea."

Sweeney told Ashworth that he did not believe in this no-win scenario and that by thinking outside the rulebook, and relying on the plane's radar-imaging techniques, he could plant the bomb near the target.

"You mean, maybe within a half mile?" asked the commander.

"Let's be a little real here, okay? With this thing, a miss is as good as a mile."

"I don't know, Chuck," Ashworth said.

"It's better than losing it in the ocean, isn't it?"

Ashworth gave the question a quick thought and replied, "Are you sure of the accuracy?"

"I'll take full responsibility for this," Sweeney said.

There was no time for discussion with the navigator or the bombardier. Sweeney had confidence that they knew exactly what to do. Jim Van Pelt checked his navigational figures, and Ed Buckley monitored the outlines of the city on his radar scope, inviting verification from Van Pelt and Beser. Buckley then called out the headings and precise closure rates to bombardier Kermit Beahan, who fed the data into the world's first portable computer—which weighed almost as much as a jeep and was connected directly to the plane's bombsight.

The new radar-imaging machinery was Iron Age crude by twenty-first-century standards, though Asimovian and still a guarded secret in 1945. The outlines of the city were fuzzy at the edges, but the river and the rail lines were reasonably easy to see. Just the same, Beahan continued looking out the viewport, searching for a break in the cloud cover.

Keeping his eyes on his own scopes, Beser, who knew Ashworth as the naval officer who introduced him to Norman Ramsey's "fusing team" at Los Alamos, tried to reassure him about the equipment: "If we wanted to—even if this plane had no windows at all—and if we had just a little more lead time, I could ride a scope in the back here and bring you right over the center of Nagasaki."

Ashworth nodded, and asked cautiously, as he had asked Sweeney, "Are you sure about the accuracy of these machines?"

"There's no reason to abort this mission and dump the bomb in the ocean. What the hell? That's ridiculous."

"You own it!" Sweeney called from the front, and turned command of the plane and its payload over to his bombardier.

"I've got it! I've got it!" Beahan shouted. He wasn't acknowledging control of the plane, but rather a hole in the cloud cover that was yawning open directly ahead, near the Mitsubishi armament factories in the industrial valley. The hole was nearly two miles upriver of the assigned aiming point—almost into the wrong district, almost into the wrong town, with much of Nagasaki now shielded behind hilly terrain. Through the opening, the oval-shaped Urakami Stadium was easy to see—as distinct a landmark as Hiroshima's T-Bridge. It looked to Sweeney as if the suburb of Urakami, and not Nagasaki proper, was going to be Ground Zero. The off-center aiming point was (and always would be) perfectly fine with Sweeney. A blast along the river valley would not kill as many people as a central-Nagasaki strike, but every major military factory and dock on Sweeney's map was located along the valley, and he was certain that this bomb would erase all of them. Thirty seconds from release, the tone signal was activated, the bomb-bay doors snapped open, and *The Great Artiste*, flying nearby and ready to drop its three monitoring cylinders, simultaneously opened its own bomb-bay doors.

The tone fell silent, and *Bockscar* lurched upward, suddenly five tons lighter.

Someone had shouted toward Beser, "Bombs away!" and then corrected himself, "*Bomb* away."

Beser watched the fusing and timer telemetry come on again, just as it had with Little Boy above Hiroshima. The bomb's radio signals showed air pressure sensors rising, and the distance between its radar-ranging beacon and the ground shrank with each passing second. Everything on the instrumentation panels was falling perfectly into place, ready to start the whole process rolling. Then all his telemetry disappeared again, and the plutonium fist seized dominion over the world below.[18]

I saw the B-29 in the sky—a plane over Nagasaki, a plane that dropped the bomb. I wonder how many of us who saw the silver plane are still alive. There must have been many who saw it. But I assume most died from direct exposure to the blast and heat rays while, with fascination, they watched the plane.

—Yutaka Kai
(Nagasaki flash-burn survivor),
Messages from Hibakusha

We have to find a way to get along, because we now have the wherewithal to destroy everything.

—Jacob Beser (atomic mission crewman, linked by a family marriage to Hiroko Tasaka Harris)

If you asked the individual [sane] people, from anywhere at all, about the bombing, I don't think anyone would want it. It's war that's bad, not the people.

—Hiroko Tasaka Harris (atomic bomb flash-burn survivor), *The Nuclear Family*

Yamaguchi-san felt the blast of nuclear fire twice, and believed that he became one of a handful of double atomic-bomb survivors for a reason, so that he could spread a message of hope and forgiveness. He became a more highly evolved human. If he could forgive, having become witness to the unimaginable not once, but twice, then couldn't anyone, anywhere, forgive wrongs, real or imagined, that drive human warfare?

—James Cameron, to Toshiko Yamaguchi and Barack Obama, May 2016

CHAPTER 6:
ALL THIS HAS HAPPENED BEFORE; ALL THIS MAY HAPPEN AGAIN

1

Ichiro Miyato's radar station was located almost halfway between John Baxter's prison camp and Ground Zero. At 11:02 a.m., Miyato had just told the anonymous controlled voice at Command Headquarters, "The object should be over Nagasaki now—" when his radar screen overloaded and went completely blank. Simultaneously, the wires inside the speaker phone were seared. During a chip of time in which the telephone at the other end of the line began to vaporize, the many miles of intervening wire swept up some small measure of the fireball's electromagnetic pulse and conveyed the surge toward Miyato at light speed. Had he been holding the telephone receiver to his ear, both he and the officer at the other end of the line would probably have died within the same sliver of a second, though they were more than fifteen miles apart.

At Camp 25, the RAF fighters fleeing overhead could only have meant that a captured island or a carrier-based strike force was nearby.

After the planes had passed, Baxter said to a friend, "It can't be long now."

Then an all-encompassing brightness filled the sky. The Nagasaki bomb blazed forth with at least two—and nearer to three—times the power of the Hiroshima device. The first weapon had flash-desiccated leaves on trees out to a distance of almost ten miles—the second, up to fifty miles. Had it detonated over the forests of California during a twenty-first-century dry season, it would have created a hurricane of flame a hundred miles in diameter, with a probable central "hypercane" reaching up through the stratosphere. And this was the power of a primitive "Model T bomb."

The sudden explosive change of air pressure and the heating of the air itself cleared clouds out of the sky, mystifying Baxter and everyone else who witnessed the disappearance. Even at a distance of nearly forty miles, the rising fireball was "an awe-inspiring sight." The glowing cloud rose almost gracefully, like one of those time-lapse films of a flower blooming. Many seconds later, a great shock wave pulsed through the ground. The airburst arrived almost a minute and a half after the tremor. Baxter happened to be standing in a small ravine. Though the blast was intensely loud, most of its force shot harmlessly over his head, and the nearest hill shaded him from the heat rays until the fireball was at least seven miles high and its energy was all but fractionally spent. Yet Baxter could feel its heat against his face. At this same prison camp, where Baxter and a few fellow slaves were safely cocooned between hills, "others of our party," he recorded, "had been emerging from the mine, covered in black coal dust." Exposed directly to the flash during its first split second, "the coal dust ignited against their skin. Others had the presence of mind (within that first critical half second) to push these unfortunates down into nearby puddles, facedown—which ensured that they were not severely burned."

Alistair Urquhart, another who was shielded between Camp 25's hills, saw something like lightning and heard a tremendous clap of thunder from the south. He had just finished watering and fertilizing plants in the commandant's vegetable garden (where, he knew, every tomato was counted, and to eat one was a sentence of death). Looking back, he would write, "A sudden gust of very hot air like a giant hair-dryer blasted me. It knocked my shrunken frame sideways and I had to drop my bamboo ladle to prevent myself from falling over completely."

He wondered whence the hot wind had come; and because it passed so quickly, Alistair did not give it much thought—until others came to him and described the huge cloud, and blistered skin, and the leaves of tall trees shriveling on the south-facing sides of the hills. Exhausted and thinking himself near death, the Scot concluded, "Something important is happening in Nagasaki."[1]

2

Just beyond two miles southeast of the hypocenter, inside the Hotarujaya Streetcar Terminal, Wada's unfortunate coworker was still being severely upbraided when a series of brilliant flashes filled the world. It seemed to Wada that the entire terminal, floor and all, was lifted off the ground and floated about knee-high into the air, then thrown down as if by a whirlwind, with one of the building's sides smashed in.

Friends pulled him out, uninjured, from beneath piles of broken wood. The survivors could hear people in multiple directions, outside, crying for help. From that moment onward, the streetcar workers self-assembled, optimistic that they still had half a building from which to work. Just as a separate group of trolley drivers and mechanics had done in Hiroshima, Wada's group set immediately about the task of digging people out from beneath debris piles, sheltering the injured, and trying to figure out how to use the streetcars as ambulances.

But from a quick look around during the first three minutes, it was clear that there was no hospital for the injured. In the direction of the main medical school, the central supports of hilltop buildings protruded like antlers of coal tossed upon a sea of thick, black dust. And off to one side, beyond Konpira Ridge, a rotating mass of smoke and fire reared up higher than Egypt's Pyramids. On a hill above the Maria Cathedral, the roof of St. Francis Hospital was beginning to burn. The cathedral itself was mostly gone, looking like an ancient ruin.

Wada's group was more essential than he knew.

The local governor had survived, surrounded by great works of art in a command bunker. He emerged physically uninjured. But once he and his aides climbed a hilltop and observed the magnitude of the devastation, and realized the rapidity with which disaster had descended on them, a kind of mental absenteeism held sway. There would be no rescue operation sent toward the trolley station or anywhere else, by anyone appointed to a position of organizational leadership. No rescue parties would be called in from outside. No medicines would be sent, as Nagasaki's entire central government retreated again to the comforts of shelter.[2]

3

"Oh, no, not again," Kenshi had cried out to his father.

Once again he was slightly more than two miles south of the explosion's center. The first time, distance combined with a voice crying out in his head kept Kenshi alive. This time, in the presence of a bomb up to three times worse, what saved Kenshi was not so much a matter of distance and response as the shielding provided by a tall hill that rose nearly a quarter mile high, thoroughly shadowing him from the heat rays and shock-cocooning him from the blast. Not very far from where Kenshi and his father stood, at the same distance from the hypocenter—and all within those same few seconds—people down in the shipyard were simultaneously flash-grilled, uplifted, shotgunned by flying glass, and hurled through walls. Even nearer, on the other side of the very hill that protected Kenshi and his father, almost everyone who witnessed the detonation was already dead. Only two miles farther north, whence came the light, people were steam and phosphorus, ashes and radioactive fallout.

Behind the hill's protective shadow, Kenshi and his father were merely buffeted by a harsh wind and saw only a few roof tiles loosened. And after the wind had passed, dragonflies still flitted about, seemingly unshaken. *But the ashes . . .* Little Setsuko's ashes, to which he had made offerings of flowers and rice and which he had held close to his chest for most of two days—the bomb had ripped the cover from Kenshi's wedding bowl and flung Setsuko out of his hands.³

4

Ship designer Yamaguchi's section chief was still trying to explain how he did not believe an atomic bomb could possibly exist when the second distinctive atomic flash concluded the argument in Yamaguchi's favor. At a distance just 10,200 feet downriver of the hypocenter, the heat that burst into the room was so great that this time, Yamaguchi believed himself gone.

During the critical first second, Yamaguchi's warnings were instantly recalled, and his listeners dived under tables and behind doorframes. In the end, the section chief did exactly what Yamaguchi had said he should do if he saw the bright flash. Given the intensity of the shock wave bearing down on them, obedience to the engineer's instructions alone would not have been enough if not for the mysterious shock-cocoon effect that seemed to accompany all explosive events. In some cases—as when the mountains on either side of a river focused part of a nuclear shock bubble on a small group of industrial buildings as if they were fleas located in the barrel of a shotgun (exactly as happened to Yamaguchi's building)—in very rare instances such as this, nearest the force of the shotgun blast was sometimes the safest place to be. Like the nose of a Von Braun rocket cutting through supersonic wind, or the trained hand that makes a karate chop through wood, a single steel-reinforced concrete stairwell behind the office where Yamaguchi stood was able to chop through the blast wave. The rest of the building flew apart around Yamaguchi's shock cocoon, and in those other rooms beyond him, some three hundred people died. Only one office, behind the bomb-facing stairwell, survived. In that office, window glass flew harmlessly over the men on the floor, and a mahogany desk became flying wooden daggers; but these men, and no one else, walked away from the building. Even the ground-level lake of instantly superheated air seemed only to

Under the mushroom cloud, within only a few minutes, a hurricane of fire taller than the Pyramids emerged from Urakami's "lake of flames." Just beyond a half-mile radius from the hypocenter, on an overlook where every living creature perished during the first five seconds, the delicate arch of the Sano Tori Shrine still stood on one leg, with the other leg knocked away.

A recovery from symphonic destruction: Upper Nagasaki's Sano Tori Shrine the day after (in 1945), and in 2010.

have eddied around the outside of the office before retreating backward toward Urakami and following the fireball into the heavens.

Nonetheless, Yamaguchi became aware that his burns from Hiroshima were now fully exposed to the increasingly abrasive and random gusts of smoke. Though the blast wave had bounced and diverged as it burst through the Mitsubishi office block, the gale that came with it had blown off all his bandages, and mahogany thorns had penetrated his skin. The young engineer merely shrugged at another strange horror and looked out from the top of the ruins, trying to find home.

In home's direction, everything had been kicked sideways and seared. Then something apparently came through and snuffed out the fires that should now be there. The ground appeared to have been scratched and raked, as if by the devil's talons. Fighting off nausea, chills, and new wounds, he climbed down and began to walk.

Tsutomu Yamaguchi discovered that one side of his house was a curiously intact box, filled with raked table and chair parts, and balcony splinters—all of it sheathed in a veneer of black carbon. The rest was ruin. As Kenshi had done in Hiroshima, Yamaguchi now searched the area and dug frantically for his family, and eventually he came upon a very young child, no longer alive, no longer identifiable. But here, as in other cases, the bomb's effects seemed to go hand in hand with the random deviations of human routines.

Yamaguchi soon found Hisako and little Katsutoshi alive. He also found an answer to what had happened at home. After he left for work on the morning of the second bomb, a cousin's wife came to visit Hisako, bringing along her own baby. Hisako had offered tea and stepped out earlier than usual for what was only to have been a brief errand before her afternoon-through-evening work shift, directing the expansion of a Mitsubishi tunnel. Her husband's injuries from Hiroshima sent Hisako along a path she would not otherwise have taken. She should normally have been at home, preparing lunch for relatives before setting off for work. As the terrible split second approached, Mrs. Yamaguchi walked away to visit a local medicine dealer who knew something about treating burns. Like most young mothers, endearingly overcautious Hisako tended to take Katsutoshi everywhere with her—even when relatives were at home willing to look after her child. While Jacob Beser prepared for the final approach, Hisako's mission to find a remedy for her husband's Hiroshima burns had brought her to the Mitsubishi tunnel-shelter ahead of schedule. Hisako sought out the coolest, deepest part of the tunnel in which to preserve the white skin cream she had bought for her husband. And this was how she and Katsutoshi came to be safely underground when the bomb detonated.

Sometimes, it worked out. "Sometimes by God's will," Tsutomu Yamaguchi liked to believe, "and maybe sometimes, we are alive just by sheer dumb luck."[4]

5

Kenshi Hirata had escaped the firebombings of Kobe and Osaka and now, after only three days, his second atomic bomb. At this point, it was becoming possible for him to wonder if the firestorms might have been following him, as if by plan. There came a certain point, he would tell history, at which one could not help but wonder if the B-29 crews had been seeking him out personally. Many months after the war, he would develop a vitamin D deficiency because he was afraid to venture outdoors and into open daylight. A paranoid reaction, perhaps, but Kenshi, more than almost anyone else during the entire parade of human life that had marched across this planet, could testify that he earned his paranoia, his "survivor's guilt," and his wish for seclusion the hard way.

At Nagasaki, he had survived in a shadow-shield and shock-cocoon zone where the grasses remained green and dragonflies were still circling and diving after prey. Kenshi and his father spent the first few minutes after the blast searching for the metal bowl and tracking down every little clump and streamer of ashes they could find, and among them something that looked like a piece of seashell.

When they reached the house, Setsuko's five-year-old brother appeared at the door and saw the bowl of ashes. The child called out for his parents, noticing that his brother-in-law seemed to be very ill, and scarcely noticing the blizzard of charred paper and clothing that was falling along the street.

The parents gazed with amazement at Kenshi and the wedding bowl.

"Oh, you had a hard time," Setsuko's father said in a calm and uniquely Japanese manner by which multiple feelings and complex messages could be represented by only a few words.

"You had a hard time," Setsuko's mother repeated, and Kenshi understood immediately the real meaning of this: *We are not blaming you. We sympathize.*

Then, in one of history's quintessential examples of how, in Japan, what was said directly and on the surface often conveyed an ocean of meaning, Setsuko's father said, "You were not registered yet with the city, as a couple. Please don't worry."

The words shocked Kenshi. Setsuko's parents were using a legal technicality as a tool for releasing him from what happened to their daughter and from any obligation to her—past, present, or future. They wished him to move forward with his life and, without looking back, find love again one day and raise a family.

Kenshi did not say anything. He simply left the porch; and even in this silent response, a rarely explored depth of emotions was communicated. He was very thankful to the parents for not reproaching him with blame, for instead understanding his situation, understanding his love, his sympathy for Setsuko. And at the same time, their words meant that this was the moment in which their relationship with him was to be terminated. Unspoken, yet said nonetheless: *Because your marriage was not officially registered, we can restart everything. You have your life. We can continue to live together as neighbors, and we will never talk about the contract of marriage.*

According to the traditions of Kenshi Hirata's generation, the wife's family was permanently bound to the husband's family because the parents of the wife either discouraged or encouraged the marriage. *We don't blame you, Kenshi*, Setsuko's father had tried to say. *Blame the parents for the hastened marriage, and for this sadness. We release you.*

"*Please don't worry.*" In that simple phrase was hidden enough meaning to carry him into the next century.

"The true sadness of the moment was unfathomable to most people," Kenshi would tell future generations as the sixty-fifth anniversary of Setsuko's death approached, in 2010. "I felt very sorry for the parents, because they had to say, 'Please don't worry.' I felt so sorry for Setsuko."

The words "Please don't worry" signified, as a rule, the end of all communication between the two families. And yet, after Kenshi Hirata eventually remarried, by 1955—and after a newspaper report mentioned that his children were fathered by a man exposed twice to radiation—Setsuko's parents would help him protect his children from a widespread prejudice and outright shunning that began to arise against atomic-bomb survivors and their offspring. They helped the Hirata family disappear and stay out of history's way.

Even during the 1970s, when an American who studied the physical effects of the atomic bombs applied all his skills as an FBI agent to finding where Kenshi Hirata had fled with his family, he failed to turn up a clue and eventually died without knowing that Kenshi had disappeared in open view. Setsuko's family, Kenshi's parents, and all their neighbors would protect his identity and the identities of his children so well that he never had to move from the neighborhood.

In the end, the same man who slept on the ground where his wife had been carbonized in Hiroshima, desiring only that her spirit not feel abandoned, never lived more than a short walk from the stone pinnacle where Setsuko's parents had buried her ashes. Even after sixty-five years passed, Kenshi continued to make offerings of water at the shrine, keeping his own private promise that Setsuko would never be left behind or forgotten.[5]

6

About the same time that Kenshi Hirata and his father finished collecting Setsuko's ashes from the street, Jacob Beser's pilot and copilot were coming to terms with the depressing mathematics of their situation.

From Nagasaki to Okinawa was 350 miles. After the bomb-drop and the forty-three-second race to get safely away by diving inland and opposite the bomb's path, *Bockscar* and *The Great Artiste* had climbed gradually from 20,000 to 30,000 feet. The way to sea and "homeward" to friendly shores was a parallel along the bomb's drop path. *Bockscar* had only enough fuel for a single flyby reconnaissance, to confirm that the target was indeed destroyed, proving that a miss really was as good as a mile. Later, Beser's de-briefers would call it a "fortuitous" miss, delivering the illusion that the US could reload A-bombs like shotgun shells, along with a narrative that the strike plane had been merciful to the population of central Nagasaki.

At this starting point for the voyage home, Sweeney's engines were burning approximately one gallon of fuel per mile. He was starting out with a total of only three hundred gallons, including a small volume that the flight engineer managed to siphon from the dead bladder. To conserve fuel, they could throttle the propellers back from the by-the-book speed of 2,000 rpm to 1,800 rpm. This would save a little more fuel but not a significantly large amount, by Sweeney's math. So he decided to throttle back to 1,600 rpm, which would, unfortunately, reduce the necessary inflow of lubrication and fail to provide the levels of cooling needed to preserve the engines in fresh-from-the-factory-floor condition. This decision was guaranteed to damage all four engines, but they would be much more thoroughly ruined by a crash on salt water and could therefore be considered a burnable resource.

The throttle-down reduced *Bockscar*'s speed by a hundred miles per hour. They were now consuming three hundred instead of five hundred gallons per hour, but the plane might still drop into the sea fifteen minutes and several miles short of its destination without the additional help of a few glide-extending lessons worked out in Paul Tibbets's math.

Fifteen minutes and more than sixty miles out from Okinawa—and over the original estimated crash point—the fuel supply, though down to barely more than a dozen gallons, was still providing food for the engines. The plane had almost two miles of glide height to spare. Sweeney gave thanks to Tibbets, Newton, and the Lord when finally, the island's runways came into view. Unfortunately, America's closest airfield to Japan was also its busiest. Even ten minutes out, Sweeney could see signs of air traffic over every glide path. He was aiming not necessarily for a proper landing, but more likely toward a controlled crash.

"Yontan. Yontan tower!" Sweeney called out to a receiver who seemed too busy to answer. "This is Dimples Seven-Seven. Mayday! Mayday! Over."

"All gauges now reading empty," flight engineer Kuharek called forward; and immediately after he said this, number 4—the starboard outboard engine—shut down.

"Increase power to number three," Sweeney called back.

The revving up of number 3 steadied *Bockscar*'s starboard wing, but by now their choices had narrowed to one: The only way to land was along a straight-in glide path. Being waved off by a flight controller to "circle 'round and try again" was not an option.

Jacob Beser felt the plane's wings pulling from starboard to port and back to starboard again as the pilot, copilot, and flight engineer tried to balance the power of starving engines on both sides. Amid repeated unanswered calls of "Mayday! Mayday! Dimples Seven-Seven," accompanied by red and green emergency flares signaling *out of fuel*, the control towers continued talking other planes into landing and takeoff patterns as if nothing unusual happened to be barreling in from the horizon.

"Do they have shit in their eyes as well as their ears!" Sweeney shouted to his crew—and then, into the mike, "Mayday! Mayday! I'm calling any goddamned tower in Okinawa!"

Not even static came back. Sweeney put down the landing gear and yelled back for the crew to "fire off every damned flare we have on board!" Every color in the rainbow flashed outside Beser's view aft along the tail gunner's windows, signaling, *Aircraft out of fuel! Aircraft crashed on water, over here! Prepare for incoming crash! Aircraft on fire! Dead and wounded aboard!*

Planes began swerving out of *Bockscar*'s path. They had no choice, because *Bockscar* came in on a swerve with two of its four engines starved to death as the wheels pounded down on the nearest runway. The last swerve banged Beser against the hull and nearly tumbled the plane onto one of its wingtips.

Barely more than ten seconds after Sweeney came to a stop, emergency vehicles were at *Bockscar*'s side. One of them began spraying down the engines, though clearly nothing was actually burning. A medic poked his head up through the nose-wheel door and asked, "Where are the dead and wounded?"

Beser's captain flipped a thumb over his shoulder, indicating the direction of Japan. "Back there," he said, and spoke nothing more on the subject.[6]

7

Time and again, odd coincidence seemed to surround the atomic bombs. But perhaps this was odd only by virtue of after-the-fact probabilities, in the same sense that every individual poker hand is equally improbable as a royal flush (though not as sought-after and, hence, not as noticed). Nevertheless, and especially when the alleged premonitions of children or their parents were involved, strangeness seemed almost commonplace under the bombs of August.

Ten-year-old Tamura Takako's older brother had been accepted into Tokyo's most prestigious school for the gifted, but his father, who was a manager in one of the city's still-functioning industrial plants, worried that Tokyo would be carpet-bombed again, and wanted to send the children away to relatives somewhere safer. Through an entire train trip, the boy cried, demanding that he be allowed to return to Tokyo and be with his father. The boy was missing now and forever would be.

"He might have had a sense of foreboding," Tamura said later. "Safer" turned out to be a nuclear hypocenter. And then there was the proverbial quiet before the storm: The younger friend of a nineteen-year-old woman known only as "Audio Disk #1, Case #1" had gone outdoors during the night before to escape her bad dreams, and would thereafter be haunted by the great many shooting stars she saw, one after another, scratching silent fire across the sky. Case Number 1's friend said, "I feel somewhat weird tonight—so weird." The old mythmakers had advised that meteor storms were to be taken as omens of a plague approaching the city. Another child, "Case #33," would record that the night before the bomb dropped was unusually still under the meteors: "There was not a noise anywhere. It was so quiet, as if every creature had died."[7]

8

Master kite maker Morimoto had emerged from his second Ground Zero, at a radius of only 2.3 miles, with scarcely a scratch. At 11:01 a.m., he was telling his wife about how swiftly the end came for Hiroshima. "First, there came a blinding blue flash—"

A double flash cut his words short, blinking first red, then blue, and then flooding his kite shop in a stark yellow glare. Acting on sheer reflex, Morimoto grabbed his child and shoved his wife bodily down the steps into what until now had been merely a supply cellar, not a bomb shelter. Taking no chances, he pulled the heavy trapdoor down behind him and shielded his wife's and child's bodies with his own. Once the lid was down, thunder exploded instantly overhead.

Close! Morimoto told himself. He did not understand exactly how close until he climbed out of the cellar. The whole top of his shop had been broken off about waist-high, hauled away, and dropped on top of a house across the street. A stove was still sitting in place on the shop floor, with a teapot still on it, but everything else—*everything*—appeared to have been scooped out of the building and taken up into the atomic clouds. Envelopes with his name on them, along with shreds of singed kite paper, were drifting and fluttering along a debris track fifteen miles long. Only much later would it occur to him that if not for his experience of the first bomb, his wife and child should never have survived the second one.

For all this havoc in his life, Morimoto could not imagine yet how extraordinarily lucky he happened to be. Of all the people who ever existed or, probably, ever would exist, only he and Yamaguchi had survived within the total destruction zone of a nuclear Ground Zero *twice*. And only Morimoto had been thoroughly shock-cocooned inside this deadliest zone both times. Moreover, his shop was located in what, by all appearances, became a hole in both the firestorms and the radioactive downpours. His wife and child had suffered no burns or injuries other than the bruises sustained while being tumbled into the cellar. Aside from nausea during the train ride from Hiroshima, Morimoto had escaped the mysterious "disease X," and so too would his wife and child.

The war had already taken many of Morimoto's relatives, and there were times when he believed that the chaos would leave him with nothing whatever. But now he settled back with his wife and child, ever so slightly relieved. The men in the palace would be surrendering by midnight, he told himself. *No doubt of it. What else can they do?*[8]

9

"In the end, all we can do is pray," one of the Jesuit brothers told Dr. Akizuki. Although he was Buddhist, Akizuki understood.[9]

Near the hospital buildings that Wada had seen catching fire high above him along the eastern hills, Jesuits helped the doctors and their students spread mats on the floor of a warehouse and move the patients there. One of those patients was a doctor named Tsunoo, the medical school's dean. At 11:02 a.m., a whole building had splashed apart around him. Students discovered their dean near the center of a wood-framed medical college building, only 1,970 feet from the hypocenter.

At a radius of 0.37 miles, this was Dean Tsunoo's second encounter with an atomic bomb. He had seen Hiroshima go up like smoke from a furnace, then traveled by train to Nagasaki. But this time, though shock-cocooned and shielded from flash burns inside a multistory wooden structure, he was too near the hypocenter. In a zone where every living thing outdoors—from people and horses down through insects and bacteria—had instantly ceased to be, layers of thick ceramic

Dr. Nagai of Nagasaki was a patient in his own hospital, terminally ill with bone-marrow cancer, when evidently just the right amount of gamma-ray and neutron spray dosing—which has a suppressive effect on cancer and other rapidly dividing cells—pushed his illness into remission. He rose from his deathbed to become the caretaker of his caretakers; and he began to organize rescue and recovery of other survivors. Located deep within a hospital so close to the edge of survivability that many people near the outer walls, on the bomb-facing side of the building, received lethal doses from the bomb's prompt radiation effects, Dr. Nagai's remaining life expectancy of three months was extended to six years. His home was located downhill of the hospital, much nearer the hypocenter, in a region where people were typically converted to charcoal and blast-ring dust. He discovered his wife's metal crucifix, with its glass rosary beads melted.

tiles and wood could no more prevent an immense dose of gamma rays from reaching the doctor than ordinary glass could prevent sunlight from shining through a window. A surge of neutron spray and microwaves likewise penetrated every cell in his body.

Dean Tsunoo's survival seemed particularly miraculous, then random, then cruel. He had been situated in precisely the right place, with structural beams aimed in just the right directions to divert the nuclear blast around and away from him. The building was essentially flattened and broken up into sticks, and the implosion of the shock bubble was evidently strong enough to put out the nearest flash fires as it hoisted most of the wooden structure's upper half into the sky and scattered it in pieces over a very wide area. Dean Tsunoo had been examining a patient when the school seemed simultaneously to compress and fly apart. After the explosion, students ran downhill from the main medical complex specifically to dig their respected dean out of the ruins, dead or alive—and then, as "a miracle," they discovered him still alive. The blast effect seemed to have parted around him so perfectly that concussive damage to the lungs—an injury typified by the coughing up of blood—was not evident at all. Though he could stand with help and even speak, and though he appeared physically uninjured, the dean's bone marrow was dead already, and most protein production throughout his body had ceased. Chromosomes were broken, scrambled, and strewn about, all in a matter of seconds, under nearly three times the maximum survivable human dose of radiation.

Outracing the approaching flames, the students ran uphill to the main Urakami medical complex, carrying the increasingly lethargic dean with them.

At first, the dean's friend, Dr. Paul Nagai, was optimistic. "Our president is here!" he shouted as the students laid Dean Tsunoo down on a straw mat. "This place is our new headquarters." Dr. Nagai did not seem to understand. No one did. No one could.

Dean Tsunoo tried, even as he began to fade, to assess the situation and to give his best possible advice for the rescue operation. Almost every cell in Tsunoo's body was leaking and shutting down, yet his brain and his iron will appeared not to recognize death. He continued for a little while longer to draw breath and animate destroyed flesh. Meanwhile, several nurses who had been clawed by speed-slung glass and touched by the rays seemed to be succumbing to a group dementia. They hurried to the dean's location carrying a white linen sheet. As Dr. Nagai continued to call, "All staff, come here," one of the nurses obsessed over creating a flag as a symbol for Dean Tsunoo, and her colleagues followed. "All of us threw ourselves almost as falling down onto [the white sheet], and painted the rising-sun symbol," one of them would record later—"using the blood on our bodies. I [gave] lots of blood [that was on] my body, to the flag."

They hoisted the flag of blood and white cloth to continuing cries of "All staff, come here!" Already, though no one would be aware of it for many months, Dr. Nagai, who on the morning of the bomb had been a terminally ill patient in his own hospital, was being pushed into a spontaneous remission from cancer by a lower dose of the same gamma rays that killed the dean. They all were surrounded by the incomprehensible. One doctor discovered that the blast had forced chips of airborne glass into several patients' lungs. He could hear the glass jingling inside their chests even without the aid of a stethoscope. "Additionally, you can't believe a twig or a leaf will pierce something as a projectile, will you?" he would write later. "Actually, however, I saw something like a twig—[it had] pierced someone's skull, just like an ornament stuck in hair. Unbelievable things could happen indeed."[10]

10

Kinuyo, the fifteen-year-old Hiroshima survivor who walked away with a steel nail embedded like an arrowhead in her leg bone, had despite such injuries assisted soldiers and a small handful of flash-burned doctors on Hiroshima's Ninoshima Island. Now, like Kenshi Hirata and Dean Tsunoo, she was twice exposed. On the second day after the first atomic bomb, Kinuyo was sent to Nagasaki. She arrived aboard the same train as Kenshi Hirata.

After transferring to a second train, she and her little brother were riding just a few minutes north of the river's east bend. They were about to pass another train approaching from the opposite direction and carrying another Hiroshima survivor (Tsutomu Yamaguchi's friend, Akira), when somewhere overhead, the sky appeared to open up—again. They were almost 2.5 miles from the hypocenter. The entire car was bathed in stark, silent white light. From experience, the two kids knew immediately to dive onto the floor. Others might have followed their example. Kinuyo could never be sure of it. In years to come, the sequence of events would shift in memory (hiding between trains, in open air—the people scattering away—then, the blast?—then, a conductor yelling, "Evacuate! Evacuate!"). Many aboard this train and the one approaching did not duck down, did not cover their faces when the sky flashed. Instead, they were moved by another reflex—which immediately, instinctively, turned their heads in the direction of the strange, horizon-spanning light. For all who looked, their irises, corneas, and retinas began to scorch even before a secondary reflex—shortcutting through a nerve arc faster than the actual pain of the scorch—tried to stop them from looking. During the next couple of seconds, being stung by the light and perplexed, some of those still standing or sitting began to crouch down for cover or dive to the floor, but when the blast struck, many more were shotgunned from waist to head by fragmenting windows traveling at more than six hundred feet per second. An assistant conductor climbed out of Akira's partly derailed train and came stumbling between the two sets of tracks. His face was a scarlet stew. After that, Kinuyo's memory of the day became quite blurred.[11]

11

Four-year-old Mami's train from Hiroshima had once again carried her family into a mountainside tunnel when an atomic bomb detonated outside. They were miles past Nagasaki in the northeastern hill country, and the tracks were still navigable, but a tsunami of freshly irradiated black ash blew quickly toward them. Many of the isotopes could last for decades and, once inhaled, would continue to shed DNA-disrupting particles over a lifetime. Mami's fellow passengers, including her mother, would lose their hair, and the child herself would survive multiple bouts of pneumonia that seemed always to stalk after her, ready to pounce the moment she developed even the slightest case of the sniffles.[12]

On the other side of the mountains, near Urakami and in a train traveling opposite Mami's direction, moving toward Fat Man's hypocenter, Yamaguchi's friend Akira Iwanaga once again walked away uninjured from just outside the fringe of a nuclear Ground Zero. He climbed out of a derailed, partly aflame, and now mostly abandoned train. Having known, the moment he noticed the distant flash, to duck and cover spared him. An actual cyclone of flames in the valley below radiated such heat that Akira was being forced uphill through a graveyard of toppled and flash-singed trees, all blown down in the same direction. He came upon five tunnels built into a mountainside, each leading down into a Mitsubishi aircraft factory and linked to subterranean launch ramps for catapulting fighter planes toward the sea. Akira continued climbing uphill, hoping that on the other side, shadowed against the bomb, he might find grass that was still green, and streams that still flowed.[13]

Behind Akira, more than three hundred feet inside one of the tunnels, sixteen-year-old Yoshitomi Yasumi had been working for weeks, deep within a huge labyrinth of interconnected factory caverns, well hidden from Allied aerial reconnaissance. Yasumi handled tools and dies and lathes, producing precisely measured parts for one-way-mission aircraft. And most chilling of all were the newly arrived aerial torpedoes called *Ohka*, a word meaning "cherry blossom."

Yasumi had been conscripted from the Imani Commercial School "to work in great honor for the emperor." The latest generation of "cherry blossom planes" (Ohka) was advertised to the kids as fantastic rocket ships. The newer models would be catapult-launched from their hiding places, and they would be given extended range, to "greet" the American ships before the enemy could come ashore. Those boys selected for training to fly the new Ohka designs were praised (or love-bombed) as "thunder gods." But being revered and granted access to great food in a time of shortages did not always quench their apprehension.

Certain bits of information had leaked out to the cavern kids. Though subsisting on a bleak ration of bean husks and radishes (and longing for the "great food" reserved for thunder gods), Yasumi learned that an Ohka pilot had to be of small stature, with a shoulder width of only fourteen inches so he could fit inside the rocket torpedo. Men had measured every new kid's shoulder width before he was conscripted and driven far from home to the tunnels. Yasumi missed his mother.

At eleven a.m., there had been radio chatter about air-raid activity near Kokura. American B-sans had been shot down. Then they had not been shot down. Then they were . . . *what? Shot down again?*

"There's some kind of confusion here," someone said.

The power went out, never to come on again. Emergency batteries flared and sizzled, and the whole mountain in which Yasumi stood seemed to dance and sway. People near the tunnel entrance were seared and mauled beyond hope of survival, even if they could stand up again. Even before an (unfinished) Ohka fell on its side and broke a wing, even before Yasumi crawled outside and looked down on the steel frame of the submarine works, converted to twisted and tangled vines *tossed upon a sea of fog that was actually fire*, the boy had a sense that *This means I get to live.*[14]

12

Later that day, Jacob Beser received news that the White House had put out an order for a "temporary moratorium" on firebomb raids. Hope sprang throughout the isle of Tinian that a land invasion—which, if not avoided, was sure to be the horror of Iwo Jima, Okinawa, and Saipan multiplied—was now a dead issue. Beser hoped that something was happening in Tokyo, and Truman was giving Japan time to surrender.

Instead of being sent on firebombing raids, the B-29 fleet was reassigned to drop millions of newly printed and distributed leaflets bearing warnings to surrender or face total destruction. The new messages were shorter and much more to the point than any that had been dropped before—"written to deliver the news like poison darts," the crews were told. Some of the leaflets were actually printed as haiku-like paragraphs. They were as close as anyone would ever come to what death threats would look like if they were written by Edgar Allan Poe or Orson Welles.

While Jacob Beser and the rest of the atomic strike force waited and hoped for war's end, a fit of intrigue, rebellion, and suicide erupted in Tokyo, and the emperor became more cut off from the rest of the world than ever before, forced to lock himself in a hidden corner of the palace with a handful of loyal and trusted soldiers.

As Emperor Hirohito secretly recorded two copies of his surrender on phonograph records, an admiral named Ugaki, who sided with War Minister Anami and Field Marshal Hata against surrender, ordered seven bombers to be filled with all the high-level explosives they could carry on a one-way trip. Targeting Okinawa as the presumed source of the atomic bombs, Ugaki contrived his own special suicide mission, using rocket-assisted planes hurriedly readied for action by Mitsuo Fuchida's work crews, while Fuchida himself set out to improve designs for his own squadron, intended to fly out against the American carriers when they approached. As for Ugaki's squadron, Fuchida did not believe that the wannabe engineer's idea of hybridizing rocketry with a propeller-driven aircraft was going to work out very well.

Lifting off with what he believed to be the largest nonnuclear blockbuster bombs ever designed, Ugaki led his planes south. On this day, Allied forces recorded no kamikaze raids of any sort. No record exists of the bombers being tracked and shot down. After Ugaki radioed out, "We have the target in sight"—meaning that the pilots were ready to light their rockets and try to dive down through the sound barrier—they died, though for a long time, many tried not to believe it. The planes simply flew away into legend as a ghost squadron.[15]

13

Joining the Nagai and Akizuki rescue operation, a sixteen-year-old boy (identified as Asahi 2010, Case 2, 77–78, a boy called "2024c") was located deep within Dr. Nagai's hospital at Moment Zero. He did not see the detonation. After the cyclone of fire eventually died away to a smolder, he would write about the revelation of a strange desert that, "all the way to distant hills, is become sticks and cold girders of steel—twisted girders, resembling snakes, and which give the land a horrible look. And it is become all black, as if someone had spilled India ink over the city."

On the night of Tsunoo's death and the blood flag, 2024c, who would in only a few days inhabit a world swarming with clouds of ravenous flies, recorded that when he slept outdoors during the first night after the second atomic bomb, there had come a total absence of mosquitoes and moths. He guessed (probably correctly) that they all must have been seared out of the air by the white flash.

C would live to regret a rescue expedition that saved no one. Near a trolley car where glass had transformed into vapor and where the shock-cocoon effect, here and there, had left carbonized figures still standing, he saw the statuesque corpses of a mother and child with the tin of dumplings they had opened for lunch. Both were flash-fossilized with the food uneaten in their mouths. At the edge of a rail line that was not twisted beyond use and along which a rescue trolley could still travel, C tried to help three volunteer firemen carry burn victims on stretchers, but the jostling seemed only to worsen their agony, and the boy returned to the place of the blood flag, feeling little except guilt.

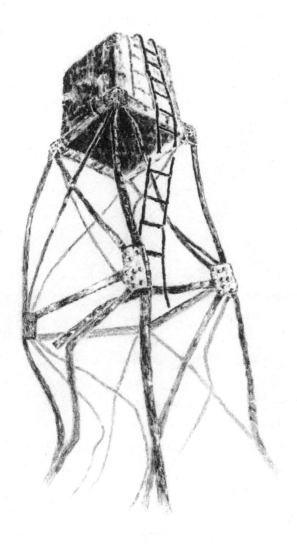

More than a mile away from the Nagasaki detonation, the atmosphere was compressed so severely that air and rods of steel, during one small part of a second, behaved indistinguishably—as if they were both compressed together as part of the same fluid in motion. A second later, the effect had passed, yet its footprints remained "fossilized" in the frame of a water tower.

At the blood-flag hilltop, patients lay on mats in a machine shop turned into more a hospice than a hospital.

"Do you know how the telephone poles fell down?" he would ask history, and would then answer, "The poles stood upright in the hypocenter but leaned more and more with distance from that point. This too was a peculiar characteristic of the destruction." Gone. A-bombed. The whole city. Left to the whim of rain and the winds.

And C concluded, "It resembled a Chinese poem: 'The country is destroyed, and the only thing left behind is nature.'"[16]

14

During the first week after Hiroshima, it had been difficult for little Masahiro Sasaki to sleep even in the imagined safety of a small shed, in a green countryside far from the fields of ashes. The four-year-old's bones still ached from the incomparably cold blackness that had reached down from more than fifty thousand feet into the half-flooded lifeboat. Though the black rain initially brought Masahiro and his little sister Sadako relief from the scorching glare of the city—which was burning brightly on both sides of the river—it arrived with the same perplexing blast of coldness that touched Tsutomu Yamaguchi in the potato field. After providing only fleeting relief, the freezing black rain terrified the two children. "Sadako's tiny body trembled without stopping," Masahiro would record years later. "Her teeth chattered. Her lips turned blue." It seemed to him a marvel that he and his sister did not freeze to death. And yet, barely more than a city block away, their adored, sacred grandmother burned.

In dead Hiroshima, a new peril was only now about to be born. Uncounted hundreds of children and young teens were suddenly orphaned. In these times in Japan, a child without parents was considered shameful, viewed only as something to be cast out from society and left to the fate of the streets. The strongest among the atomic orphans would soon begin to organize, to emerge from the ashes and the black rain as the next generation's crime syndicate. In the decade to come, Masahiro's childhood would be haunted—terrorized by a severely scar-faced and merciless postatomic apparition who, with his teenage henchmen, was going to invade the house and extort from Masahiro's parents everything they tried to build. The gangster orphans would invade everywhere and unceasingly, like locusts.

This was the kind of future that projected itself toward Masahiro like a leering, flash-burned sadist. The recent past was bad enough; and yet, he managed to find beauty even in horror. To each person who witnessed the last moments of the old world, the sound of the blast, the color of the flash, and even the duration of the detonation seemed to be recalled individually, uniquely. Masahiro remembered dozens of lights twinkling and hanging in the air and would write later that they filled the atmosphere with "a magical sparkle, unlike anything [we] had ever seen before. The beautiful brilliance of the glistening lights overhead transfixed [everyone] . . . then . . . it sounded like everything in the whole world was being destroyed."[17]

15

Although President Truman had quickly threatened to follow Hiroshima with a nuclear "rain of ruin," his real feelings might have been a little different from what most people would suppose then and for decades to come. After receiving news about the second atom bomb, a senator had sent a telegram cheering the "rain of ruin," and he called on the president for the more expansive use of atomic weapons. Harry Truman's reply was written the day after Nagasaki, with still not a whisper of surrender coming from Japan. On this day, Truman knew (and certainly did not want anyone else to know) that America was fresh out of atom bombs. The president also knew that at least two new bomb cores were in the manufacturing pipeline, scarcely more than two weeks from completion. And the first news of radiation bursts recorded and transmitted to the planes from Luis Alvarez's parachute-mounted monitoring devices, combined with Paul Tibbets's brief report of silver fillings crackling and melting in his teeth almost ten miles from the blast, hinted that new and unexpected horrors must now be playing out on the ground for people located many miles closer to hell than Paul Tibbets's teeth.

Knowing this, and embedded in one of history's loneliest moments, Truman replied to the senator:

> I know that Japan is a terribly cruel and uncivilized nation in warfare. But I cannot bring myself to believe that because they are beasts we should, ourselves, act in the same way. For myself, I certainly regret the necessity of wiping out whole populations because of the pigheadedness of the leaders of the nation. And for your information, I'm not going to do it [a third time], unless it is absolutely necessary. It is my opinion that after the Russians enter into the [Pacific] war, the Japanese will very shortly fall down. My objective is to save as many American lives as possible. But I also have humane feelings for the women and children in Japan.
>
> Sincerely yours,
Harry Truman

As history would have it, the letter was to be discovered and revealed in 2015 by the president's grandson, Clifton, and by Clifton's friend—a child of Hiroshima named Masahiro Sasaki. And for reasons no one in 1945 could have anticipated, seven decades after the bombs of August, Clifton and Masahiro would place beside Harry Truman's letter a tiny paper crane folded by Masahiro's sister, Sadako.[18]

To every man is given the key to the heavens. The same key opens the gates to hell.

—Buddhist proverb,
about AD 700

With rockets and nuclear power we can reach out to the planets, and beyond . . . if we can stop making ballistic missiles . . . if we can stop World War III.

—Arthur C. Clarke,
while scripting *2001: A Space Odyssey*, AD 1965

Houston, Tranquility Base here. The Eagle *has landed.*

—Neil Armstrong,
after landing a rocket named
Eagle on the moon, AD 1969

You live in the shadow of the third great shaking of the world. Look to the eagle, for you will see her fly her highest in the night, and she will not stop until she sits upon the moon. When this sign is seen, when the eagle has landed, it will mark the [time]—in which we must learn to live correctly . . . as one human family, or the shaking of the world will begin—and the houses of mica, seen in a great city, higher than the tallest tree and gleaming in the sun, are smoke and ruin . . . The keepers of wisdom watched as the warning of the first shaking was forgotten. The second shaking has come and gone, and still there is hatred among the family of human beings. They spoke of the warriors in the sky who dropped the gourd of ashes upon the land. The nation who dropped the gourd of ashes must be warned, for if the third shaking comes, it will fall upon its makers.

—The Cherokee Proverbs of
Twisted Hair, recorded AD 1880

CHAPTER 7:
THE FALLEN SKY

1

The day after Nagasaki, four days after *Enola Gay*, a curious calm settled over Hiroshima. The normal human responses to mass-grave funeral pyres and roving black fog banks of flies were much dulled. On August 10, Haruno, the sixteen-year-old streetcar engineer, was making semi-regular stops near the Prefectural Girls' High School—which, minus most of its roofing, had also become a makeshift field hospital. She had "a tough time" there, trying to come to terms with the vagaries of disease X: "Friends were now patients. In the auditorium, even people who looked energetic and healthy were suddenly staggering and dying one after another. I didn't see anyone shedding tears at the school. We must have been too busy to cry."[1]

In Nagasaki too, even as major portions of the city still burned, streetcar drivers had quickly begun to organize rescues. No medical supplies were being trucked in under orders from Government House, even though Dr. Nagai's team had confirmed that numerous requests to the governor's mansion were received and acknowledged.

Kinuyo Fukui, the fifteen-year-old volunteer medical assistant who had survived both atomic bombings and who still carried an iron nail bone-embedded in one leg, was nonetheless offering help wherever she could between searches for her mother near the newer hypocenter. She was also fighting against the realization that she and her brother were now (without doubt) orphans, and fighting just as hard against early symptoms of what others were beginning to describe as a mysterious disease associated with "death sand" from the bomb. "But don't worry," someone said. "You and your brother will be okay."[2]

Streetcar engineer Wada had accepted that his mother vanished the day before, and now he feared that worse things might be coming. As in Hiroshima, survivors who had seemed well were suddenly lethally ill. Others were badly flash-burned, but there were no antiseptics except those that could be distilled from local weeds. Wada felt that he could do little more than comfort the dying with his words. He lied to people who were carried to his streetcar with hideous burns: "Stay with me. You're going to be okay."

Despite all that was plainly visible, legend would have it that in the flash-burn zone, all the people who left shadows on the ground were instantly carbonized and desiccated like burned paper and died painlessly. This was true only near the two hypocenters, in places like the vanished wooden schoolhouse where Wada found children "lying or sitting in the hypocenter circle like little black rocks." Farther afield, the reality of the shadow people was much worse than this. Two miles out, every person who was severely flash-burned on one side of the body had left a shadow on a wall, or on wood, or in the grass, or along whatever else stood nearby. Usually, they staggered away from their shadows burned and slowly dying. There were also shadow cats, shadow clotheslines, shadow horses, and shadow birds.

"Stay with me," Wada had said to people whose skin along one whole side of their bodies had been converted to something like blackened parchment. "You're going to be okay." In all but a very few cases—the thirteen-year-old Hiroshima girl who would eventually marry into Jacob Beser's family being one of the rare exceptions who actually survived—the people who walked away from their shadows lived only two or three days.[3]

Despite the horrors, ordinary people thrown into extraordinary history (among them the streetcar drivers) continued coming to the fore and setting about the task of rescue.

The OSS man, Walter Lord, would find nothing unusual or even remotely paradoxical in this phenomenon when he heard of it. He already knew that essentially the same thing had occurred after the 1906 San Francisco earthquake. While Frisco's government authorities proved effective at little except afterward denying and covering up the number of people killed, there too it had been the cab drivers, a few doctors, and even a traveling theater group that organized and became first responders in the rescue effort.

Looking back with the twenty-twenty hindsight of 1993, Walter commented to former secretary of the army Stanley Resor, "There have always been natural leaders who never, under normal circumstances, get a chance to lead. They are all around us. Under normal conditions you may never notice them. They probably don't even know, themselves, how they will behave until the day they are needed."

"And the ones in authority are usually there just because they're good competitors," added Resor from this same point in futurity. "When havoc strikes, it is the ones who are officially in charge who often freeze or become unhinged. That's when the true leaders, who might not be near the top simply because they have the good sense to avoid competitive, backstabbing people, rise to the occasion and assume the role of hard, risky leadership that no one else, in time of crisis, really wants."

Stanley Resor had witnessed, and understood on a deeper and more dangerous level than almost anyone alive, the leadership paradox. During the Nixon administration, he had so admired his commander in chief that he became a framer of the White House "enemies list" and put his own son (an antiwar activist) on it. Resor was present one day, trying to console his old friend as the 1974 Watergate scandal reached crisis level. President Nixon, seeking council between bouts of talking to paintings of Lincoln and Eisenhower, said, "Do they not realize that

I could get on that phone and in ninety minutes, seven hundred million people could be dead?"

Resor did realize something then. He really did. It astonished him that this man could even be harboring such thoughts over what was, at bottom, nothing more substantial than a bad career move. Nixon became a walking nuclear time bomb, its fuse lit initially by an obsessive belief that presidential candidate McGovern was colluding against him with the Russians and must be spied on by any means necessary. During the height of the Nixon crisis, with the aid of General Alexander Haig, a plan was put into action making doubly and trebly certain that no branch of the American military would obey a presidential order to launch missiles without visual confirmation and radiologic surge evidence of nuclear detonations on American soil. Until the crisis ended, even if incoming missiles were detected, America was in a nuclear "stand-down-delay" mode. The Russians (presumably) never knew. Resor believed that Nixon left the White House and was fated to die without learning the truth. After the incident, Resor became an effective advocate for massive reduction of nuclear arms—to deeply limit the odds of a nuclear war occurring, whether by blunder or by depravity.[4]

Ever since Moment Zero in Hiroshima, through and beyond the moment of Nixon's threat, perhaps the most important question facing human civilization has been not how inadequate leaders got that way, but what characteristics of human nature cause civilizations to so consistently choose the most dangerously inadequate and elevate them to positions of authority where they can inflict the greatest harm.

2

On August 10, 1945, although the emperor had by now decided to send out a message of surrender, some of the higher-level warlords had other ideas. Only their belief that the emperor was sacred and could not be harmed kept him alive.

As Japan's spotter planes were permitted by Allied forces to see and call home about a gathering storm of American ships in groups five across and twenty deep, War Minister Anami refused to believe that the armada spelled Japan's defeat. Along with three other warlords, he insisted that an all-out bombing raid on the convoy "might make the Americans rethink their actions."

A general named Mori was ordered by one of Anami's officers to join him in the coup against the emperor. When Mori refused, he and his aide were shot and hacked to pieces.[5]

3

At Prison Camp 25, only one day after Nagasaki, Baxter and the other slaves could see immediately that the commandant knew much more than he was letting on about the fiery dragon that had risen above the highest clouds and breathed hot air on the camp from nearly forty miles away. There had been no rousting awake of POWs the morning after. Instead, the commandant declared a day off from work. "A holiday," he had called it. All mining operations, all equipment repairs, were shut down. The next day too was a day of no activity—unprecedented. Rumors began taking root around the camp, then taking flight and often becoming fantastical (albeit not quite so fantastical as what had actually occurred).

Tamie Ekashira was a resident near Camp 25 on the day Nagasaki exploded. She traveled on foot toward the mystery in the south. In the Urakami hills, during the camp's third day of rest, she discovered a blast-flattened forest. Descending from the forest into the center of a new desert, its bricks swept by sheets of shifting "death sand," she came upon telephone poles, blackened but still pointing at the sky as if somehow protected from the blast. Not very far from the silent school Koichi Wada had visited, a streetcar stood eerily intact. Here, people must have been instantly vaporized all the way down to their bones. Particles of sand-mist—rising into the air at more than fifteen times the boiling point of water—would have cooled the moment they encountered the comparatively cold streamers of vaporizing blood, so that a trillion microbeads of molten glass and the air that enclosed them spontaneously imploded against, and solidified around, the bones and tendons of the passengers. In this manner, if a man in the trolley happened to be speaking, his skeleton was flash-fossilized in mid-word—"the dead-alive effect." Tamie beheld a skeleton woman bearing a skeleton child on her shoulder. The woman of bone and black glass was still holding onto a glass-veneered streetcar strap. The skeletonized driver's hands were still clasping the wheel. During an instant of paradoxical mercy, he and the passengers all appeared to have been killed before they could flinch.

At night, from high in the hills, one could actually see the danger to which Tamie had exposed herself by venturing so deep into the desert, so soon. A faint bluish glow emanated from the central ruins, here and there outshining some of the stars. The worst of the radioactive isotopes were already fading from existence; but the nightglow would last for several weeks more, and people would continue to die in ways that people never imagined people could die.[6]

4

Near the southern fringe of Nagasaki's Ground Zero, ship designer Yamaguchi, his wife Hisako, and their child were among the few creatures still moving. Though inexplicably alive after two atomic blasts, Mr. Yamaguchi was becoming increasingly lethargic and depressed.

The engineer side of his brain told him, logically, to be grateful that his burns from Hiroshima had sent his wife along an improbable path, at just the right moment, to the tunnel she had been constructing for her employers. Nevertheless, Yamaguchi's heart told him that his siblings were dead. His cousins were dead. A cousin's wife and their infant child lay dead in what little remained of home.

Hisako's family was near the hypocenter—gone. Yamaguchi and little Katsutoshi were all she had left, and she began to fear that even this would not last. A tunnel had become their only home, and as

Mr. Yamaguchi's depression grew, his left arm and one whole side of his face had begun to swell like balloons inflating, turning purple and quite painful. The burns on his arms became gangrenous and started sprouting nests of fly larvae, at which point Yamaguchi passed out and could not be roused awake.

Hisako tried to remove the maggots, but someone who seemed to know something about medicine arrived at the cave and insisted that she leave the maggots living in her husband's skin, for they removed only dead and putrefying tissue. The idea sounded to Hisako like an old wives' tale, but she put her faith in the visitor and decided that even if it was only a myth, if it healed her husband's burns and he recovered she would believe in it. She helped the newcomer feed her semiconscious husband strange new concoctions made from persimmon leaves, dried rose hips, and any other sources of vitamin C that could be found, and she was instructed to cook him helpings of liver from any animal—even from rats, if they could be found. She became convinced over time that had she taken Mr. Yamaguchi to one of the woefully overwhelmed and undersupplied first-aid centers near Governor Nagano's side of central Nagasaki, he would surely have died.

Little by little, the blisters stopped discharging blood; and the maggots, hour by hour, removed dead and gangrenous flesh until Hisako believed that the bones in her husband's arms might soon be exposed. But in the end, the fly larvae left behind only living tissue that still had a healthy blood flow.

The visitor had sprinkled a powder of crushed grape seeds and talcum on the wounds to dry them out and prevent further infection. He also suggested attaching live leeches to the still-living flesh that surrounded the worst of the burns, explaining to Hisako that leeches (their mouthparts exuding anticoagulants) would keep blood circulating through her husband's wounded hands and prevent his fingers from dying and having to be amputated.

It would all have been dismissed as witchcraft by her ship-designer husband, but he was semicomatose and now living under the advice of the only house-calling doctor in town, so Hisako obeyed the "witch doctor" and spent uncounted hours searching for leeches and gagging on the bitter mineral water given her by the visitor. The concoction reeked of chalk and something mixed with miso that tasted how iodine smelled. In years to come, Hisako would leave physicians perplexed with assertions that except for irritability and brief bouts of vomiting, she and the baby did not get sick at all during their stay in a tunnel on the edge of a radioactive no-man's-land. And except for permanent blast-induced swelling that left him mostly deaf in one ear, and flash damage to his hands and scalp, Yamaguchi would make a full and equally perplexing recovery.

The strange visitor Hisako would forever regard as her guardian angel refused her offers of thanks and devotion. In later years, Tsutomu Yamaguchi would become certain that these were the remedies of his favorite pre-war basketball teammate, Dr. Nagai. He could never be sure whether Nagai himself had made the visit. Like most true heroes, Yamaguchi's rescuer simply walked away from history's stage.[7]

5

Since returning to Tinian Island, Jacob Beser had seen the promising news of August 10 come and go with no word of the hoped-for surrender from Japan actually coming through. The moratorium against bombing with anything worse than printed leaflets of harsh language had continued through the nights of August 11 and 12 and through Yamaguchi's fever.

In Washington, no one knew yet how a deadlock in Tokyo had evolved into a palace revolt that, in essence, muzzled the emperor. On the evening of August 13, President Truman authorized General George Marshall to resume firebombings against Japan. During the predawn hours of August 14, every one of the more than 2,500 aircraft within striking range was sent against the Japanese mainland. The palace and one or two other places were to be spared, at least temporarily. Aside from these, even a cow farm came under consideration as a mission objective, given the increasingly apparent scarcity of targets.

6

In Tokyo, General Tanaka and his staff received and compiled reports of air raids that appeared to be taking place virtually everywhere. By lunchtime, the general had confirmed to his own satisfaction that the approaching armada—which Anami insisted on dismissing as "only a phantom fleet of rumors"—did indeed exist and was slowly, surely preparing to take aim directly at Tokyo. With the advance of the Soviet army into Manchuria, combined with the armada, and finally the massive firebomb raids of August 14, the palace deadlock was broken. Tanaka withdrew his support for the military coup, and most of its leaders promptly ended their own lives on the palace lawn. War Minister Anami wrote, "I apologize to the emperor for my great crime," wandered off to get drunk, and committed ritual suicide with a ceremonial blade. Here too, Anami proved inefficient. It took him three hours to die.

Three hours . . . some justice, John Baxter supposed when he eventually received the news.

Jacob Beser's Nagasaki pilot, Charles Sweeney, after hearing about the broadcast of Emperor Hirohito's surrender recording approximately twelve hours after the last August 14 raider dropped its bombs, noticed that the emperor had scripted a reference to America's use of "a new and most cruel bomb" into the recording. To Sweeney, the real power of the atom bomb, insofar as quickening the war's end, was to give the emperor something to use as an excuse for surrender, yet allow him to save face while doing so, by referring to the victor's unfair use of an overpowering weapon.

And yet, behind the scenes, the emperor knew everything about Dr. Nishina's atomic-bomb designs and foresaw the path humanity might have followed if both Japan and America and maybe one or more other countries developed the weapon. In the very next sentence of his surrender, with perfect hindsight on his own country's wartime nuclear program, he said atom bombs might ultimately lead "to the total extinction of human civilization."[8]

7

At Camp 25, Baxter and the others had noticed the extraordinarily large numbers of B-29s going to and returning from bombing raids. They did not hear the emperor's surrender. On that day, a camp overseer broke down into tears, saying only, "This is a day of mourning."

For another five days, nothing happened. Nothing at all. Food remained scarce, but the mines were idle. The prisoners were allowed to rest. On the morning of August 20, Baxter later recorded for his family, "We awoke to an unfamiliar silence from the officers' guardroom and discovered that the entire garrison had departed overnight—rather hurriedly, leaving all of their rifles and equipment." Hyato remained at his post. The commandant had also stayed behind, in his office. He emerged to read an announcement that the war had ended, then turned himself over to his POWs, as *their* POW. Baxter stepped forward with his repair team and offered that they would assume responsibility for his safety until Allied troops arrived—a sentiment that might never have prevailed if not for the humanity of the commandant's guard, Hyato.

The only postsurrender killings in the camp involved the officers' pigs and chickens. The same tomatoes that, if eaten only a week before, would have led to a prisoner's summary execution were now plucked at will.

There was no shouting or cheering among the prisoners. Those who had survived were too weak. There was no feast, either. The camp's medic warned that eating too much too quickly, when so near to starvation, could prove very uncomfortable and even deadly. The commandant cut free his officers' food hoard—large enough to provide one small can of meat or fish for each of nearly three hundred men. Baxter supposed that whatever had been happening outside the camp must be really frightening to cause a bug-out so hurried that the officers and soldiers left such a precious hoard behind.

"We're not out of the woods yet," Baxter announced. "We're still surrounded by a potentially hostile Japanese community." That night, sentries were posted around the perimeter, armed with guns left behind by the bug-out crew. They kept watch against locals trying to enter the camp.

There were no attacks.

Two days after that, a Red Cross team arrived with a two-way radio, then opened up direct contact with Okinawa. From the island's command headquarters, Baxter and the other ex-POWs were instructed that they were now the front line of an army occupation force until General MacArthur arrived to organize a new administration for Japan.

"We have an urgent need for food, medical supplies—even clothing," the camp's Dutch physician radioed out. MacArthur himself called back, instructing them to mark drop zones for B-29 supply runs and assuring them that the drops would commence within hours. Of just over 250 POWs still alive at the Camp 25 mine, only seventy were strong enough to help with the recovery of supply crates as they parachuted (or sometimes meteored) in.

By August 23, the B-29s had delivered an overenthusiastic oversupply. Meanwhile, the POWs learned, for the first time, that nearly three thousand Chinese slaves needed help at a second camp nearby. In trucks that were now working perfectly, Baxter set off with a convoy of supplies. The Chinese POWs were "a ragged multitude of scarecrows who cowered away from us as we dismounted our trucks . . . having survived cruelty and forced starvation that made our own experience pale [by comparison]."

That night, after the Dutch physician determined that many of the Chinese POWs were too far gone to survive, a desperate Japanese soldier who spoke some small amount of English approached Baxter and begged—"all but demanded, as if still a prison guard"—that Baxter assist in writing a job recommendation to work for General MacArthur's approaching forces.

Baxter and two of his friends enthusiastically completed the forms, signing their recommendations as "Donald Duck," "Hey, Moe!" and "King George VI." Baxter added a final instruction at the bottom: "To whom it may concern. Please kick this man's ass as far as Kingdom Come, and back again."

Hyato appreciated the sentiment.

During the next two days, B-29s continued to drop supplies. Weapons also arrived, along with four medics. The repair shop team learned from Hyato that there were hospitals nearby with many malnourished children, along with civilians injured during firebombings of the towns. "It was the Christian thing to do," Baxter decided, "to return them an empathy rarely felt for the POWs." They set out for the hospitals in trucks, offering Camp 25's oversupply of food and medicine, with Hyato assisting as a fluent translator.

During one of the aid excursions, Hyato invited some of Baxter's team to his home in a nearby village—"for a meal and green tea with his wife," Baxter would tell *The Japan Times* in 2010, after Hyato's death at age eighty-nine. "He was twenty-three years old when I first encountered him." Baxter remained perplexed about an enemy who "never had a hard word for us"—*and who fed us, even as we sabotaged some of his machinery!*

Only after he visited the village and Hyato's house did Baxter finally realize how great a burden the extra food rations they supplied to the POWs must have placed on the prison guard's family members.

"I believe they were moved to their actions by their faith. They were Buddhists, but Buddhists had to hide their faith during the war."

And that little meal at the house really did turn into the beginning of a most unusual friendship between a POW and the guard who saved him.

The date was August 25.

As the clock touched midnight on September 2, a typhoon began to sweep through the area, washing much of the Nagasaki ash layer out to sea, along with Ground Zero's nightglow. Days later, the former POWs began an expedition to Nagasaki, where ships were arriving to bring them home. The sights that confronted Baxter were difficult to comprehend: "The midair burst had created an effect that I could only compare to a giant scythe. Almost everything seemed to have been cut off about three feet from the ground—and everything still standing above that level had been scorched as if by a giant blowtorch."

Reinforced concrete buildings and chimneys had retained some of their original shape, but the steelwork skeletons of the factories that surrounded them resembled crushed birdcages, with the occasional jigsaw piece of brick and mortar still adhering. The iron girders of a water tower were reeds bending in the wind. At the river's edge, a quarter-mile-long Mitsubishi factory was a mountainous tangle of steel. In the river beyond, sunken ships and unrecognizable debris spread across the entire water surface.

Baxter learned that on the morning of August 9, "Several survivors from the hell ships had been sent to dig shelters and Ohka launch [tunnels] in the hills . . . A ship carrying two hundred [new] POWs was crossing the bay, toward the excavations, when the ship burst into flames under the light of the bomb and could afterward be seen from the shore, slowly sinking. There were no survivors."

At dusk, the Camp 25 crew had crossed the ruins and reached a harbor in the south, where the aircraft carrier *Cape Gloucester* was in port. John Baxter and Alistair Urquhart climbed down from their trucks. Since his first year in captivity at age twenty-one, the Scotsman had been reduced from 135 to 82 pounds. During the journey across the black desert, apart from the occasional civilians picking their way among broken foundations, there was little sign of life. No birdsong. No cicada buzz. "Everywhere, an eerie silence."

Only as they approached the *Cape Gloucester* was the unbearable silence of the streets broken. Someone had hooked up a phonograph to what was on the verge of becoming the emerging technology of concert-quality loudspeakers. They had been invented in a hurry only months earlier, in a partly successful attempt to convince civilians at Saipan and Okinawa, in clear, amplified, and only minimally distorted words of Japanese, that rumors of American cannibals were lies from the warlords, and to "please, *please* stop killing yourselves and your children . . . No one is here to hurt you. We will help you."

Now, from the flight deck of an aircraft carrier, those same amplifiers and speakers—equipment directly ancestral to hard-rock concerts from Tokyo to Shea and into the next century—sent history's first electronically amplified music across the atomic wasteland. For Baxter and the stubborn Scot, this marked, at last, the reality of war's end. The end was announced with Glenn Miller's "Moonlight Serenade."[9]

What-about-ism?—including denial *that segregation camps based on race were really all that bad—because "What about Auschwitz? Wasn't that worse?"* So, to hell with us, then . . . *In the camp, my parents did their best to make life seem normal. As a child, I very readily accepted our new circumstance and adjusted to it. As far as I was concerned, it was normal to line up to use the common latrine or to eat wretched grub in a common mess hall, prisoners in our own country. It was normal for us to share a single small barrack with no privacy whatsoever. And it was normal to stand each day in our makeshift classroom, reciting the words of the Pledge of Allegiance, "With liberty and justice for all," as I looked past the U.S. flag out the window, the barbed wire of the camp just visible behind it.*

—George Takei, nephew of Nobel Laureate Setsuko Thurlow

This year [2010] came the rise of radiation denial and shadow people denial, and even claims in America [in its media] that I, and my experience of Hiroshima, did not exist. The realities of nuclear war are so horrible that there are people who claim Hiroshima and Nagasaki did not happen this way and what I lived to tell is all lies. What do they want? Do they really want a sleep of forgetfulness? So the whole world becomes hypocenters? Don't forget. Never forget. I saw it. We all saw it. No one should ever see it again, for any reason whatsoever.

—Keiji Nakazawa, Hiroshima artist

The truth does not change just because the wolves are howling at it, any more than the moon stops shining.

—Rip MacKenzie and J. R. Finch's First Law

CHAPTER 8:
IS IT DUSK ALREADY?

1

The history of civilization is written in humanity's perversion of nature.

In 1945, the two hypocenters were merely the latest examples. Uranium-235 was, in all essentials, the still-active remnant of supernovae and their colliding neutron-star corpses—which gave our solar system and its emerging human denizens life. Thinking creatures sought out the uranium, coaxed it to beget plutonium, and taught a dead star how to scream out against humanity—twice.

2

In a shelter on the southwestern fringe of Urakami's Ground Zero, Mr. Yamaguchi had remained, at best, only semiconscious after reuniting with his wife and child. Twigs were still embedded in his skin from the Hiroshima blast, and a pebble had gone into his arm like a shotgun pellet. In Mitsubishi's Nagasaki office, one arm had been splinter-blasted with a sampling of all the debris that had whirlwinded through the room.

At one point, Mr. Yamaguchi's wife had tended to his wounds for nearly three days without sleeping, struggling to keep him alive. There was no actual medicine in the shelter, except for miso and the skin cream Hisako had brought with her on the morning of August 9. Nonetheless, a mysterious visitor's odd ideas about allowing the maggots to nest under his infected skin, and about plant remedies and lightly cooked liver, seemed to be working. Unfortunately, Hisako encountered an unexpected difficulty in keeping the chickens under control. They were continually seeking out her semiconscious husband, and from time to time he remembered being awakened by the hungry birds.

"Behave yourself," Hisako warned, "or my husband will have your liver."

And it seemed that every time Hisako turned her back on the chickens, one or two of them managed to sneak past her. They went to Mr. Yamaguchi directly and began pecking and plucking the maggots out of his wounds. One of them apparently pecked too deep, and a half-conscious hand reached out, still with enough strength to crush its neck. Hisako made the bird's liver into a very strong, iron-rich porridge.

The Yamaguchis were living with four or five other families, inside the very same tunnel Hisako had been building for the Mitsubishi offices under the governor's "emergency preparedness protocol."

Aside from feeding the chickens, the next thing Mr. Yamaguchi clearly remembered was awakening in a dark cave one afternoon to the sound of two dozen people weeping. They were listening to a radio on August 15, and the emperor's voice had just announced the surrender.

The tunnel itself was all the evidence anyone really needed to know that the war had been clearly perceived, by those in charge, to be drawing toward its final battle. Yamaguchi's mind had already accepted the fall of Japan, so he went back to sleep and continued to bleed from his nose and bowels.

During the next week, soldiers were sent, under orders from a new deputy governor, to assist survivors from the Mitsubishi offices. By then, all surviving engineers who knew anything about ships or steam-catapulted planes, about submarines or bomb shelter construction, were of keen interest to the American occupation's scientists and engineers. The soldiers, under the advice of Professor Shirabe and Dr. Nagai's house-calling nurses, brought a rich supply of tangerines and cans of peaches.

As Nagai's team had predicted, once Hisako began feeding her husband substantial quantities of fruit, Yamaguchi's health improved to such an extent that by the first week of September, he was able to return with Hisako and little Katsutoshi to their half-destroyed house and to begin thinking about reconstruction. Nonetheless, he was still a long way from being able to make effective repairs. Even if the house had not been cracked and scorched by the bomb ("Oh, that's bad," Hisako said), he would not have been up to the task. Even the saving grace of having the flames blown out by a great wind ("Oh, that's good," Hisako said) left Mr. Yamaguchi overwhelmed; for even if the same fire-snuffing wind had not blown the house in two and bounced it off its foundations ("Oh, that's awful . . ."), he would not have felt like working, no matter that repairing the roof was a straightforward engineering problem.

"I was quite able physically and in terms of basic knowledge," he recalled. But family members had vanished, and none of the neighbors seemed to have survived. "And now, spiritually, I wasn't really quite human anymore. I moved around, day by day, like a machine and not like a husband or a father at all."

The engineer knew that he should be thankful for being alive, but an undeserved guilt started to gnaw at him anyway over the loss of so many friends and family. There was always the sense that somehow, he could have done more. He began to drag guilt and depression behind him like Jacob Marley's chains.

In September, when the rains came, he and Hisako hid under umbrellas in the house. Hisako laughed. Yamaguchi did not—*could* not. He began to think that his soul, if not his life, had been ended by the two bombs. And then he began to think about the fate of Father Maximilian Kolbe, a Franciscan known to Yamaguchi by the more personal nickname of "Simcho." The two met in the early 1930s, when Yamaguchi was still a teenager, while playing basketball with their mutual friend, Dr. Nagai. Being of Polish origins, and because there was suspicion about his sect, Simcho was arrested after the war began. Yamaguchi had learned only recently that his friend was murdered in a place called Auschwitz. The story, as received in Nagasaki, was that a man in the concentration camp had been accused of stealing and hoarding food. He was going to be either "sent to the gas" or hanged until dead and decaying, as an example to the rest of the prisoners.

In actuality, what transpired was a prisoner had escaped from the camp in July 1941. As punishment, the deputy camp commander ordered that ten men be selected to be starved to death in an underground bunker. It was then that one of the ten cried out, "My poor wife; my poor children!"

"Father Simcho made a remarkable decision," Yamaguchi later taught all who were willing to listen. "He actually took the position of [another man] . . . The accused man had a family out there, somewhere beyond the prison walls. Simcho stepped forward so that children might have their father." Father Kolbe survived nearly two weeks of forced starvation, one of the last of the ten still alive. The Germans ended his life on August 14, 1941, by lethal injection. In 1982, Pope John Paul II canonized Father Kolbe for living what he taught: "Love is greater than hate."

With Simcho on his mind, Yamaguchi told his wife of the decision he was finally coming to: "If my life ended on August 6 and August 9, then whatever might come afterward, I should perhaps consider to be my second life?"

As the September rains came to an end, a strange, pearly-white rainbow manifested over Nagasaki. *Like a promise*, Yamaguchi thought. And the rainbow firmed his resolve. What meaning was there in Simcho's example, he wondered, if someone did not remember the missionary and carry on after him and send forth acts of human kindness in his memory, hoping that they might spread like ripples on a pond— *anti*-ripples, perhaps, against humanity's dark half?

Mr. Yamaguchi eventually walked away from engineering, especially

The ruins of Urakami Cathedral, in a suburb of Nagasaki (based on a painting by Dr. Nagai). A reason General Douglas MacArthur made sure the much more powerful Nagasaki bomb became "the forgotten atomic bomb" was that its hypocenter, in the town next door to Nagasaki, occurred above the largest Christian community in all of Japan. Most Americans did not know that something so familiar to them even existed, and MacArthur wanted to keep it that way. And mostly, he did (mostly). In 2022, on Long Island, New York, a small paper container of once highly Classified color slides and movie film turned up at a local flea market (asking price $20, bargained down to $15). One of the films included audio, on a three-minute reel, memorializing American military travels into the remnants of the two cities. Two men came upon Urakami Cathedral in December of 1945. The cameraman describes bringing his soundman and a tripod uphill with him toward the skeleton of Urakami Cathedral, and toward what sounded curiously like singing—a disconcertingly peaceful singing. Both men arrived at the rubble-cleared floor in the skeleton church; and they saw, and they recorded, and they broke down in sobs. The focus of the congregation was a statue of Maria, half melted, her eyes looking skyward, streaming metal tears. And the people were singing "Silent Night."

anything connected to machines of war. As he saw it, his second life gave him only one choice: to regard himself as a victim and nurture hate, or to regard himself a survivor, walk in Father Simcho's path, and treat others with humanity.

And so Yamaguchi decided that his second life would be devoted to the children of Nagasaki. He made a plan to shift from engineering to carpentry. Then, after helping rebuild schools along the Urakami River, he resolved to go inside the buildings and become a junior high school teacher.[1]

3

Kimiko, the seventeen-year-old schoolgirl who had fled the safety of a rescue boat to set out in search of her mother, was among the few in Hiroshima who succeeded in gathering the family back together.

After camping with Mother in the northwest corner of Ground Zero, she found her sister at about the same time the palace revolt ended and Emperor Hirohito broadcast his surrender order.

"My sister's clothes were in tatters and she was wearing a different shoe on each foot," Kimiko would record, adding that if one did not know what happened, it was easy to mistake her for a hobo or a woman who had gone mad. "Her hair had fallen completely out and she coughed up blood. She coughed up a lot of blood. Although I walked through the middle of Hiroshima (and the black rain), I never suffered any major ailment from the radiation. The problem was that A-bomb illness could occur at any time. So even if you were healthy, the worry never went away."[2]

4

Like a desert wanderer of biblical times, Mizuha had done much walking since the day her father found her alone and unharmed near the school where only one other had survived. It was plain that she had much to think about. Even the indoor-shielded child was beginning to feel the side effects of exposure.

Father no longer possessed either the strength or the ambition to assist at the nearby Communications Hospital or at any other rescue center, or even to continue patching broken windows in the home. On the day of the surrender broadcast, he could no longer leave the house. At age thirty-eight, on the morning he returned from a Hiroshima suburb uninjured and shifted immediately to the work of saving lives, it would have seemed to Mizuha or anyone else that no fewer than twenty years more of a healthy existence lay ahead for him. But during the second week after the black rain, Mizuha feared that the remainder of her father's lifespan might really be down to months. When urine turned to blood, it was all too clearly down to weeks. And then days. And then . . .

In October, he was a pyre.

Father had been taking care of his siblings before the war and up through the bombs of August. The two houses still existed, but the family was breaking. Uncles abandoned ship. Food was scarce, and aside from small buried hoards of prewar foreign gold and silver coinage (which, to avoid persecution, had long ago been melted or hammered into unrecognizable five-gram bars), money no longer meant anything.

Glass still scratched at Mother's insides. And not until the first unbroken microscope arrived in the city would anyone be able to see that her white blood cell counts, from week to week, had come to resemble a strange self-limiting leukemia. And no less alarming than her receding physical strength was the emotional withdrawal. At times, she seemed even to recoil from her own children.

Mizuha's sister, Futaba, still had all her hair, and the purple stars were staying away from her, but carcinogen's dark angels, sneaking past a shocked, distracted immune system and having already alighted, were taking a keen interest in meiosis and in Futaba's rapidly maturing ovaries.

At age fifteen, the girls' brother Kunihiro was the oldest child in the family—which, by tradition in Japan, meant everything. From the moment Father died, the boy became responsible for taking care of the whole family. But the damage to his spine left him unable to walk, and it made him essentially unemployable outside the home.

Thirteen-year-old Gyoji became the breadwinner, even as carcinogen's angels began to plow tiny furrows in his liver and plant the first seeds. Gyoji had a talent for making jewelry and fine clothing, which he bartered in Hiroshima's emerging black market.

Kunihiro, whose nervous system overall continued to take damage, had little dexterity remaining with which to help his mother and his siblings. Mizuha, at age twelve, was as gifted with "book smarts" as Gyoji was in the arts and "street smarts." To help her older brother and ailing mother, Mizuha continued to learn first aid and was recommended for a college path toward medical school. But she aimed to remain close to home and take care of her wounded family.

And her aim made Kunihiro believe he had at last become the shameful burden of the family. And in the end, he would decide to set Mizuha and the others free by leaving his life behind.

Kunihiro did not understand that those who continued through life in the aftermath could never heal from that kind of choice. Mizuha, who would become the longest-lived of them, could not stop grieving for him. Ever.

And all around her, as the human tribes forged straight ahead, intimidating one another with nuclear testing (first the Americans and soon the Russians), and as new species of atomic nuclei were detonated into existence like summoned spirits and set free, and as the atmosphere spread quanta-spewing atoms from polar ice cap to polar ice cap and settled them in the teeth of every new child, the people could not discern whether it was they or nature, or both, that had really changed under a young electronic civilization's newest instruments of darkness.[3]

5

Tak Furumoto's exposure to Hiroshima radiation came through a spasm of postwar confusion every bit as strange as the behavior that had sent his family to the Tule Lake prison camp in the first place. There were factions among American authorities. Some proclaimed that no segregation-camp prisoners should be deported. They personally told the families it was unsafe in Japan and they should refuse to go, while others insisted the "No-no" internees *must* be shipped away, and their children along with them, because it was the only way to be sure.

Having refused four years earlier to renounce the emperor, for the very real fear that signing such documents for public release would cause relatives trapped in Japan to be rounded up and executed, Tak's parents were criminalized for now having the temerity to openly denounce the US government's destruction of their home, their business, and four years of their lives without anything even remotely resembling the US Constitution's guarantee of due process. Spoken or written expressions of anger against injustice should normally have been protected under the concept of free speech, but technically, if freedom of expression was committed on internment camp property, America's First Amendment would be deemed *not relevant*. Even expression of a desire to visit Japan and learn what happened to relatives in Hiroshima could lead to an immediate stripping away of American citizenship, without trial.

As Hiroshima's first winter approached, the army transport ship *General W. H. Gordon* also approached, carrying the Furumotos and many other families of "No-no people," deported to Japan and no longer Americans.

The Japanese people did not want the deportees, because these new arrivals were, to them, technically Americans, next of kin to the enemy. There were few places for deportees to live. Many pointed them toward the hypocenter cities. Fortunately, some of Tak's relatives owned a small farm just over two miles north of where the two Sasaki children had survived in a lifeboat under intense downpours of black rain. The farm was located a mile outside the worst of the oily cloudbursts, but the soil nonetheless received a misting of unstable isotopes, many of which had a tendency to bio-concentrate in plants and animals. The more common poisons had continued to mimic calcium and were just as continually absorbed in the bones and teeth, and especially in the rapidly developing bones of children. Not coincidentally, all but three of Tak's family members, who raised their food in the Hiroshima soil and who ate of it, would end young by cancer—typically spreading out from the bones and pancreas.

And yet, because they had been born far from Hiroshima, Tak and his siblings were spared the bomb's "prompt radiation" effects. Even before the two Sasaki children were made thirsty by the fires of August and began to lick the icy black rain from their lips, a hospital in the southeast of the city—located at the very same distance from the bomb's detonation point as the Sasaki house—recorded what happened to the two children and to everyone else at their radius during the awakening of the bomb. On the ground floor of the hospital, a lead-lined cabinet designed specifically to protect unexposed photographic negatives from the X-ray machine nearby had survived perfectly intact, still holding nearly a hundred unused X-ray plates. But upon those plates had fallen the gamma rays—upon them and through them, thoroughly overexposing the films, all during the first three seconds. As for the X-ray plates, so also for Masahiro Sasaki and his sister, Sadako.

In time, though they were of different ages and from different families, Tak's path would eventually converge with Masahiro Sasaki's path, even though the two families lived miles apart during the days of ruin.

For more than a year, Tak's youngest uncle attended a school that was little more than a partially rebuilt outdoor roof on stilts. The original schoolhouse was a mound that had absorbed most of the blast, coming apart around Tak's uncle, in one sense protecting him but, in that same moment, scratching him badly. Only as he began to grow older did Tak notice, *There's something strange, because a lot of people have scratches and burns.*

First had come the horrors of the bomb itself—which Tak, as he grew, began to hear about from his family. Then, as the survivors started to rebuild their lives and move forward, they discovered that they were moving toward the most disheartening horror of all: Though they had often survived against overwhelming odds, their fellow Japanese, beyond the hypocenters, began to fear even being touched by the A-bomb–exposed and would not allow the survivors to truly live.

Emerging businesses did not want to hire people who might become sick or pass the radiation sickness along like a contagion. Those survivors who did not have permanent scars and who could easily hide their exposure often did so behind a lifetime of self-censorship. This was the only way to avoid what was about to become at least two generations of injunctions against employment, marriage, and even higher education.

Tak had a cousin whose intellect and beauty were exceptional, but in a time when most marriages were arranged between families, she was universally rejected. Some A-bomb survivors made an exodus to the cold wilderness of the northernmost islands and changed their identities—which was, fortunately, easily accomplished in a country where the records of more than sixty cities were burned out of existence. A voluntarily forbidden history suited General MacArthur, who wanted to keep a lid of censorship over what people had seen and experienced in the two cities. Self-censorship worked so well that not until the second decade of the next century would many children and grandchildren learn what their ancestors had survived.

More and more, the Furumotos began looking toward America and drawing plans for a way to sneak back among their prior oppressors. Despite all that had been summoned against them under Order 9066, the family included American patriots.

From a few relatives who were still in the United States, occasional "care packages" came to the Hiroshima Furumotos through California's Japanese Family Association—packages with clothes, coffee, candy, and evaporated milk. Tak had four older sisters who would swarm over the candies, but what he wanted most was the little bag of colorful marbles that came with each package.

"I was very happy with just the marbles," Tak remembers. "In those days, when we came back to Japan, we were outcasts. We came from the country that won the war, and there were kids with scars from the American A-bomb. The other kids did not realize we were in a California prison camp the whole time. Food in the prison was scarce. Food in Japan also became scarce during the war. We were having a hard time all the years they too were having a hard time. The neighborhood kids would not play with me, because I came from *that place*.

"But they liked to play marbles. It was a complex game, with lines and obstacles—a kind of betting game. And when I arrived with all these colorful marbles, it was the only time the other kids would play with me. And after thirty minutes or so, I would lose all the colorful marbles; and my mother would see me with the empty bag and feel sorry for me. But I was smiling. I was so happy to lose them—so happy that the other kids let me play."

Then one day, a package came from America with a cowboy hat, a leather holster, cowboy boots, and two cap guns. Tak's mother dressed him up and sent him outside for what became one of his best days of play ever with the neighborhood kids. But the next day, the boots and cap guns were gone. Mother had to take them to the black market, near the T-Bridge and the Dome, to sell for bread, rice, and some dried fish.[4]

6

Almost four hundred miles northeast, in Tokyo, Mitsuo Fuchida was growing impatient with repeated summonses from the MacArthur committee, at least once every few months, to answer essentially the very same questions as the year before. There was nothing new for him to report on his participation in Pearl Harbor, Midway, or the initial scientific investigation of Hiroshima—nothing that the general did not already know. Many among the scientific crew that had landed in the ruins with him were already succumbing, in varying degrees, to radiation-related aftereffects (including lack of employment). After his 1948 interview, all Fuchida wanted to do was return forever to his little piece of land, not very far from the spot where Kenshi Hirata had cheated death during the firebombing of Osaka.

"I started my new career from practically nothing," Fuchida emphasized for the committee, like a parolee hoping for a final release. "At first, it seemed so insignificant, something like an ant's progress. Nevertheless, as time went by, I built myself a house and dug a well." He considered himself "a star that had fallen." Yet eventually, he had come to like living in association with the Earth, through the plants and the animals and every other aspect of farm life.

"I want," he explained, "to be like your George Washington—and like Cincinnatus, whom Washington admired—and just go back to my farm."

His interrogators crossed their arms, shook their heads, and said no.

Angered by revelations that the Americans had imprisoned Americans of Japanese ancestry, angered at somehow being accused, because he was Japanese, of having some level of responsibility for the hell ships and the slave labor POW camps, he blurted, "You know that war is war—and there can be no question that your people committed heinous, equally evil acts against Japanese POWs."

Fuchida awaited a reprimand. It did not come. Afterward, he began seeking out Japanese POWs, returned from captivity under the Americans. They told him that life had been difficult, but they never feared starvation or summary execution. He did not want to believe it. Among the lists of detainees, he found the name of his former flight engineer, Kazuo Kanegasaki—the same man who, by a curious swerve of history, had come directly into the crosshairs of a particularly angry orphan named Peggy Covell.

"Yes, there were hardships in the camps," Kazuo told his friend. "And there was one event, especially, [near] the end of the war. There came to our camp a certain American girl named Peggy. Her age, I would judge, was about twenty. Our army had beheaded her parents."

"And the Yanks put her to you?"

Kazuo nodded. "But it's not at all what you'd expect," he explained. She came with a blood oath, but by the time she arrived at the camp and had her chance, something inside her broke. "Peggy looked after our sick with such tender and conscientious care that all of our hearts were touched."

"What the . . . ? How can this be?"

"We asked her, 'Why are you so kind to us?' And she replied, 'Because my parents were killed by the Japanese army.'"

Fuchida sat back hard in his chair, amazed.

"Yes. That's how I felt. The moral code that you and I had been taught was, *The murderers of one's parents are the sworn and irreconcilable enemy*! We did not understand how anyone could return kindness for that!"

At first, Kazuo continued to explain, Peggy *wanted* revenge. A camp full of disarmed Japanese captives, each of them rendered helpless like her parents, presented an opportunity to get away with it and claim temporary insanity as a defense. Peggy had mentioned that her parents asked for and were permitted a half hour to read their Bible before their execution.

Kazuo said he always wondered now, *What was the last prayer her parents came to, and stopped at, before they died?* The question had haunted Peggy too while en route to the camp. Her parents had pleaded confusingly (to the Japanese commander, who surely knew they were innocent of any crime) for "forgiveness."

After many a summons more before the Tokyo inquisitions, Fuchida encountered other men like Kazuo, who continued to frustrate him with reports that while life was tough under American captivity, there was nothing remotely like the death railway over the River Kwai, or Camp 25 and the Chinese POW camp nearby. Then he met Jake DeShazer, a Doolittle-Raid survivor of hell ships and slave labor. Jake handed Fuchida a Bible and befriended him.

One day, Fuchida came across a strange passage in the Gospel of Luke, in which a scourged-nearly-to-death and crucified prophet so hated *no one* that he begged forgiveness even for those who had flayed his skin to the bone and nailed him to a tree.

Suddenly, Fuchida believed he could understand the story of the American girl whose parents had been slain. Later, he would be drawn toward religion, but during that moment of discovering the strange passage in Luke, it ceased to matter to him whether one was Shinto,

Buddhist, or atheist. *Her parents' prayer,* Fuchida told himself, *must have been* that *passage. Their confusing last-minute request for forgiveness was not for themselves, the accused, but for their executioners. And the young girl's inexplicable love for the Japanese prisoners must be the answer to the prayer of her parents.*

During the years to come, Fuchida would be haunted and even guided by this realization every day, every night.[5]

7

Double survivor Kenshi Hirata, who had carried his wife's ashes from Hiroshima to Nagasaki only to be on a convergent path with Jacob Beser a second time, was hardly a unique convergence. Aboard that same B-29, Beser belonged to a family that was fated to become forever linked to Hiroko Tasaka, the eighth grader who had been pointing out the diving *Enola Gay* to a friend when the bomb flash-burned her arm and melted two of her fingers together. Hiroko would never quite forgive Jacob Beser. Through an odd swerve of historical coincidence, her marriage to Harry Earl Harris eventually bound them as family. And though Hiroko would ultimately befriend Jacob's grandson, Ari, she chose never to speak with Jacob in person. The only time they were ever in the same room was at the funeral of a family member beloved by both of them.

There were other strange and seemingly impossible coincidences, connections, and mirrored tribulations, as if nature were conspiring to mimic Thornton Wilder's novel *The Bridge of San Luis Rey,* as if to ask, "Is there direction and meaning in lives beyond the individual's own will?"[6]

About the time Mitsuo Fuchida's inquisition finally began to wind down, Kenshi Hirata started a family. When a local news report identified him as a man twice exposed to radiation who was now a father, during a period in which discrimination against the exposed became next of kin to the discrimination against lepers in prior centuries, he contrived a plan to hide the children from such history.

Time seemed to have its own plans for all of them.

Nine years after war's end, Sadako Sasaki, the two-year-old who had nearly been frozen by black rain, was growing up to be an unusually athletic child. Her teacher, Nomura, began to see an Olympic hopeful in her, but what Sadako dreamed of most was to become a physical education teacher when she grew up. During interschool sports day events, fleet-footed Sadako dominated all the speed records and helped pull her class relay team from its previous standing in last place into second, then first.

As a reward, the class won a field trip to Miyajima Island, where eleven-year-old Sadako promptly challenged her teammates with a race to the top of Mount Misen. At the peak, everyone laughed when Sadako called out to her exhausted friends, "Well, that was fun. But now I'm hungry, so when do we eat lunch?"

Another classmate cautioned that it was not safe to joke near the mountaintop gardens, because a jealous goddess was rumored to dwell there. Sadako looked her friend in the eye with feigned severity and said, "We've lived in Hiroshima too long to be afraid of ghosts. Just look around you."

Fully one-third of the children in their class were survivors, and more than half of that third had lost parents or grandparents, brothers and sisters.

Sadako continued, "We've lived through the atom bomb, you and I. Nothing else as bad can happen."

Indeed, it did not seem possible. Sadako, her mother Fujiko, and her brother Masahiro had been shock-cocooned and shadow-shielded in a region where almost everyone else died.

So how, Sadako wondered, after escaping the flash burns and the blast effects herself, could anything unlucky ever happen? The postwar years had been, if nothing else, a difficult struggle—two steps forward, one step backward, a faltering step or two forward, and again backward. Mr. Sasaki was the first to become ill, having exposed himself to fallout in and around central Hiroshima as a member of a rescue team. Mrs.

Sasaki then sickened so severely that it became possible to believe that the children might become two more among the city's many atomic orphans. Eventually, the bleeding under the skin had abated and they gradually recovered their health. The parents were thankful that at least Masahiro and Sadako had been spared bouts of disease X.

As Mr. Sasaki's health improved, he began building a new house on the foundations of their old home. He also rebuilt his barbershop and helped his neighbors rebuild their homes and businesses. Each year, in fits and starts, Japan's economy, and the lives of people in general, started to improve. The Sasakis had gone from feeding on kebabs of locusts during the year after the war to having actual meals of fish and sweet rice, and even the occasional luxury of candy. Nonetheless, Sadako and her brother Masahiro still recalled fondly the *inago*, or fried grasshoppers. These they had eaten regularly when food was scarce. They tasted like popcorn, but some of the kernels had fed upon isotope-laced plants, had bio-concentrated the contaminants in their flesh, and were crawling with death.

Throughout the neighborhood, there had come black rains. Every vacant lot where houses were flattened out and burned away was being used to grow food. Not very far from the barbershop, the ruins of a canning factory became a favorite playground. From their platform atop steel and concrete rubble, the children liked to survey the city. Not all the bridges were repaired yet, and most of the cars on the road were jeeps driven by Allied soldiers. The steel arches of one bridge were still bent outward from the direction of the building they called "the Atomic Bomb Dome."

As 1954 approached, while neighbors' health tended to suddenly fail and sometimes just as unexpectedly recover, their good fortune rose and fell in accordance with their health. The owner of a dry-cleaning business next door to the barbershop had fallen on hard times. With the disappearance of the city's banks, along with whole offices full of deeds and records—burned to cinders on Day Zero—few people had any proof of property ownership, and they had little or nothing to offer as collateral.

Feeling only recently back on his feet himself, Mr. Sasaki felt compassion for his neighbor and agreed to cosign a loan for the dry-cleaning shop. As a rule, such loans were given at loan shark interest rates—and were, in fact, managed by loan sharks. Throughout Hiroshima, the strongest of 1945's atomic orphans grew up quickly and were surging forward as the next and most powerful generation of the Yakuza syndicate. In this case, the neighborhood boss was a cold and cheerless personality who seemed to derive a malicious joy from using his scratched and severely scarred face to frighten the Sasaki children. About the time the owner of the dry-cleaning shop fell behind on his loan payments, Sadako began shaking off mild but stubbornly recurring cases of the flu. This was a common annoyance for those who lived along the dusty streets. Meanwhile, the neighbor and his family either fled or were robbed and slain in the dead of night, leaving behind nothing with which the Sasakis could repay the local sharks—nothing except the full responsibility of settling the debt.

For Mr. Sasaki, the extra financial burden loomed as a threat against keeping the house. Disruptive visits by the scar-faced young man began to put shivers into the Sasaki children and customers alike. The family business suffered from the intrusions. Mother began sewing clothing together as quickly and perfectly as she could to meet the loan's interest rates and the country's escalating income tax rate, hoping to keep the family financially afloat.

Year by year, the parents had managed to make the home incrementally more pleasant with such improvements as broad windows sustaining indoor gardens. At the local school, though blast-damaged classrooms still leaked during storms and grew every variety of mold, at least the gymnasium finally had a new roof. Athletic competitions and practice sessions were Sadako's favorite parts of each school day.

But atomic-bomb disease remained in the city—a ghostly predator, lurking everywhere. During recent months, thirteen of Sadako's classmates were stricken with a rare childhood leukemia.

As 1954 came to its end, Sadako began arriving home from

after-school track practice complaining of being unusually worn out. Over the course of only a few short weeks, her dinner-table conversations became more and more dominated by murmurings of, "Tired . . . tired . . ." In late January, going to bed early no longer seemed to help. Gradually, she was becoming tired even at breakfast. The bad times really began gathering force during the first month of 1955, when a new family photograph revealed, purely by chance, the first clear signs of swollen lymph nodes on one side of Sadako's neck.

That was when Father took her to a doctor for blood tests. The results were horribly apparent. The doctor bowed his head. "Acute marrow leukemia," he said in a voice that cracked from having given this same diagnosis to far too many other parents.

For a little while longer, Sadako felt well enough to attend school, play jump rope with her friends, and live at home, but on February 21, 1955, she was hospitalized. The disease seemed to strike like a lightning bolt. During a span of weeks, her white blood cell counts climbed to seven times normal, and most of those cells were rogue—cancerous. Instead of defending her body from invading bacteria and viruses, they were turning treasonous and joining the other side. Judging from the rate of her decline, a doctor told Mr. and Mrs. Sasaki that their daughter probably had less than a year to live, more likely only three or four months.

Sadako's mother was bewildered. Only seven months earlier, during an annual physical at the Atomic Bomb Casualty Commission clinic, doctors had said that both children's blood values were normal. Even now Sadako did not look sick to Fujiko—merely a little sleepier than usual.

"How is this happening?" Mr. Sasaki said. That first night in the hospital, though they needed to be up early for work the next day, Shigeo and Fujiko stayed in chairs at Sadako's bedside until sunrise. On any given night, Sadako went to sleep knowing that when she awoke in the morning, one of them would always be there. And each night as she slept, each parent prayed, "If it is possible, let me die in her place. Please, give the disease to me instead."

While he prayed, Mr. Sasaki tried to form for himself a plan for something—*anything*—he could do to help raise Sadako's spirits and maybe give her a little more time. Yamaguchi's old basketball buddy, Dr. Nagai of Nagasaki, had famously reported that receiving even the simplest "gifts of the heart" from loved ones could keep a patient's will to live intact, even when the body was saying, "It's time to give up and move on."

Shigeo and Fujiko had an idea for a gift from the heart. Mr. Sasaki had dreamed of one day buying their little girl a fine dress-up kimono in another year or two. The new responsibility for a cosigned loan rendered the purchase impossible. But Mr. Sasaki realized that a gift from the heart would become even more powerful if, instead of buying the kimono, he and Fujiko made one with their own hands. They bought silk fabric decorated with a cherry blossom pattern, and at night, while Sadako slept, Mrs. Sasaki and the rest of the family took turns cutting and fashioning the sleeves, belt, and all the other individual parts of the kimono, which Mrs. Sasaki checked and double-checked for quality before assembling them into the completed garment.

On the day she opened the box and ran her fingers over the silk, Sadako broke into smiles and tears at the same time.

"You did too much for me," she said. "You spent too much."

Fujiko said, "Please, model it for us," and she withdrew a camera from a large bag. She also withdrew a little silk pocketbook and a pair of zori sandals, and Sadako seemed to fill with joy and swell with life's surge even as she wiped tears from her eyes.

"I'm not a good daughter," Sadako told her brother Masahiro. "It's a bad situation because Mom and Dad will be having to spend so much money for my sickness."

"There was very little income for anyone in those times," Masahiro would tell history.

> Even the doctors were poor. They and the nurses gave my sister everything they could, including vitamin B injections and anti-inflammatory drugs that kept the swelling of Sadako's

body under some kind of control. But all the nurses and all the doctors could not fund the blood transfusions beyond a monthly donation of their own blood—and there were many other leukemic children in the wards.

So my parents had to pay people for the blood transfusions. Father was making a living by cutting hair, and in order to fund each transfusion, he would have to serve five customers. My little sister knew the situation and told me that she would accept it and deal with it somehow. She understood that if she received a transfusion of healthy blood, she would feel better only for about ten hours; and she saw also that economically and emotionally, it must have been getting bad for us. Here lay a grade-school girl who saw that her parents wanted to help her—a girl who also seemed to know that except by a miracle, she really could not get better. She guessed she could probably live a little while longer if she received transfusions and medicine, but she knew at the same time that her parents' support for her was making them poorer. Emotionally, she was being torn in two directions.

"I just have to find a way to deal with it," Sadako told her brother repeatedly. "We have to get by somehow."

By March 1955, Sadako's white blood cell count seemed to stabilize at about six times the normal value, but her abnormal red cell structure brought her close to oxygen starvation and made walking even short distances difficult. A severe drop in platelet counts was causing bruising from even the gentlest touch—a sign of internal bleeding that raised fears Sadako might be killed by a simple hug.

In early May, local schoolchildren brought a box of colorful paper cranes to the hospital's nurses and showed them how to fold paper cranes themselves. Throughout the day, Sadako observed the staff carrying around the pieces of multicolored origami art. When her father arrived, she pointed to a folded bird someone had left at her bedside, and asked, "What is it about these paper cranes?"

Her father replied, "Why, someone probably sent the cranes as a wish for wellness to all the children here."

Shigeo had recently read something about the pain-relieving and potentially healing powers of concentrated enthusiastic thought. He also knew of a myth dating back to antiquity, about the crane and about what it meant to fold a thousand of them, and this gave him an idea.

"Sadako-san," her father said cheerily, "there is a legend that the crane lives for a thousand years. And they say that if you fold a thousand paper cranes, putting your heart into each one, they will help you with your wish for wellness."

And so it began: Sadako's first three or four cranes were large and lopsided, and the heads did not bow down quite right. After her first twenty, they became perfectly symmetrical, although when nurses came to take blood samples, the slightest movement sent two or three pieces of origami to the floor. So Masahiro brought a long, long string to the hospital, pushed a pin through the twenty paper cranes, and threaded them together.

The first twenty averaged about the size of a sparrow. Among them was a large silver crane fashioned from a piece of protective paper from an X-ray plate, which had been given to Sadako by one of the doctors.

"Now I have only nine hundred and eighty left to fold," Sadako announced. The difficulty now lay in acquiring enough paper, which was expensive in those times. She traveled to other patients' rooms asking for paper wrappings from get-well cards and candies. By mid-May, more silver X-ray cranes had joined the strand. Red cellophane from medicine wrappings followed the silver cranes, in addition to any piece of colorful paper that Sadako's family, the doctors, and the nurses could scrounge from anywhere—including squares of color that had been cut from eye-catching magazine advertisements. It became a quiet group effort, with nearly a dozen people straightening all the wrinkles out of paper scraps and leaving them under Sadako's bed.

Sadako soon discovered that conserving paper by folding smaller cranes required greater effort to make each fold. This suited her. By the end of May, the cranes were down to the size of hummingbirds. Sadako's blood abnormalities were also down—from six times a normal white cell count to only twice normal.

She now felt well enough to go home for a weekend, and when she returned to the hospital on Sunday evening, Sadako told the doctors, "I think I have enough strength, these days, to be a good roommate."

The nurses nodded agreement and moved her into a double room with a junior high school girl named Kiyo, a recovering tuberculosis patient who happened to be relatively energetic and very widely read and who introduced Sadako to all sorts of fantastic, forward-looking novels ranging from romances to stories about Isaac Asimov's utopian robotic societies.

The two girls began corresponding with other readers of fiction through hospital-sponsored pen-pal programs, and throughout their spring-season surge of activity, Sadako still had enough reserve energy to show her father and Masahiro a continuous strand of paper cranes and to announce proudly, "Only five hundred and fifty to go. I'm almost halfway there!"

By this time, the cranes were smaller than the tiniest known hummingbird species. "Her eyes were shining while she was folding the cranes," Sadako's mother observed, "showing that she wanted to survive by all means."

She was twelve years old now and had picked up a new title from Kiyo, who said, "Sadako, you know everyone in the hospital. I'll call you *mayor of this hospital*." Through Sadako's frantic activity, through her socializing with nurses and doctors, children, and their parents, the normally shy and "bookwormish" Kiyo became acquainted with all Sadako's new friends and began "emerging from her own shell."

Still, as May had phased into June and as the cranes continued to shrink in size, Sadako's white blood cell count climbed from twice the normal value to three times normal. She began to run high fevers. Sadako's body was at war with itself, prone to infection and to an attack by her own blood against her internal organs.

The doctors offered painkillers, but she waved the needles away. At first, Masahiro thought this was because the opium-based substance was rare and expensive. He heard Sadako reiterate to her father an earlier fear: "I'm a bad child to you, aren't I? I've used up so much money being sick."

Masahiro told a relative, "It was the cost of the morphine that made her turn away whatever comfort the painkillers might have brought." But even here, he eventually came to understand that he had underestimated his sister. By now, no one could escape noticing that as her little body was slowly breaking down, the paper cranes continued to grow progressively smaller. By late July, after white blood cell counts climbed above six times normal, and fevers began spiking so high that the doctors resorted to bathing Sadako in cold water, the cranes were down to the size of bumblebees. She had only enough energy to fold five or six per day.

In August, Sadako's white blood cell count improved to only four times normal, then to three times normal. Though her gums began to bleed and the threat of infection became a dark companion, her crane project picked up pace again: Fifty in a day. A hundred. *Finished*.

The thousandth crane was barely larger than a honeybee.

During her low point in July, when Sadako's paper-crane project had slowed down to only five or six per day, her blood values were absolutely deadly. Now, with renewed strength, she began a second string of paper cranes—which continued to diminish steadily in size. Soon, she could no longer fold the cranes with her fingers. No one could, as they diminished again by nearly half, from the size of honeybees into the realm of the smaller varieties of houseflies. The folds became so delicate that she used sewing needles to score and shape each wing. "As if it were a prayer," Masahiro would remember. "A prayer. Inori."

Shigeo warned his daughter, "Soon they'll be smaller than grains of rice. If you keep up that pace, you'll wear yourself out."

Sadako said, "It's okay, Papa. I have a plan."

"The reason for this," she told her brother Masahiro, "is that I still have hope of getting well." Even if hope itself appeared to be diminishing—

for her body weight was shrinking as if in a kind of resonance with the cranes—Sadako decided, "I must put more of my heart and soul into each one. The smallest cranes are the most difficult of all to create. So if I'm going to continue to do this thing, I'm going to put more and more of my spirit into each one."

"*All* of my spirit," she confided to Masahiro as her father's prediction of cranes smaller than rice grains became prophetic. "*All* of me, because in time, the smallest cranes may be all that's left of me."

On August 19, 1955, it began to look as if Sadako could hope again for a miracle. Her appetite was improving. Though she was still quite anemic from deformed red blood cells, her white blood cell count was now only twice normal. She displayed for her roommate, Kiyo, and for her family more than a hundred miniature paper cranes on a bedside table.

"You intend to make another thousand of these?" her father asked.

"The number isn't important anymore," Sadako replied. "What matters is the act of putting all of my concentration into each crane."

"You can't keep doing this," Shigeo said. "Save your energy. Just rest."

"Father, don't worry about me. I have my own plans. A new idea."

"But she never said exactly what that plan was," Masahiro told the children of a friend, fifty-five years later, as he placed in their hands three paper cranes, each folded with pins, down to the size of mosquitoes and gnats.

> Maybe she did not have an idea consciously, of what her paper-crane project might become. But maybe subconsciously, she glimpsed the future and she knew. Maybe she saw, that day in August, the paper crane growing into a symbol of hope, carrying the message and the spirit of the word *Omoiyari* (or what began as a word symbolizing such empathy as to make one always think of the other person first, and which was evolving into what Americans would one day come to know as "paying it forward"). *Omoiyari*. Sadako had grasped this word, this

principle . . . and maybe she saw it spreading outward into the world until, hopefully—*carried on the backs of a thousand paper cranes, and then billions of thousands*—it reached enough people to stop something terrible.

One evening, she explained that, more important than her own health, "I'm praying for Papa's debt to be repaid soon." During one of Sadako's brief visits home, in the middle of August, the scar-faced young man and two of his fellow loan sharks showed up at the door and confronted her parents. When their leader noticed Sadako and saw how pale and thin she had become, he decided to leave. Likely, his face was scarred by the bomb, and perhaps he had a moment of understanding about Sadako's plight, and this was why he left. No one would ever know for sure. They did not see him again.

By now the family home that Papa had so lovingly rebuilt was forfeit. "Home" had become a very small rental, and Sadako noticed her father's prized wristwatch—gone. What Masahiro could never forget was that in those days Sadako prayed more for her father's debts to be cured, more for her family, than for her own health. Having clearly grown in wisdom far beyond her years, she began emphasizing the need always to think of the other person first.

One night, Papa arrived at Sadako's hospital bedside and tried in vain to hide the fact that he was suffering from a terrible headache. In spite of the exhausting hours he kept, working at any job he could find, he made sure to be in the chair next to her bed even if headache and sheer willpower could not keep him awake. After he passed out, Sadako crept away to the nurses' station. "When he awoke," Masahiro would write later, "Sadako was folding cranes in her bed. She smiled at him and handed him some aspirin and a cup of water. 'Here, Papa, take this,' she said. Even in her enormous suffering, she found the strength to care for others."

During that same August 1955, a delegation of students from China arrived at the hospital. At the reception, patients heard an unfamiliar song, sung in Japanese: "*Genbaku-O-yurusumaji*" (Never again, the A-bomb).

"Something in that song seemed to resonate with Sadako," Kiyo remembered. "She sang it to me over and over, up on the hospital rooftop, until I learned it." They made other visits to the rooftop. A six-year-old girl named Yukiko had been born and raised on hallowed, contaminated ground, and like most families, she and her parents must have eaten black-market food grown near the city center, along with locusts that grazed on local vegetation. Sadako befriended her. Leukemia took her. According to legend, when children died, it was said that their spirits went to the stars. One night, on the hospital roof, Kiyo said, "The brightest star we find will be Yukiko's." They chose a star and embraced. Kiyo would never forget how bony Sadako's back felt.

In September, climbs to the rooftop decreased in number as Sadako's white blood cell count doubled. Too soon, the count increased by another multiple of two . . . and another . . . and another.

Masahiro knew that his sister was now living with a great deal of pain. Something was spreading outward from her lower spine, and her left leg began to swell so large that the flesh was rupturing under the skin and turning purple.

"She never said the words 'it hurts,'" Masahiro recalled.

> Although, when a leg swells up to one and a half times its normal size, the throbbing alone has to hurt. Yet she continued to refuse the painkillers. For a long time, I believed she did not want our parents to bear the expense. But later she gave us two reasons completely different from this. First, she believed that the dreamlike state that the morphine put her into might become permanent and kill her. Second, Sadako did not like a dream state in which she could not feel the touch of her mother's hand. She wanted to be aware of our presence when we were in the room with her—wanted to be acutely aware of the

people she loved most. She did not want to lose even a minute with us by floating away into a painless dream.

In mid-October, Sadako's fevers reached 105 degrees.

About October 20, a dozen paper triangles lay under her bed, each prefolded into a starter triangle no wider than one of Sadako's fingernails. She had by now folded 1,600 paper cranes. Using two pins, Sadako put the greatest concentration of dexterity and thought yet into the smallest crane, into a reddish-violet bird no larger than a gnat—the last one she would ever fold.

"She was fully conscious till the very end," Masahiro would record later. "And I do not believe she had any idea, that morning of October 25, that she was about to die at any moment. I remember my father waking me and explaining that a doctor had said the time was near. I remember my mother looking at all those pieces of paper on the string and asking, 'Why didn't your thousand cranes sing? Why didn't you fly?'

"But most of all, when I think of that morning in Hiroshima, I remember my sister just slipping away, suddenly and without suffering, as if drifting off to sleep. Only minutes before, I heard Father urging her to eat something, and she responded, 'Tea or rice, please.'

"A nurse brought a bowl of white rice. Sadako swallowed two spoonfuls and, smiling, she said, 'It's good.' That was it. She drifted away with those words—'It's good,' and then 'Thank you.'

"The last words she left for us, even after such suffering, were 'Thank you.'

"Before she left," Masahiro explained, "my sister and I had [the] one-word saying between us, just that one simple word: *Omoiyari*."

Masahiro had heard it said that when a person comes to a place where he or she is reduced to nothing, that's when we begin to understand the value of all things.

For Sadako, the lesson became *Omoiyari*, which meant "In your heart, always think about the other person before yourself."

According to Masahiro, after Sadako wore her first and last dress-up

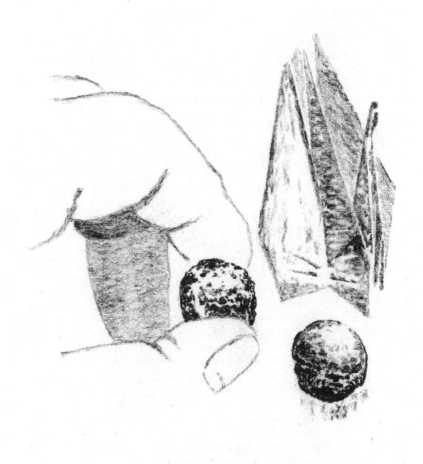

Toshihiko Matsuda, whose shadow was found on his aunt's garden wall, also left behind his toy marbles. The marbles were made of glass, and they had melted. Ten years later, another child of Hiroshima left behind sixteen hundred paper cranes, and folded her prayer of *Omoiyari* into each of them. *Omoiyari* translates in the West, roughly, to the principle of "paying it forward," in the hope that random acts of human kindness can spread and, perhaps without us ever knowing it, will prevent something horrible. *Omoiyari* comes with only one simple commandment: "Be kind."

kimono, she had imagined and defined the perfect, one-and-only future marriage for herself as one in which both husband and wife treated each other by the principle of *Omoiyari* and yet neither took it for granted.

More than a half century later, Masahiro said, "That's what I want to pass down from her to young people. I do not want the next generations to think only of paper cranes and a twelve-year-old girl dying from atomic-bomb disease. I want them to think, in their hearts, always about the other person.

"You start *Omoiyari* from your family members, and from your friends. Sadako thought—and taught me—that if the principle of *Omoiyari* could spread even a little, into the right places, it might ease the world toward never seeing another *pika-don* ['never again that terrible flash-bang, never again the A-bomb']."[7]

8

During the tenth anniversary of the bombs, as Sadako taught her brother *Omoiyari* and as China sent children with a song of peace to its former enemy, Tak Furumoto's family was dreaming of going back again to America. His parents had their citizenship permanently blacked out—"Adamantly: 'Do not come back. You are blocked even from a visit to the United States, under the law.'" Yet this was, of course, a government program. And, as happens with most bureaucratic procedural games, someone, somewhere, stuffed it up. Tak's eldest sister, Mary, was able to immigrate to the United States because the bureaucrats had left her citizenship intact. Then, at age twenty-one, she had been able to recall two of her sisters to the West Coast, and now her father.

Tak was still with his mother in Hiroshima. While he and Mother awaited their turn, other kids were finally befriending the ten-year-old. A few posed for photos with him. Because Tak's father loved photography, the family's photo diary included "postapocalypse" Hiroshima, along with illegal shots that could have brought Father much unpleasant treatment during the war, memorializing daily life at the internment camp. By now, among the children of Hiroshima, even Tak's practicing of English brought no trouble to him. Japanese had become his primary language, but preparation for a return to America required him to develop bilingual skills. In a manner no one could anticipate, this would serve him quite well more than a quarter century into futurity.

Tak's sisters had worked diligently for two years, saving money from their jobs, to bring Father across from Japan. Because in the 1950s better and higher-paying jobs were reserved for men, with Father's arrival the family could begin to rebuild, as they had built once before. During the 1930s, they had climbed upward from migrant farmers to Father driving trucks, then working at the produce market, and eventually becoming a produce business partner with twenty-six employees. He even came to own a house, and a car, through the end of the Great Depression and up till the "Great Confiscation" that followed December 7, 1941.

In 1956, Tak's family was together again in California. Father had sought out his old friend and business partner, with whom he had run the once-famous Oka Produce Company. He learned that Mr. Oka's family had been taken away to the Manzanar prison camp. After Tule Lake and Manzanar, most families seemed to have dispersed and hidden themselves, having already seen too much history and wanting to experience no more of it. Some changed their names and forbade their children from learning even the simplest Japanese words. Mr. Oka's produce company was gone. He had traveled away from Manzanar, adopting a similar but just different enough name, Ooka. Mr. Furumoto could not find his friend, could not learn whether he was even alive. Gone was the hope of reuniting and rebuilding their produce company.

"If one plan does not work," Father believed and taught, "then make sure you have another plan." Seeking out jobs in new directions and building anew, Mr. Furumoto settled his family in South Central Los Angeles.

"In those days," Tak later recorded, "discrimination was still rampant, and not even considered wrong by the majority of the people. We had been looking at a new home and were blocked." Sometimes, the discrimination could turn bloody at the drop of a hat; other times, it got downright, two-plus-two-equals-three stupid. On the East Coast, a friend of Tak's—a kid growing up in a white suburban neighborhood—could never forget what happened when a Korean family bought the biggest house on the block. A WWII veteran next door to Tak's friend did not like this—especially since the parents were an interracial couple. The veteran had a few souvenir kamikaze flags from the war; they were headbands with Japanese writing on them. One was stained everywhere with blood. The man announced that he was going to place the flags on the neighbor's front lawn, and the kid said, "Not for nothing, but they're not even Japanese. They're Koreans. During the war, the Japanese *killed* Koreans." The man shot back, "K's, Japs—same thing!" and went about the deed anyway. In those days, the local police regarded it as just a veteran's harmless joke and told the new family on the block that they should simply "lighten up."

For Tak's part, though his family was segregated in South Central LA, he discovered that his experience of living with and going to high school with Latino and Black kids really worked for him—especially as the Vietnam War era loomed ahead like a giant flyswatter.[8]

9

Here and there throughout Hiroshima, camphor trees, believed for years to have been killed by the rays and the flames, sent out green shoots and came gradually back to life. Around the ruins of Hiroshima Castle and along the river's edge, the cherry trees that began to blossom each spring were surviving witnesses to the A-bomb.

As trees healed (sometimes after many a summer), so healed the people.

In the suburbs of Nagasaki, Setsuko Hirata's parents chose to regard such changes as a tribute to their daughter's love for her husband, and what she would have wished for him. After their sorrowful release of

Kenshi (based on their own expression of *Omoiyari*), love had come again for him. By the time Tak Furumoto returned to America, Kenshi was raising two healthy children. After the Mitsubishi Corporation allowed its records of his "twice A-bombed" status to be published by a *New York Times* writer in 1957, he had no choice except to all but completely disappear with his new wife and their "contaminated" offspring. Setsuko's family participated in hiding the Hirata family's identity so well that the children themselves did not know exactly who they were.

Kenshi's daughter, Saeko, grew up to study journalism in college and was working for the Nagasaki Broadcasting Corporation when she learned, quite by accident, that she was born of what had turned out to be her father's second marriage. Though perplexed and wanting answers, a young Japanese woman could not, in that era, simply ask her father what happened. Instead, she asked her mother, who explained for the first time about the remarriage. She learned about her father's first wife, who had died in a terrible firebombing. Saeko's mother did not mention "double *hibakusha*," (twice exposed) or even the word "atomic." She told a strange story about how the second true love of Kenshi Hirata's life was actually his first love, and how his first love (Setsuko) was actually his second.

At age twenty-three, about the time Japan engaged America in war, Saeko's father had been sent to the battlefields. He returned with his legs all but destroyed by malnutrition and disease and was thereafter assigned to a desk job.

Before the war, three children—Kenshi, Saeko's mother, and Setsuko—had grown up in the same neighborhood. Kenshi knew Saeko's mother from the time they were toddlers, and almost from the start they had become inseparable childhood sweethearts. Yet when Kenshi approached Saeko's grandfather in 1943 to ask for his daughter's hand in marriage, he was refused. No one knew for certain why the father had blocked the marriage, but in the militaristic atmosphere of the day, men fighting and dying in the Pacific arena gained honor, whereas a man who was returned safely home by the army and placed out of harm's way behind an accountant's desk would likely have been viewed as dishonorable even if the desk job was born of battlefield injuries.

Two years after the refusal, love came to Kenshi Hirata a second time, and he married his childhood friend Setsuko and brought her from Nagasaki to the city where she died.

More than a year after Kenshi lost Setsuko and Japan lost the war, Saeko's grandfather had a change of heart and allowed Kenshi to marry her mother. Saeko learned that Kenshi wept and "confessed" to her mother everything that had happened to him, including the story of Setsuko and how he recovered some of her ashes from the fire and saw them placed in a tomb that he continued to visit.

Saeko's mother had told the story—minus the part about her father sleeping on Setsuko's radioactive grave in Hiroshima, minus mention of the city's name and the part about the second atomic bomb. And she believed that Kenshi had needed to "confess" out of some inner shame. But his first love did not hold him to any blame at all for loving Setsuko or for losing her to a fate that seemed as much beyond all human control as it was beyond all prior human experience. Saeko's mother explained that she had long ago accepted these events. Indeed, it occurred to Mother that had Grandfather allowed her to become Kenshi's first wife, fate would have dealt them all a very different hand. She came to regard Setsuko as a sister, as the gentle, kindhearted young woman who traveled to a doomed city and died in her place. And so she made regular visits to Setsuko's tomb, pouring water over a shrine stone, honoring her.[9]

10

In South Central Los Angeles, life for the Furumoto family had been difficult but steadily improving. Yet nerves were frayed. Time was short. 'Nam was coming.

For those who did not know how to play the system, the draft was already here. Tak's friends were being taken. Normal plans for the future were scrapped. Tak graduated with a bachelor of science degree and volunteered in 1968 as an engineering officer candidate. After finishing the required aptitude tests, Tak Furumoto, the former deportee to Hiroshima, with "No-no" ancestors, was assigned to military intelligence and counterinsurgency training. In November 1969, they tapped him for a dangerous and increasingly chaotic program called Phoenix. Tak landed in a strange tongue twister of a place called Hậu Nghĩa, Đức Hòa District, Long An Province, on the border of Cambodia. There, under senior advisor Major Ebby, he became Đức Hòa's second in command for Operation Phoenix, where they were visited regularly (at least in the beginning) by the innocuously named program's architect, William Colby. And so, as an intelligence officer and advisor to the National Police and as part of a "Parrot's Beak" III Corps team that grew to become A-list targets of the insurgents, First Lieutenant Furumoto was taken under the same agency of the US government that Walter Lord (Mitsuo Fuchida's interrogator-turned-friend), had a hand in helping create with Colby. The OSS of World War II was now the CIA.

As Tak departed for 'Nam in February 1970, actor Takahiro Tamura appeared on the big screen, playing the role of Fuchida in a film based on Walter Lord's interviews: *Tora! Tora! Tora!* The film portrayed the beginning of a nightmare for Tak's family, and now, going back again to Asia, he traveled toward a new species of nightmare. There were the uncountable miles and miles of underground tunnels, from which ambushes typically commenced after sunset. Each tunnel entrance was ringed by webs of expertly hidden trip wires linked to land mines. Huge limestone caverns along the rivers hid whole fleets of attack boats. The caves were camouflaged behind curtains of trees and vines. As a countermeasure, the Americans concocted new chemical defoliants to push back and strip away the rain forest and reveal hiding places. In this manner, Tak became the first person known to have been exposed to both Hiroshima radiation *and* the toxic brew called "Agent Orange."

As defoliants withered the forests, the enemy's subterranean endeavors grew more sophisticated and sent their roots deeper. Not even the CIA would know that during the United Service Organizations' concerts, on at least two occasions, the insurgents had extended feelers from their system of underground hospitals, lodgings, pumping stations, and supply tunnels right up to the edge of the performance area and enjoyed the concerts right under the feet of perimeter guards and the skids of helicopters.

"They could come out at will, from anywhere, as if from nowhere," Tak learned. He also observed,

> This was the first war in which [it was an everyday experience for] American Blacks and Caucasians to be fighting side by side. Potentially, this situation within could have been as intense as the attacks against us. Even with African Americans beside Asian Americans, there was a potential for trouble. But I was able to get along with everyone, and get almost everyone to get along—and this was because of South Central LA. I went to elementary school, junior high school, and high school with Black kids, and *they* helped *me*. They basically protected me from other kids who did not like Japanese.

In 'Nam, it perplexed him that there were more minorities than Caucasians along Đức Hòa's front lines. As more of the deadly tunnels were discovered, there arose a shortage of officers, and Tak would not send his team members near the Cambodian border without joining them, exposed to the same danger. The land in that direction was literally honeycombed underfoot. In the town of Củ Chi, Americans bought goods during the day, unaware that huge weapons depots and even recreational facilities existed beneath the market floors. Every night, after the Americans departed, the enemy emerged from its subterranean world and shopped at those same markets. From other underground habitats, they would surface near American perimeters and bait soldiers toward booby traps. When the rescue helicopters came in and were shot down: more bait. "And our body counts, terrible—sometimes you go crazy with the bodies—and fright . . . and you get used to the fright . . . stop caring . . . numb."

Tak held it together through 'Nam. But "this was a hell of a time for coming home." He learned of a high school kid named Doogie who had waited for his brother to return home at a local train station. His brother was assailed the moment he stepped off the train. Ostensibly in the name of "fighting for peace," a group of bullies his own age spat all over the young man's uniform. Doogie's brother said to him, "Wait a minute," walked into the train station's washroom, and stopped the rest of his own life. The bullies laughed and even cheered. Doogie never recovered. Within a family, the end to which his brother was driven had a way of becoming contagious. The bullies laughed.

Tak was also spat on. Being decorated for heroism only force-fed his being tarred with the then-popular moniker "baby killer." There was no doubt that the bullies derived a malicious and self-righteous joy from this. A few had made their way into the ranks of Hollywood and were eagerly creating the stereotypical Vietnam-veteran-as-lunatic-rapist for such films as *Earthquake* with Charlton Heston. Tak came home already with the beginnings of post-traumatic stress disorder. Dealing with a hidden enemy, and the awful spasm of Phoenix itself, only provided criteria for comparison with what he had seen of the refugee surge created after President Nixon ordered illegal bombing raids on Cambodia—ultimately amplifying the chaos that increased the power of Pol Pot, a Cambodian Hitler who eventually built pyramids out of human skulls. All this was horror enough. The bullies at home became the proverbial icing on the cake. He began to feel a strange kinship with other veterans—with the men he'd seen being spat on in Japan. During the post–World War II haze, Japanese women whose husbands and sons had disappeared in battle often spat on soldiers who returned home alive. Though many bore ghastly scars, merely being alive was a dishonor. To the spitters, the men were dogs because they survived, and survived because they were dogs. For an entire generation gaslighted under the unceasing propaganda of palace warlords, reality had been distorted if not altogether canceled.

Tak Furumoto believed that as a child of Hiroshima, he now understood perfectly how it must have felt to be one of those soldiers he had seen being spat on. As an American veteran of 'Nam, he felt like a beaten dog retreating into a corner. Friends and family wanted to help, but, like that dog (as he self-described it), he sometimes lashed out from that corner, as if to bite. And he knew that none of those people deserved to be bitten. The last thing in the world he wanted to do was to bite the people he loved. So he isolated himself and moved to New York—a city John Lennon had said one could love "simply because in New York, people leave you alone."

After a while, Tak's wife, Carolyn, traveled east to be with him. Postwar life (post–internment camp, post-Hiroshima, post-'Nam) continued to be difficult. Working side by side with other, often gossipy workers at Mikasa, a chinaware manufacturer, was the worst situation for him. The approach of an office Christmas party threatened rage in a china factory and sacrificing the last bits of hope for peace he could see in his future. The path ahead was looking like a storm of firings. All things considered, the young Mrs. Furumoto agreed, saying, "Tak, you need to work alone."

And as it turned out, he was now in the right place, at the right time. Like Tsutomu Yamaguchi and Kenshi Hirata, Tak began to consider himself always unlucky and, at the same time, lucky. When he decided to work alone and obtain a broker's license to start his own real estate business in New York—a business born out of trauma—he discovered quite by accident that because he spent his early childhood in Hiroshima, he was virtually the only Japanese person in New York who spoke both Japanese and English. The rest of his generation, growing up with parents and relatives who were locked up in the camps for *being* Japanese, were warned, "Don't study Japanese language; don't study Japanese culture." In America, all the traditions—even the *words*—were being driven into extinction.

During the next decade, as the only Realtor in town who spoke both languages, Tak would have no competition at all when Japan's economy began to boom and the investors came to New York. He assisted with the sale of a large building across the street from the New York Public Library, and with much else that Japan's nouveau riche came around to purchase. He was there when rising real estate star Donald Trump needed a translator. The new arrivals bought casinos and portions of Tennessee. Tak also assisted in the sale of several golf courses and Donald Trump's yacht. Trump sometimes commented—*outwardly as a good-natured joke, but*, Tak would recall, *perhaps not so jokingly*—"You Japanese won't have to invade anyone next time. If this buying keeps up, all you'll really have to do is throw us out of your country."

It was a good joke, maybe. But other jokes, decidedly less friendly, arose from other quarters. One day, near Penn Station, a pair of Japanese nationals asked an elderly and somewhat disheveled lady, "Which direction to Radio City, please?" The woman shouted, "You fucking found Pearl Harbor! Go find Radio City!" The visitors found it; then they bought it.

The shouting woman was what would, in those days, be called a "bag lady." Even those who experienced it were able to laugh, in hindsight, about having apparently gone up to a gravelly voiced alcoholic, asking for directions. But very soon, and with astonishing rapidity, the little jokes began to lose their charm. As Detroit's four-year-self-destruct style of car manufacture started to fall behind Japanese car sales, Lee Iacocca began talking about tariffs against the emerging "Japan peril," while the comedian Andrew Dice Clay added, "Didn't we drop a couple of bombs on those people? Maybe we ought to send them a little reminder . . ."

After a Chinese American couple known to Tak were denied service in a New York restaurant ("Go back to Tokyo—Ching-Chong!"), the picture began to look dangerous.

Chinese Americans were beaten with baseball bats in Detroit. Then Tak and a friend were accosted outside a restaurant. The friend was the president of Nissan.

"Are you Japanese?" a young man asked.

Tak replied, "I'm American."

"We saw you speaking Japanese."

"My friend here came from Japan."

"You guys are buying up America!" the ringleader of the bullies said. "And you take our jobs!"

"Look!" Tak said firmly. "I'm American. I did fight for this country in Vietnam." He backed his words up with a stance that let them know that if they were looking for trouble, they had just found the local distributor. (Item: It's not wise to threaten someone who survived Vietnam's subterraneans.)

The bullies crawled into their car and, once they were a safe distance away, shouted back, "A Jap is a Jap, and you're no good!"

Once again Tak was made to think, *My face was my crime*.[10]

11

Mizuha's house divided stood on the edge of a grass-and-wildflower-strewn field near the divide in a river where, only a few years after the bombs of August, the waters flowed clean again. In the south, buildings were clustered around the Hiroshima Dome and the T-Bridge like greenery around an oasis. The buildings had evolved from the original post-holocaust shapes of tin-roofed scrap-wood shacks into more the appearance of prewar houses. They evolved in parallel with the shift away from systems of barter to the return of government-backed currency.

During the years when Tak Furumoto's father earned wages as a jeep driver for American officers, and while the spate of makeshift homes and shops quickened its spread along both sides of prewar avenues, Mizuha lived and studied in the old house. She learned medical skills as nimbly as humanly possible despite the postwar condition of the city, and despite a deepening reluctance in towns beyond Hiroshima to invest in education and employment of anyone who, even if not really carrying the rumored (and feared) "contagiously acquired disease X," might be felled at short notice by their exposure, becoming "a sink of wasted resources."

At age seventeen, Mizuha had attended the city's reviving Jogakuin School and College alongside Setsuko Thurlow, the girl who lived because pattern-recognition test scores and a talent for codebreaking had placed her inside an army bunker at Moment Zero. Theirs was a school for advanced placement, but the bomb and its cascade of consequences continued to be the pollutant of Mizuha's dreams.

During months that passed too chaotically to fathom, a brother was lost, and in sorrow and illness Mizuha's white blood cell count declined to half the normal value, and even a common cold flared demonic and life-threatening.

And then Mother, who was already turning (emotionally) more into an absentee landlord than a parent, simply walked away from the home. Ahead of the walk-away, her health had taken a turn for the worse, with slivers of bomb-injected glass becoming internal scalpels that started to migrate with merely a shift of position in her sleep, or the raising of an arm, or even a deep breath. A sympathetic surgeon probed after and then removed the most dangerous slivers. Before anyone knew or understood what was happening, she was in love with the doctor, and married him, and left her children behind.

After the arrests and the torture, Mizuha's mother was never able to return to the world of everyday life whole again. There was no healing from what future generations would have recognized immediately as post-traumatic stress disorder. And layered on top of torture by the soldiers, the death of her husband, and radiation sickness moving through the home like a silent assassin, the same siblings Father had taken into the property's second house, instead of helping her, "began coming 'round and bullying her," granddaughter Shiho would record nearly eight decades later. "She was incredibly sweet, soft-spoken, beautiful—the kind of person who really wouldn't consciously hurt a fly. With the bullying and no husband to protect her, she felt she had no choice but to leave. Mother Mizuha forgave her. But my mom's sister never spoke to her mother again."

Young Mizuha again put schooling aside to aid a (youngest) family remnant who was too shocked to react. Yet, much like Tak Furumoto, her thoughts began turning occasionally, and eventually more and more frequently, toward a Japan real estate industry that was, sooner or later, bound to break open and sprout opportunities.

(*If I can just get enough good mileage out of this body*, she told herself.)

Mizuha would tell future generations how the Atomic Bombing Survey physicians were tirelessly involving themselves in her life, always seeking her out for blood samples—"but never offering medical care. Just candies." And whatever those doctors learned from her, the family would be unable to find a record. Even in 2024, with the eightieth anniversary of Hiroshima approaching, the record was going to remain sealed. In the year 1950, Mizuha knew only that her white blood cell counts continued to roller-coaster, mostly plunging down and staying down for long periods. And this she learned only because her mother was then married to a doctor, whose sons were also doctors. But none of the medicines they prescribed were helping.

Still, as an owner of a rare property deed that had not been lost to the fires, she had a foundation for the trading and uptrading of land—at least until 1954's *Godzilla* climbed out of the sea as metaphor for the atomic bomb and its radiation, and until a new generation of family doctors told Mizuha that she was terminal and that medicine could do nothing to save her.

Defiance again.

Mizuha had enough medical knowledge in her own school background, even before she was seventeen, that she could navigate medical libraries with ease. She firmed a resolve to face death along her own path, shifting toward what future generations would recognize as a vegetables-and-nuts-and-fruits-centered "Mediterranean diet," backed up with everything she could learn about Chinese herbal and root-extract medicines, buttressed with an indomitable will to live.

In defiance of medical prophecy, Mizuha lived.

The doctors who prophesied her death—well, they died.

And still, the bomb's power to harm a family had been but fractionally wielded. Mizuha found love, married, then suffered four miscarriages and a stillbirth. Each time, she survived a crippling anemia "by too frighteningly thin a margin."

And then, while monsoons and isotope decay returned Hiroshima gradually toward normal background radiation levels, while rockets shot to the moon and Tak Furumoto fought for sanity under talon and wing of the CIA's Operation Phoenix, and while Mizuha's family real estate business prospered, she knew, finally, the hope and joy of a pregnancy that took root—and which had progressed successfully through the first three months without degrading her blood. Yet her sister, Futaba, became fearful that the pregnancy would become (again) too great a stress on an already lurking bone-marrow disease and that her kidneys would (again) be stressed to the edge of uremic poisoning. Futaba did not want both her sister and the baby to die.

Mizuha smiled and guaranteed her, "Everything will be all right."

The doctors were not so sure. Though the space age had arrived, in 1973 there were no such tools as high-resolution sonograms and genetic testing. So the condition of a gestating child could not be determined. In prior decades, fetal bone structure and skull growth had been commonly monitored using X-rays, but with the post-Hiroshima and post-Nagasaki world came the realization that deep-penetrating, short-wavelength photons of light (X-rays and gamma rays) were harmful to fetal development. And so people stopped the folly of X-raying the unborn and counting finger bones.

The doctors told the forty-year-old mother-to-be that given her Hiroshima exposure, she had a 90 percent probability of delivering a significantly handicapped child—"if it survives."

This mathematical judgment was based almost entirely on what happened to first-trimester fetuses exposed directly to the bombs of August 1945. By 1973, the "90 percent" figure had become a self-perpetuating textbook dogma, based on supposition and fear rather than actual data.

No one in authority quite understood yet that almost all the alien-appearing fetuses in the Atomic Bombing Survey's embalming jars had been exposed during nature's crucial first trimester, when the genetic software that sequenced tissue layers into human beings happened to be most easily shaken up and shoved off course, such that layers of the brain ended up in the wrong places, or parts of the digestive system sometimes developed outside the body, as the too-common result of overwhelmed RNA feedback and DNA repair systems. Occasionally, "ontogeny had recapitulated phylogeny" late into development, with some December 1945 stillbirths resembling prehuman mammals and even, in one worst-case example, an amphibian.

Knowledge had been so slow to come (and acceptance of knowledge generally slower) that among the exposed, who now called themselves *hibakusha*, nature's self-correcting nucleic acid monitors were normally so vigilant that postwar second- and third-generation children were already proving the expected "monsters" to be just another bit of dogma. Healthy and fully human children should have been the expected norm.

When the molecular biologist Francis Crick insisted in 1953 that the chromosome was not a triple helix, and then helped define the structure of DNA, and when Mizuha became pregnant twenty years later, although technology was finally rendering strips of DNA readable, the best that the biological sciences could provide happened to be no more reliable than trying to read Egyptian hieroglyphs before the Rosetta Stone made decoding possible. No one knew yet how surprisingly efficient their own body's molecular watchdogs and repair systems could be. No one knew that the transmission of genetic instructions and the control of protein production in a person's body proceeded with unimagined accuracy, in almost any given cell, faster than machine-gun fire.

No one knew. Few had even guessed.

And so the obstetricians and the family doctors of 1973, and even Mizuha's sister Futaba, advised her to stop the pregnancy.

"But my mother heard a single dissenting voice," her child, Shiho, would tell historians a half century later, in the year that paleogeneticists would bring an ibex from extinction to the brink of "de-extinction" and dream about using genetic Rosetta Stones to cure most any disease, while forging a new technological path of both promise and peril on their way to dinosaur daydreams.

"The dissenting doctor," said Shiho, "though no one knew what the outcome would be for me, and though everyone except my mother was very afraid of her refusal to abort—this one doctor said to her, 'I know you. I see your kind soul, and if you're going to have a child with a disability, you will take care of and you will raise that kid.'

"And my mother's sister was very angry with her because she didn't want her to die, as she almost had during all those other pregnancies that ended only in sorrow. And my mother said, 'I'm going to give her birth (she somehow felt, *it's a girl*), and if I die, then it is what it is.'

"And that's what I tell my own kids: 'Life. It is what it is. Just think,' I tell them, 'how your father's father's father was on his way to the Pacific, and to the war, when surrender occurred. So if anything happened to him—if all of these coincidences and close-call calamities had not played out exactly as they did—you would not be here.'"

The child, Shiho (who married as Shiho Burke), had met filmmaker Tengo Yamada after she traveled to America as an exchange student in 1985. Yamada was part of the manga and anime art movement and had helped Keiji Nakazawa, the author of *I Saw It*, turn his manga story into the live-action film *Barefoot Gen*.

In 1985, he was at work on another film, *White City Hiroshima*. Recognizing how closely the "tween" Shiho resembled photos of her mother at the same age, and having learned that she was the daughter of the evacuation camp escapee who really did run home for two days toward the imagined safety of Hiroshima, Yamada cast young Shiho in the role of her mother, Mizuha.

Shiho remained in the United States, always keeping active her dual citizenship so she could continue working with her family's real estate investment business in Hiroshima.

Two of her three children went on to graduate with honors. A third child appeared to have been harmed by the legacy of black rain. But it only appeared so. Much as hemophilia in Queen Victoria's family could be traced to what was likely a spontaneous mutation, the specific translocation that Shiho's daughter received was completely absent in maps of parental DNA. It had occurred spontaneously, independently of Hiroshima.

At a very early stage of embryonic development—likely within the very first days, hours, or even minutes—a muon or other highly energetic particle-ray reached down from the heavens and lanced through a chromosome, releasing most of its energy across a field of radiation no wider than the very tip of a human eyelash.

This sort of encounter is happening all around you and in you, and it's the reason your nucleic acids have evolved (and still are evolving) defenses against radioactive particle-rays, including those emitted by that big fusion reactor in the sky, the sun. Only rarely (and improbably) do such effects manage to pinpoint target the first diploid cells of the yet-to-be-born. Some of those particle-waves (the most powerful of them) were shot from smash-ups between black holes or neutron stars (or sometimes a combination of both).

And in this one case of Shiho's child—if a light-speed rifle shot was indeed the source of the dislocation—in such a case, it becomes a shot aimed at a particular spot in the universe, a spot not quite so wide as an eyelash, into which the Earth would carry Shiho at the end of a journey that began perhaps eons before the first dinosaurs were evolved. Such is the fantastical quantum chessboard on which everything in the universe is forced to play, bound by the same rules of mass and energy and relativity and probability curves that made the stars, the iron in your blood, and the poisonous black ash in Hiroshima's rain.

When the first atomic bomb was birthed from heavy, neutron-emitting metals, humans were working with an understanding still so primitive that no one knew what a neutron was made of or how they, the bomb's creators, succeeded at igniting the device. They knew this no more than the first *Homo erectus* fire makers, a half million years earlier, had any understanding of how oxidation worked against carbon in wood. Oppenheimer, Szilard, and Urey had scarcely a clue to how the quark-and-gluon microverse below the diameter of a proton operated by rules quite different from one's common-sense experience in the universe of the very large (things wider than the diameter of a proton). So strangely different, the large and the small, that in one sense the Schrödinger's-cat microverse is cut off from everyone, yet in another sense, it's at the root of every atom, every chemical, and every electrical pathway in your body, every breath you take.

"It is what it is," Mizuha had said.

"My mother, Mizuha, was an extraordinary person," Shiho had said, and called on futurity to remember. "Black rain had fallen upon her, but she chose not to dwell on anger, not to walk through life darkly. She thought, 'I don't want to talk too much about what happened. I don't want to hate Americans, either. Hate instead the bombs. Because to hate people—that's going to create more orphans.'"

And Mizuha had thought often about teachings from the Buddhist side of her family, and also from the Christians who came out of Nagasaki and married among them—both sides needing to keep their beliefs hidden during earlier centuries, and again during the war. What she took from that was the need for humans to build "a bridge to forgiveness."

For Shiho, her mother's bridge to forgiveness was a way of thinking, which (with a lot of hard work) might become the hope of a civilization that was beginning, more and more, to behave like tigers with nuclear-tipped claws.

"My family," Shiho said during the 2024 summer when Russia and then Iran first threatened a new dawn of atomic death and America resumed underground testing of nuclear weapons—"the sad thing is, they were a so, so very happy family. Wars take everything away from people. Safety. Peace. Sanity. Family."[11]

12

About the time Tak Furumoto immigrated back to America from Hiroshima, workers in Nagasaki had begun designing and building a permanent memorial museum. Like many other survivors, Mr. Yamaguchi avoided looking back over his shoulder at the past. As one of American baseball's newest fans, he took Leroy "Satchel" Paige's warning to heart: "Never look back. Something might be gaining on you."[12]

He did, however, make very rare visits to the museum during the decades after it was completed. One day, more than a half century after the atomic bomb, Yamaguchi saw a child from another city filming the exhibits. He walked up to the boy and asked him, "What are you going to do with this video?"

"When I go home, after vacation," the boy said, "I want to edit this together into a film and show it to everyone in my school."

"I think what you are doing is very important," Yamaguchi said, and bowed with his two scarred hands held together, as if in prayer. He never did explain how his hands came to be burned, nor did the boy ever suspect that the man bowing to him was a survivor of both Hiroshima and Nagasaki.

Were it possible, Mr. Yamaguchi would have preferred to remain anonymous forever, living peacefully in the forested countryside beyond Nagasaki with his children and his grandson, quietly sending forth little ripples of Father Simcho Kolbe's teachings. But history had charted an altogether different and more conspicuous destiny—"urging me," Yamaguchi recorded, "to turn a bad thing on its head and try to bring something good from it."

The course change began when his wife, Hisako, developed cancer. Then his son Katsutoshi developed cancer, suffered, and died a week short of his sixtieth birthday in 2005. Katsutoshi appeared to be part of an emerging pattern. People who held radiation in their bodies from childhood often developed tumors by age sixty, especially if their families had fled into the paths of wind-driven fallout and black rain or eaten contaminated fish and vegetables. Adolescents who were exposed at the age of fourteen or older and who survived were generally living full life spans. But for those exposed at a younger age, while their bodies were growing and their cells were rapidly dividing and differentiating, any chromosomal snaps and breakages (a primary pathway to cancer), if not immediately recognized and corrected by the body's often overwhelmed DNA repair systems, were not only passed onward to developing organs but also were often copied and mass-produced. A fractured, ruined gene became a lost chord that resonated and rippled through entire organ systems. Just as severely, the chemistry of human bodies continued all too often to confuse the bone-building and enamel-building metal calcium with some of the worst residua of the bombs. And from the decay of strontium-90 alone, thus did every child of Hiroshima and Nagasaki emit very fast electrons and antielectrons from his or her teeth. On every breath, Tsutomu Yamaguchi's son had exhaled antimatter.

The positrons (or antielectrons) born of strontium-90 almost immediately encountered the matter of tooth enamel or atmosphere and emitted submicroscopic flashes of gamma photons. And so it began for the children of Hiroshima and Nagasaki: Even in death, their teeth leaked gamma rays.

Yamaguchi started asking himself, more and more each passing day, *Is it time for me to speak up?*

"And when 2006 came around, I should surely have been dead," Yamaguchi told history. "Yet there I was, going into my nineties and somehow still walking around after being burned by the atomic *flash*—twice. Maybe, by God, or fate, or the universe (call it what you will)—maybe I was put right where I was supposed to be in those moments."

For a long time, the engineer-turned-carpenter-and-teacher wanted simply to stay out of history's way. Yet after his son died, and after he learned what was really happening to the children of a nuclear war, it became possible for him to believe there was truth behind the old saying that one sometimes meets his destiny on the road he takes to escape it. Perhaps, the time had come to shed his hard-won anonymity and tell the story of the two cities.

"I feel that I am allowed to live for that reason," Yamaguchi told his family. "To live long enough to do what needs to be done and say what needs to be said."

"They will *use* you," his daughter Toshiko warned. "You are almost ninety, and some of those who want to deny the effects of long-term radiation will point to you as an example for their agenda. If one can survive two atomic bombs and live so long, then why shouldn't even the Chernobyl meltdown be looked at as mostly harmless?"

Toshiko did not have to wait very long for someone to turn her warning into at least the very stubborn illusion of prophecy. After her father came out from seclusion and began to talk, a science book titled *The Violinist's Thumb* devoted a chapter to Tsutomu Yamaguchi, in which the author argued that radiation hazards had been grossly exaggerated to the public, because Yamaguchi was exposed to the radiation of both atomic bombs and lived to advanced old age.[13] No mention was made of what happened to the rest of his family or to Tak Furumoto's family (felled, one by one, by cancer), or to Sadako and all the other children who perished in a postnuclear leukemia epidemic. Nor was it mentioned that during both of Yamaguchi's exposures, in the moment of detonation, he was far enough away for the air and the humidity between himself and the bomb to provide the equivalent of at least six feet of shielding by water—from gamma rays, from the bomb's neutron spray, and (in Nagasaki especially) from most of the microwave surge. Only rays within the visible spectrum of light surged through the shield to scorch his skin. Nor was it mentioned that in Hiroshima, he was located *south* of the hypocenter and that only a slight misting of fallout ever reached him, cold and yellow like olive oil—while almost all the deadly black rain blew to the *northwest*. In Nagasaki, he was located south*west* of the hypocenter, and the fallout was driven away from him—*east* and north*east*. By improbable circumstance, the average CyberKnife cancer patient probably received a higher radiation dose than Tsutomu Yamaguchi on both those days. And most relevant of all, at Moment Zero he was a fully grown adult; it was his loved ones who faced the most frightful effects of radiation, as Father Kolbe might have anticipated from a reading of the Gospel of Matthew, had he lived to see the bombs.

(But woe unto those that are with child and to them that give suck [of milk, to their infants] in those days.)

The children of the bombs were most endangered of all, and young mothers who were inhaling and ingesting even small doses of calcium-mimicking isotopes could not have known that their bodies were concentrating white death in calcium-rich milk glands.

"I have a job that needs to be finished," Yamaguchi told his daughter, "regardless of what others will say." When a pair of documentary filmmakers asked him if he would speak at the United Nations, he looked to the past for signposts to the future and said the core of his message would be simply this: "We cannot let an atomic bomb be used a third time." And so, for the first time in his life, Tsutomu Yamaguchi applied for a passport and traveled to New York, at the age of ninety.

At the United Nations, Yamaguchi struggled to hold back tears. He was looking out on the faces of too many young people. They brought him down into recollections of encounters with aimlessly wandering children blinded by the flash—recollections that caused him to worry about this next generation's future.

"Until there was war, nobody knew of an atomic bomb," he told an audience that included students from an American high school, about the same age as a group of broiled and disfigured bodies he had seen floating in one of Hiroshima's rivers the day after.

"Please," he said, "everyone, study history with earnest and think about the nobility and the importance of peace. Together with you all, the good-hearted American youth, I now pray . . . for an understanding that we are one and the same, all of us."

He recalled that he had it on the word of several scientists—one of them working on the interplanetary flight potential of nuclear fusion—that if some aberrant suicidal faction of humanity decided to create a mass extinction, it was possible to detonate two or three easily redesigned hydrogen bombs in just two or three specific places. One scientist had called them collectively the "*On the Beach* bomb," after a novel and two films of that title. The scientist explained that it would take about six years instead of the six months in *On the Beach*, noting that while it was possible to nitpick little details in either of the films, the result, six years after, would be simply this: No whales, most fish extinct, many invertebrate species lost. No deciduous trees. Most flowering plants gone. No birds. No mammals. Life becomes good for fungi and putrefactive bacteria. Flour beetles will survive the radiation if they can find anything to eat. Bedbugs will go down with their human prey. Rats will outlive humans, at least for a little while. Cockroaches will mostly die off, because they are tropical insects and require the heating systems of human habitations in all the high latitudes, wherever snows develop. He knew that Einstein said a nuclear war would knock civilization back to the Stone Age. But the new reality was that life on Earth would be knocked back far beyond the Stone Age, back more than 500 million years to the early Cambrian.

"One and the same, all of us," Tsutomu Yamaguchi said again. "All for one and one for all. One humanity, or none." He felt that the point could never be overemphasized:

"*Each of you*," he began to teach, "though you may only be a single human being—each of you can, on your own, help us to start understanding each other. That's all it takes: small steps. That's all you have to remember. Send simple acts of kindness outward, from person to person. Send forth kindness like a contagious disease."

What could be easier? Yamaguchi wondered. He realized that his hope of

Approximately three hundred people are known to have traveled by train from Hiroshima to Nagasaki. Ninety percent of them, including Dr. Susumu Tsunoo, died in the second atomic bombing. Kinuyo Fukui (shown left, in 2021) and Tsutomu Yamaguchi (shown right, in 2008) each survived the atomic bombings of both Hiroshima and Nagasaki. Mr. Yamaguchi is one of only two (the other is Shigeyoshi Morimoto) known to have been shock-cocooned within the zone of Ground Zero damage, both times.

change through individual acts of mutual human tenderness might sound simplistic—completely naive, even—"but if we follow such principles, then we must emerge from the experience of war not as Japanese or American, not as Christian or Buddhist, Hindu or Muslim, or Jew or Shinto, but simply as . . . human beings. We have to start somewhere. *Have to.*"[14]

13

Time and tides always have the final say, or so the poets claim.

Though more than a half century had passed, John Baxter remained in contact with the prison guard to whom, he told his family, "I owe my survival." When his son, also named John, was grown with children of his own, they made a pilgrimage to a Japanese town called Inatsuki. There, once again, Hyato invited his former prisoner—and this time the POW's family—for green tea and a ceremonial meal on fine porcelain. "And there," Baxter would say later, "a chance to recall a very different time in both of our lives."[15]

Haruno, the heroic streetcar driver who gave up the search for her mother to transport and nurse the injured instead, emerged from Hiroshima as an atomic orphan. She moved far from the city, married at age sixteen, became the mother of three children and grandmother of seven.[16]

Fifteen-year-old rescue worker and double survivor Kinuyo Fukui, like Haruno, chose to move as far as possible from the cities—all the way north, beyond the land of the snow monkeys. She married a Northerner and started a strong business; but about 1967, a recurrence of atomic-bomb sickness, from which she had quickly recovered in 1945, almost cost her the business and her life. Gradually, with her husband's help, she became mobile again, and finally quite active again. Her little brother, Kuniyoshi, never quite recovered from being witness to nuclear war. The Hiroshima Memorial Museum displays the sketchbook he left behind—"Brutal memories," she said. "Things you wouldn't want to recall. But I became painfully aware of the feelings of my brother, compelled to keep records of us surviving with all of our strength."

In the year 2021, Kinuyo mourned for her recently deceased brother, whose childish bickering had changed her schedule and saved her life on the day of the first bomb. The year her brother passed, Kinuyo attended Hiroshima's August 6 memorial for the first time. She imagined 2021 would be her last time. Recalling how Kuniyoshi got lonely easily, Kinuyo explained, "I'll probably go to be with him soon. When that happens, we two siblings will start bickering again."[17]

In America, Leo Szilard left nuclear physics behind and switched to the field of molecular biology, unable to quite surround the fact that they had indeed dropped "that horrible thing" on two cities. In 1960 he developed bladder cancer and moved to Memorial Sloan Kettering Cancer Center in New York, where he began perfecting the then-experimental cobalt-60 radiation treatment on himself and (somewhat in the manner of Dr. Nagai of Nagasaki) brought about a sustained remission from cancer, until a heart attack felled him in 1964.

H. G. Wells, whose 1914 science fiction novel about the development of the atomic bomb was, as Szilard saw it, the start of "the whole damned mess," lived until 1946—long enough to assist Eleanor Roosevelt in penning a section of the United Nations' Universal Declaration of Human Rights.[18]

After learning about Peggy Covell, Mitsuo Fuchida became very religious. He eventually traveled to America preaching forgiveness, sometimes even asking forgiveness for himself. He would leave Walter Lord perplexed (especially about requests that Lord "be born again"). Along the way, Fuchida had a son, Joseph, who grew up to become an American architect. During the early 1980s, like Tak Furumoto, Joseph Fuchida became an extreme rarity in New York real estate circles—able to speak the two essential languages for Japanese land buyers. Though Tak was still slowly coming to terms with PTSD, he and Joseph teamed up for a while, at just the right moment for both of them. Many months passed before the kindly, soft-spoken architect revealed to Tak who his father was. During the anti-Japanese rants of the 1980s, there was no predicting whether Tak's occasional business associate, Donald Trump, would "freak out" over the possibility of some shoddy reporter trying to go full Salem-witch-trial mode by associating the Trump organization's Japan dealings with "a Pearl Harbor family." So Tak kept Trump blissfully unaware. There was already enough PTSD in the world.

For Tak Furumoto, it sometimes seemed that history never wanted to be quite finished with him. More than a half century after his family was imprisoned, a letter arrived from President Bill Clinton. Frustratingly, not until most of the people who deserved to see such a thing had passed from this Earth—not until July 2018 (too late, for most)—would Tak live to see the US Supreme Court finally declare, officially, that the internment camps were unconstitutional. His family's imprisoning home state of California would resist agreement with the federal court until 2020. These declarations began a quarter century after President Clinton's letter of October 1, 1993:

> Over fifty years ago, the United States Government unjustly interned, evacuated, or relocated you and many other Japanese Americans. Today on behalf of your fellow Americans, I offer sincere apologies to you for the actions that unfairly denied Japanese Americans and their families fundamental liberties during World War II . . . In retrospect, we recognize that the nation's actions were rooted deeply in racial prejudice, wartime hysteria, and a lack of political leadership. We must learn from the past and dedicate ourselves as a nation to renewing the spirit of equality and love of freedom. Together, we can guarantee a future of liberty and justice for all.

For Tak, though a president had said in 1993, "We must learn from the past"—*even with this*, he thought, *nothing is guaranteed*. He told himself again: *Nothing is guaranteed. It's up to you. We have to be vigilant. All of us.*[19]

His family knew better than most. And so it had come to pass that one day a most sickening human aberration turned the skyscrapers of lower Manhattan into a crater. During the weeks afterward, on a gray deathscape of toxic dust, paper cranes arrived in multicolored bundles of one thousand, each bundle held together by delicate threads. Many bundles were sent to the "miracle firehouse" on Liberty Street, in which nearly three hundred injured people were being sheltered at the moment the South Tower of the World Trade Center shotgunned the earth, frighteningly near, with much of its force deflecting around the three hundred. The little firehouse became one of history's largest known shock-cocoon events. By Christmas 2001, one of the firehouse doors was draped in thousands and thousands of paper cranes. Within the crater rim, except for American flags drawn gently over baskets being raised from the ruins, the paper cranes were the only color inside Ground Zero. They seemed the only traces of color in the world. Some who saw them wept. A marine wept.

One of the firefighters, after helping uncover a terrible sight in a building next door, asked a forensic investigator, "What is it about all these colored paper birds?"

"I don't know," the scientist said. "I've asked about that. They're from Japan. I heard from one of my kids that it has something to do with Hiroshima."

When the streets were cleared of rubble and reconstruction began, two buildings near the firehouse became a gathering place for 9/11 family members and survivors. One of the buildings evolved into the first "Tribute Center" and museum.

("We must learn from the past" . . . *"We have to be vigilant.")*

By then, many Americans, among them some of the 9/11 family members, were calling for Muslim Americans to be deported or even to be "put away"—notwithstanding the reality that many people of the Muslim faith had died in the towers during the attack. Tak Furumoto had seen this sort of ugliness before.

"We have to watch out," he said to anyone who would listen. "America is a great place in the world. I've seen many other countries. It *is* a great place in the world. And you've got to guard it (and its Constitution, and its Bill of Rights) to make it stay great." A friend's daughter came home for winter break from college, where she was being indoctrinated with the increasingly common idea that "the Constitution isn't really relevant anymore." Her family had been hit hard by 9/11.

The father replied that those who were declaring constitutional rights "irrelevant" seem to covet the power to repeat what was done to Tak's family, and maybe on a wider scale than was done last time. "The Constitution is like a life-giving river. We must protect it, every mile, every inch along its course. Read it; then ask Tak."

Through 2010, Masahiro Sasaki made several trips to New York. He spent time with Tak Furumoto's family. And he met many 9/11 families. He taught them the origin of the paper cranes. He taught them *Omoiyari*. Not all of them understood, or wanted to hear it. But a few did. And a few were enough. And *Omoiyari* would, in time, spread among them until the Tribute Center itself came to be symbolized by the paper crane and the word that came with it.

When Masahiro met with Tak, he brought not just the word with him, but one of his sister's actual paper cranes, as a presentation to the emerging museum.

At dinner the day before he made the donation, Masahiro explained that a changed way of thinking did not need to start out like a shotgun blast. "Even a single snowflake can bring about change. For what is the mightiest glacier but a [river] of snowflakes?" Send forth enough of them, Masahiro believed, and one individual, somewhere, has a chance of reaching some person, somewhere, who might become pivotal in history. ("Do I advise my commander to attack or to talk? To launch or to hold back for a while?") Like Tsutomu Yamaguchi, Masahiro hoped that out-branching acts of kindness might, without anyone ever knowing it, reach into the heart of a child who has perhaps lost all hope and who thinks there is nothing good left in humanity, and was it then possible to believe a random act of kindness could change the path of someone who might otherwise grow up to create another night of black rain and strange blue light?

Masahiro withdrew a reddish-violet paper crane from a special box. Clearly, it had been folded from a medicine label in the Hiroshima hospital all those years ago.

"So small," said Tak's wife, Carolyn.

Masahiro placed it in the center of her palm. Tak was surprised at how it could be so small—could be folded like this, tinier than a mosquito.

"From the children of Hiroshima to the children of New York—and the world." Being among the smallest, it was also among the very last paper cranes Sadako had created. And a larger origami bird would emerge from the ashes, all so tragically too soon. In Manhattan, Tak Furumoto had become the only person on Earth exposed to Hiroshima radiation, *and* to Agent Orange in 'Nam, *and* to New York City's months-long "snow flurries" of toxic 9/11 dust. After 3/11 happened—Japan's day of earthquake, tsunamis, and the creation of a nuclear lava pool (March 11, 2011)—Sadako's cranes came full circle. From New York's Tribute Center, impromptu counseling and aid reached back to Japan. Survivors and first responders of 9/11 reached out to survivors and first responders of 3/11. Some members of the 9/11 Family Association flew to Japan directly.

One came from the opposite direction. Shiho flew her mother out of Japan and permanently to the United States. She decided that Mizuha had already been exposed once to radioactive fallout, in Hiroshima, "and once was enough."

One who flew *toward* Fukushima, a firefighter who had undergone a heart-lung transplant as a result of intense dust poisoning in New York's "WTC crater," personally escorted a large origami crane, folded and welded from World Trade Center steel. It was mounted in Japan's Kaiseizan Park, some fifty miles from a still-active nuclear volcano that used to be part of the Fukushima reactor system.

The steel "paper crane" marks another place on Earth in need of healing.

Writing for *National Geographic*, Ari Beser described the visitors from New York, the day a folded bird of steel was dedicated, "as a symbol of hope and resilience in the face of disaster." Ari, the grandson of Jacob Beser, had been befriended by Sadako's brother. "Consoled by Sadako's crane," Ari recorded, "they [the New Yorkers] dedicated their own crane."[20]

The lessons of the origami crane and its sacred word would not (and could not) ever be finished. As a matter of fact, they were only beginning to spread.

14

A boy's marbles. That is what you would have found in 2011 if you visited the suburban retirement home for the nurses and physicians and one or two other witnesses of Hiroshima. Nenkai Aoyama lived at the home, keeping alive the memory of a mother who had shooed him out of the house and away to his work detail perplexingly early on the day of an experiment in death that severed the human species' past from its future. Nenkai Aoyama's mother was near the "Atomic Dome" when it happened. She vanished. The Aoyama boy and the other retirees had dedicated a whole room on the ground floor as a memorial museum. In one corner, surrounded by paper cranes, little Toshihiko Matsuda's glass marbles lay on a bed of cotton.

A boy's marbles, melting. That is how the great human divide began. On that day, molten green glass had resolidified into strange new shapes.

We are tactile creatures. Hold one of the Matsuda boy's marbles in your hand, and your mind is shoved back to the war that changed everything, back to that bisecting moment.

Not very far from the retirement home and its museum, little Tak Furumoto's toy marbles had brought him gradually to friendships with the children of his farming community in Hiroshima. Some of the boys eventually made it into his father's photo album. The marbles they won from Tak probably passed down through children and grandchildren of the 1950s and '60s and the year that internment camp witness George

Takei performed voice-over for a scene in the movie *Rodan*, and the glass beads must have continued circulating throughout the city until video games and smartphones became ascendant. Future generations will occasionally find them in forgotten storage closets and in garden soils, rarely if ever suspecting their actual history.

And so the dice of history kept rolling. And probability curves kept running amok and against one another. In the west, ancient Romans would have said it was the Fates toying with humanity—taking certain families as pets, setting them apart on divergent paths, stepping back for a while just to watch, then coming back, even more meddlesome, to intertwine them again: Walter Lord, Mitsuo Fuchida, Tak Furumoto . . . stepping back (the goddess of mischief and her Fates) . . . stepping back for a little while longer, then mixing the names Furumoto and Fuchida again, with Trump . . . then Sasaki and Furumoto . . . Peggy Covell and Mitsuo Fuchida's flight engineer . . . and there are thirty double survivors in the mix . . . and the "premonition" cases . . . and Baxter and Hyato . . . Jacob Beser and Hiroko Tasaka . . . Kenshi, Saeko, Setsuko . . . Yamaguchi and Nagai . . . Tengo, *Barefoot Gen*, and Mizuha . . . Yamaguchi, Cameron, Obama . . .

And so on.

And Walter Lord again, baseball, and Heisenberg.

At war's end, after the fall of Germany and before he met Fuchida, Walter had participated in the interrogations of Hitler's architect, Albert Speer ("the swine-hund only pretended at being the repentant Nazi") and German physicist Werner Heisenberg ("an unsung hero, perhaps, who sabotaged the German atomic-bomb project from within . . . and who, when secretly recorded with surrendered colleagues, could not believe we actually built and dropped the thing"). After the war, after his "Heisenberg incident," the polymathic Walter Lord would so obsess on baseball that he could have written one of the great histories on the subject. During the war, he had come to know another polymathic genius, retired baseball home-run slugger Moe Berg—valued by the OSS for his photographic memory and fluency in multiple languages. He was a brilliant conversationalist, informal and disarming. As an ambassador for baseball, he appeared to be merely a layman who could listen to scientists (while pretending mere curiosity), but most of all, he understood them. In late 1944, Berg had been assigned to kill Heisenberg at a Zurich conference where, at the last moment, during a dinner discussion, he declined to complete his mission. The decision left Walter and others puzzled, even if Heisenberg did appear (and perhaps *only* appeared) to be leading Germany's atomic scientists in the wrong direction. Walter did not understand the meaning of the reactor cross section Heisenberg had drawn for Berg, sketched during just a few seconds in what appeared to be childlike scribble. Walter and his British counterparts were angered by Berg's decision, but he had asked them to trust him, and let Heisenberg continue what he was doing.

And in those days, during what few snippets of daydreaming time existed, Walter Lord and his British colleague, Ian Fleming, carried on a friendly competition, betting on which of them would be first to pen a postwar bestseller. Walter still carried in mind, since age fourteen, the seeds of *A Night to Remember*. Ian was drawing up plans for *Chitty Chitty Bang Bang*, before eventually deciding on a real-life composite-but-fictional spy named after his and Walter's favorite ornithologist, James Bond. In 1992, when a *New York Times* writer approached Walter Lord about a biography detailing the birth stages of the CIA and MI-5, Lord said, "Never want to relive that. It's too depressing a story to tell."[21] Moe Berg, when asked to write an autobiography, had said the same thing.

And so on.

In 2012, an American woman named Elizabeth was rising in the real estate industry. Her family had come originally from Japan, so in her travels through New Jersey, a drive past a Fort Lee real estate office with a Japanese name out front aroused her curiosity.

Maybe there's some sales potential here, she thought, and stepped inside, and was greeted by Carol Furumoto.

"My name is Elizabeth Ooka," she said, and pronounced it *Oka*.

Elizabeth recalls: "Carol had this look on her face, where she kind of cocked her head over to one side, and her jaw dropped a little bit, and she was just looking at my business card. (The card gave a California address.) I was telling her about all the products and services that my company provides, and she couldn't—she just couldn't take her eyes away from the card."

Strange . . .

Carol did not say anything about the products Elizabeth was offering. Certainly, there was no indication that this could be the beginning of reacquaintance (or convergence, or negative entropy, call it what you will)—no, not the beginning of an oddly more beautiful kind of chain reaction.

"I think my husband will want to meet you," Carol said at last. "Can you come back to the office tomorrow, around twelve thirty?"

Elizabeth put the appointment into her calendar and drove away wondering, *Maybe her husband makes all the business decisions, and I'll just have to go back and repitch.*

The following afternoon, Tak greeted Elizabeth and walked her into a conference room. A large book lay on the table, closed.

"You may not know who I am," Tak said. "But I know who you are."

Elizabeth laughed. "Who am I?"

Tak opened the book to a group photo of some twenty or thirty employees standing in front of a building in California. A sign above their heads read Oka Produce Company.

"Ohhh . . . That's a photo of my grandfather's produce company."

Tak smiled and asked, "Where's your grandfather, in this picture?"

Elizabeth pointed to a tall man at the center of the photo. "*Here.* That's him."

Tak said, "My *father* is in this photo."

"He is? Where?"

"Here," Tak said, pointing. "Standing right next to your grandfather." And, he explained, they were in business together. "My father had only a third-grade education, but your grandfather gave him a chance. And they were quite successful."

The large photo celebrated the company's grand opening in 1938. Elizabeth had seen this same picture in her own family album. Both families had been deported initially to a California racetrack. They never did see one another, as they waited with thousands of others for transport to individual camps. Yet the oral histories of both families told of finding the same kind of shelter in vacated horse stalls, where they were obliged to sleep on floors of manure-slicked straw.

Elizabeth's family knew of only one photo documenting their time in prison: journalist Toyo Miyatake's classic 1944 image of three Manzanar camp children behind barbed wire. Tak, like millions of other people across America and around the world, knew this image.

Elizabeth mentioned the "*Three Boys*" photo and said, "The one wearing a white shirt, the one whose hand is reaching out toward the wire—your dad surely knew him: just a little kid helping out with the groceries, way back at the Oka Produce market. That boy is my father."

Although the photo was already famous by the time Elizabeth went to college, she had been deep into her twenties before she learned of her family's connection, "because Dad never talked about the internment camps." She did not learn of it until the turn of the century, when her parents attended a friend's fiftieth wedding anniversary dinner and took Elizabeth along.

"And for some reason," Elizabeth recorded for history, "they started talking about the *Three Boys* picture. And Mom said, 'Do you know, my husband's one of those boys?'"

People who knew the photo looked at the man whose father had given Tak's father his first chance, and the resemblance was unmistakable.

Elizabeth looked at him in shock and saw it for the first time.

A man who had been standing nearby walked over to Elizabeth's dad and said, "I overheard that you're one of the boys in the picture. Do you know anybody named Bruce?"

"Well, I knew him also from his Japanese name, but yeah. I know him."

"And it turned out," Elizabeth explained to futurity, "that Bruce and his wife, Linda, were living in Hilo, Hawaii, only about five minutes out the backyard of my brother's house. And then we learned from a park ranger in California that the other boy, the third boy, Bob, had just made a visit to the Manzanar camp."

And so it was decided: back to Manzanar—back seventy years to 1944, in 2014.

A cinematographer friend went with the boys, their families, and some of their fellow prisoners. The six-minute documentary that began to take shape, initially just for a private family memoir—*Three Boys Manzanar*—would go on to be awarded an Emmy in 2022.

Most everything that had stood in Manzanar in 1945 was long ago bulldozed into the earth. A park ranger navigated an old paper map to find where the Oka family's barrack had stood, somewhere near the middle of a mostly featureless field of scrub grass, rocks, and weeds. But Dad corrected her on the location. He recognized a pear tree in the distance. Their barrack was much nearer that tree and the garden that had surrounded it.

"You know," he said, "there was a street here. Just down this street, there's this woman who had the craziest garden. There's something like a moat—Japanese-style, with a bridge."

And a remnant of the bridge could still be seen. From the reference point of the garden, they found all that remained of the barrack where the Oka family had lived: a distinctive arrangement of shapes that the elder Furumoto's business partner had carved into a doorstep threshold stone. "This is how I know that this is my home," said Elizabeth's father.

Archaeological traces of basements were still there. The three boys explained to park rangers that fathers had dug the basements because it was cooler down there during the summer, warmer in the winter. Ten and twenty feet long, the features of rectangular depressions in the ground were softened by bulldozing and erosion; but they were still there, waiting to tell their story.

The three boys spoke about how they used to play games in those chambers beneath the floorboards.

It was a ghostly place. "The streets and barracks are gone, but there's still something of the people—there's still fragments of cups and glass plateware in the fields," Elizabeth recorded. "The rangers leave it all untouched now, as much as possible. And it was so crazy, because while we were walking around, Dad and Bruce were talking about how they played marbles. My sister saw a little ball on the ground and asked, 'What is that?' There was another nearby. And another. They sent chills up our backs—that Dad and Bruce are talking about how and when, as kids in the camp, they played marbles. And here they found, weathered by decades of wind and rain, marbles on the ground."[22]

15

Thurlow, the thirteen-year-old girl who had been assigned to what turned out to be a protective chamber within Hiroshima's army headquarters during Moment Zero, had grown up to become a nuclear weapons abolitionist. In May 2015, in New York, she unfurled an approximately four-foot-wide, very long ribbon of yellow silk, covered with beautiful examples of Japanese calligraphy.

"Tonight," she said, "I want to show something very precious to me. People stumble over the big numbers. When I say that by the end of 1945, a hundred and forty thousand people perished in the city, it's too huge to visualize. And I thought, 'How better, how effectively, can I help the people to grasp the idea I am trying to convey?'"

She ran a hand across the rows of Japanese characters.

> Well, let me explain. You see four rows from right to left, and hundreds of names of the girls that I studied with at the Girls' School in Hiroshima. And altogether there are three hundred fifty-one names of the girls who perished. There are several names of the teachers, but the girls are grades seven and eight students. One of these belonged to my good friend Setsuko Morimoto. She was in the center of the city together with many other students as part of a work crew, right under the

explosion of the atomic bomb—which, by the time it reached the ground level, generated four thousand degrees Celsius (forty times the boiling point of water, four times hotter than molten lava, three times the temperature of steel emerging white from a furnace).

"It was summer and people dressed lightly, and some of the boys must have had their shirts off . . ." Thurlow looked down and went quiet for a moment. Just for a moment. "They're the ones who melted. Vaporized. Some, carbonized. I don't know which term is the most appropriate one. People argue it today. And these girls . . ." Thurlow touched several of the names with a hand. "They died in that moment. But they happened to be in the center of the city, and I happened to be in the army headquarters about one mile away from them. That's all. Therefore, I'm alive and standing here before you. I just want you to remember, on this long ribbon, each one, each name, represents one human being, most quickly vanished from the face of the Earth. We cannot let them be just disappeared."

A scientist who was present quickly ran through some math regarding Thurlow's ribbon of just over 350 names, twenty feet long, and told her that if all the 140,000 she mentioned could be named, the ribbon would have to be a mile and a half long—the names of human beings, reaching more than halfway across Manhattan Island.

Touching the small sampling of just 350 names and looking to the city beyond, Thurlow concluded:

> As we talk about nuclear weapons, we are finally talking with a humanitarian perspective. In the past, people were always talking about statistics and military doctrine—of deterrence and things like that. But now we are refocusing on humanity, on human beings. *That* is a great change. I have lived in North America for many years, but I am lately meeting the agents of change and feeling the emergence of change. We have to

rejoice. But we need to work hard to make sure that no human beings will have the experience of a most inhumane, immoral, and cruel nuclear war.

She began rolling up the ribbon, touching the names as she did so. "Well, I made the vow to them," she said. "That is my vow. That is my prayer."[23]

16

In January 2010, Tsutomu Yamaguchi succumbed to what appeared to be the fate of most *hibakusha*: a prolonged battle with cancer. He survived years (to age ninety-three) with a form of stomach cancer that was often lethal within six months of discovery; and long ahead of the cancer, as far back as his daughter Toshiko could remember, his hair fell out every summer and the scars on his hands seemed to worsen temporarily. Two or three times each winter, a simple common cold progressed to pneumonia.

In a suburb of Nagasaki, Kenshi Hirata's daughter Saeko, who worked for a TV news organization, was both moved and fascinated by the story of a double *hibakusha* who had lived nearby. She did not know yet that another survivor of both atomic bombs lived much nearer or that he was her own father.

In late February 2010 documentary filmmakers Hidetaka Inazuka and Hideo Nakamura finally located Saeko and gently revealed who her father had been.

"Had been," it turned out, was not the correct term. Kenshi Hirata was still alive. He was ninety-one years old, but like many of the survivors, he did not want to remember. Even those who did speak of it, as Yamaguchi had, did so with great difficulty. Especially, Kenshi did not want to speak about his beloved Setsuko and what happened to her in Hiroshima.

Only slowly, between March and August 2010, did Kenshi Hirata begin to reveal what, for most of his life, he had hoped no one would actually learn about him. A contributing factor moving him to think of "coming out" was a report in the American press claiming that he might never even have existed—and that his long-ago recorded experiences, and the experiences of others in and around the two cities, should be suspected as "possibly fabricated."

And so he confirmed for his visitors, "Yes. I am Kenshi Hirata," and volunteered for facial-recognition analysis against surviving photographs of himself in the Mitsubishi archives.

"Being a double survivor was a shameful dishonor," he said enigmatically; and for many weeks afterward it appeared that he would never say anything more about it. Hideo Nakamura and Nagasaki Museum historian Tomoko Maekawa tried to comprehend what sort of survivor's guilt must have accompanied being shielded from the atomic bomb twice while his wife and more than 200,000 people died all around him in two cities.

In time, Kenshi explained that part of his shame came from the demands of Japanese society during the 1940s. Even remarriage of a widower, in those times, came under the shadow of "the district gossip committee" and was considered a dishonorable act that somehow stained the children: "So I was not only trying to protect my children from radiation discrimination; I did not want society to carry rumors and scandals about my daughter as a second-marriage daughter. And so I eliminated the secondness of the marriage."

"How can you keep it in your heart?" Saeko asked her father. "I'm amazed that you kept it secret, like a clam, for sixty-five years."

"I am relieved to finally speak out," Kenshi said.

"I am sorry for him to now have to expose this secret after so many years," Saeko recorded for history. "In that inferno, my father was trying to find his wife. Sacrificing everything—without complaining about the pain—to find her. I am amazed. For two full days, he was searching for his wife. This is something he has been hiding for a long time. But I am delighted to see my more real father."

"I did not wish to be a double *hibakusha*," Kenshi said, emphasizing for all humankind: "This is not my wish. It just happened because they built the bombs. So everyone has to think about it. If we really think about each other, this should not be. Nuclear arms are not [compatible] with civilization. I think such a thing should not be existing."

And he concluded, "This is the first and last time I will speak to the world about it. These are my last words on the subject. Do with them what you may."[24]

17

Once upon a time, there were only three atomic bombs—only three, in all the world. The humans tested one on a platform in the New Mexico desert, to see if the machine would work. They dropped the other two on themselves.

In May 2016, as President Obama was headed toward Hiroshima, Tsutomu Yamaguchi's daughter Toshiko was called upon for some words, and she asked James Cameron and a scientist friend to prepare, with her family, a paragraph as an accompaniment for the president's speech at Hiroshima's Memorial Park.

The plan for the statement had developed on short notice, and Cameron's colleague happened to be sitting in a New York Supreme Court jury pool when the email deadline arrived. He and Cameron started corresponding back and forth, determined to have something ready in time for Obama's presentation.

In Manhattan, the courts typically allowed potential jurors to bring laptops and conduct business in the courthouse waiting area, except during moments of particular importance. According to instruction, at such moments, "Not even if it's the president of your corporation calling (and not even if your corporation is Apple) will you keep your phone on or your laptop open." The friend did not hear the call for one of those moments, so hurriedly was he jotting down (and crossing out) sentence fragments on pieces of paper and trying to shoot notes off to Cameron. He received a swift reprimand from a no-nonsense Tina-Turner-in-*Mad-Max-Beyond-Thunderdome* doppelganger.

"I'm awfully sorry," the friend tried to relate, while dropping the paper scraps onto his keyboard and closing the laptop screen over them. "I didn't hear because I'm working on this paragraph for the president's vi—"

"*You were told*, it doesn't matter if it's your boss or the president of your company yelling, '*Urgent!*'"

"Not *that* president," he said as softly as he could, to keep the attention on the incident minimal. Then, asking politely to move nearer and to whisper, he was allowed to explain about a president who was visiting Hiroshima and about the drafting of a letter honoring the family of a man who had survived both atomic bombs.

"Honey!" the officer said. "Here's what's going to happen: I'm finishing your jury duty right now so you can just get your ass right home, *right now*, and do your job!"

An hour later, Toshiko Yamaguchi had her joint statement:

> In Hiroshima there is a "Tree of Hope," which survived the first atomic bomb and which is prophesied to continue growing until the day humans banish nuclear weapons from the Earth. One day, the tree will be forgotten, either because human civilization has changed its way of thinking and eliminated nuclear weapons, and the tree becomes just another tree, or because nuclear weapons have eliminated us, and there is no one left to water it.[25]

A whip-like flash. The building, all around me, exploded away. From a ditch, somebody called my name, so I turned toward the voice. It was someone whose ears, nose, and head had melted. A neighbor? I couldn't tell who that person was. As I stood there, the person fell down. It seemed the neck was broken. To this day, I do not know who that person was.

—Kanji Fukahori (age 12),
Messages from Hibakusha

When I was about to give up, I came across my father. He did not recognize me.

—Mitsuko Masuno (age 7),
Messages from Hibakusha

EPILOGUE:
ISLAND IN THE STREAM OF STARS

After stumbling upon and studying Morgan Robertson's strangely prophetic "Beyond the Spectrum" tales, Walter Lord and a colleague sought out everything they could learn about the author's personal history. Even with a renowned private detective pitching in to help, there wasn't much: Robertson had almost drowned during a boating accident (believed to have occurred on Long Island Sound, age at the time of the event unknown). For a time, he went to sea aboard merchant ships. He drank heavily of wine and rum, often to drown out nightmares about a monkeyish muse that told him what to write. This is how Robertson explained his novel about a ship named *Titan* that struck an iceberg and sank, fourteen years before the *Titanic*. For a while, he was befriended by Henry Sleeper Harper, who published one of his stories, then stepped into history by boarding the real-life 1912 version of Morgan Robertson's science fictional steamship. Harper might have had Robertson's 1898 *Futility, or the Wreck of the Titan* in mind when he hurried into one of the first lifeboats to leave the *Titanic*, early enough to allow space for his dog. After that, the sci-fi writer and his monkey muse became virtually unpublishable. Dulled by drink, Robertson's style deteriorated from borderline "penny dreadful" to the pits. Even after his fictional global war really did shake the Earth, even after Pearl Harbor and Manila really were attacked by the Empire of Japan on a December morning, even after the president really did succumb to jingoism and herd Japanese Americans from their homes like cattle, and even after the bombs of August unleashed invisible radiation and the power of the sun over Hiroshima and Nagasaki, his stories never did come back into print. The war ended thirty years after Robertson himself ended, in 1915. On mid-century backroom shelves in libraries across the land, even autographed "Beyond the Spectrum" volumes remained unborrowed, visited only by book lice and mice feeding on the bindings' glue.

Walter learned that Robertson died young, raging to anyone who would listen against publishers who refused any longer even to read his expanding collection of chapter-stories, much less actually print the chapters. Robertson's nightmares pursued him till the very end. Sometimes, they came upon him while he was wide awake. He may have been suffering from schizophrenia or delirium tremens, or some combination of both.

Weeks after the Twin Towers of the World Trade Center fell, news anchors, looking for anything they could even *pretend* to report as sensationally new, started poring over the old Nostradamus quatrains. Walter, who always preferred to stay out of the public spotlight and who in any case was feeling too exhausted on most days, had told only one close friend how he awoke one morning to a wondrous and frightening realization:

"Morgan Robertson wrote another book."[1]

THE SHADOW PEOPLE PROJECT

The real horror of the "shadow people" phenomenon is that only rarely, only within the small radius of instant carbonization at temperatures hotter than lava emerging white from Kīlauea, hotter than the "surface" of the sun—only to a radius of about eight hundred feet in Hiroshima—only there was death a matter of instantaneous nonexistence. Beyond that radius, flash-burned people walked away to slow death, leaving their shadows behind.

The Shadow People Project is in memory of them, and it should involve young adult artists. It is in remembrance, and for widespread teaching.

Education. There is no substitute.

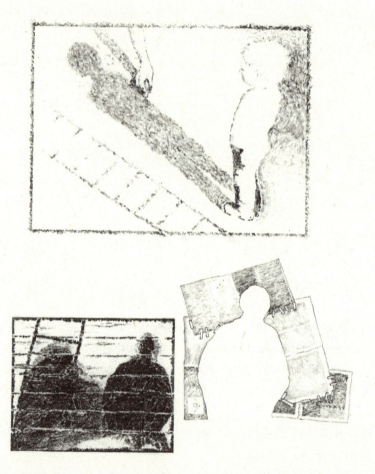

The Shadow People Project—which asks that you use non-vandalistic chalk (never spray paint)—is something art students, parents, and even children can carry out around the world: education through art. As illustrated here, chalk images can be produced either by creating new shadows as they would appear around the fringes of nuclear detonations in the modern world, or by creating a stencil (as in the lower half of this illustration: a newspaper-and-tape cut-out, for chalk spray; in this case, the figure is based on an actual "shadow man" burned onto a wall three miles from the Nagasaki detonation). Yoobi is just one of the easily available, washable, nontoxic chalk sprays. Black and (for dark walls or dark pavement) off-white chalk are the preferred colors. If you or a friend does not own a smartphone attachment for projecting figures onto walls (to make stencils), there are effective tutorials on YouTube for how to make cell phone projectors from shoeboxes—as, for example, on the "d'Art of Science" page.
If you wish, you can begin by using shadows illustrated in this book (these are provided free of copyright).

Six miles from a modern nuclear detonation—up to 330 kilotons (Russian warhead, relative to Nagasaki's approximately 27 kilotons)—people caught outdoors and unshielded would leave little more than shadowy traces behind (this, too, can be copied for a Shadow People Project). In Japan, the survivors of August 1945 call themselves hibakusha. Between the years 2009 and 2019, at the Nagasaki Memorial services, a dwindling number of them sang, "Hear the Voice of the Hibakusha." As the clock ticks toward the 2045 centennial, the day approaches when there will be no one alive who can tell you what they saw and experienced under an atomic bomb. And this is as they wish it to be: That you and your children will never know anyone with a new hibakusha story to tell, about a new city hypocenter.

"Never Again, the A-bomb" was a song brought by ambassador children of Japan's WWII enemy China to a hospital where children who survived the flash and blast effects of the bomb were dying ten years later from the effects of radiation. To a few who witnessed this suffering, people and animals "who vanished utterly in the searing white flash, leaving behind only ghostly images on walls and sidewalks" were the lucky ones. (This is another image suggestion for the Shadow People Project. The images can be accompanied by chalk captions: for example, "6 miles from Ground Zero," with distance to a city landmark added—"Empire State Building" or "The Pyramids" or "The Eiffel Tower," or any other location.)

And with each image, for the hibakusha wish and for the teaching of Omoiyari, please leave behind a paper crane.

APPENDIX: KEY EYEWITNESSES (ALPHABETICAL GUIDE)

JOHN BAXTER: A "hell ship" survivor, sent to a slave labor coal mine outside a city targeted for nuclear attack. Baxter and dozens of other prisoners lived to see war's end through the lifesaving efforts of a young Japanese prison guard named Hyato.

JACOB BESER: A twenty-year-old engineering student who, after scoring high on an aptitude test, was recruited to design the atomic bomb's radar-triggered altitude sensor (a concept subsequently used in everything from the Apollo Lunar Module and robotic Mars landers to safety systems in cars). Because of this device, Beser became the only crewman assigned to fly aboard the atomic strike planes during both the Hiroshima and Nagasaki missions. He is the man who essentially pulled the detonation trigger on both bombs. In subsequent years, his family also became strangely connected by marriage to a survivor, over whom he had detonated the Hiroshima bomb.

PEGGY COVELL: A childhood survivor of Japan's occupation of the Philippines, at war's end she emerged from the slaughter of her family with a plan for revenge, and eventually encountered an imprisoned Japanese veteran of the Pearl Harbor attack.

MITSUO FUCHIDA: A Japanese pilot/engineer, recruited as a child into "The Catechism of War." He led the air attack on Pearl Harbor and survived several plane crashes, the sinking of an aircraft carrier at Midway, a revolt at the emperor's palace, and Hiroshima radiation exposure.

KINUYO FUKUI: A fifteen-year-old rescue worker, fated to survive the atomic bombings of both Hiroshima and Nagasaki.

TAK FURUMOTO: Born in a Japanese American internment camp, Tak was deported to Hiroshima at war's end, along with his parents and his two sisters. Thus began one of history's strangest life-journeys.

HYATO HIRANO: The young prison guard who saved the life of John Baxter and many others at the slave labor coal mine (Camp 25) near Nagasaki. Facing execution if caught, Hyato and his wife smuggled food to the camp's prisoners. By allowing equipment to be broken, he ultimately saved the lives of more than 125 prisoners of war.

KENSHI HIRATA: A newlywed who had narrowly survived the massive firebombings of Kobe and Osaka, he returned home to the imagined safety of Hiroshima. While he was at work, just outside the zone of Ground Zero, his wife of only ten days was located in a house near the A-bomb's detonation point. After excavating fragments of her bones in the ashes of their home, he boarded a train, with the intention of bringing her remains home to her parents—in Nagasaki. He arrived just in time to survive the second atomic bomb.

HARUNO HORIMOTO: A sixteen-year-old engineering student, she joined other students in organizing the conversion of Hiroshima's streetcars into ambulances.

KEY EYEWITNESSES • 259

AKIRA IWANAGA: A Mitsubishi engineer who, after surviving Hiroshima, returned to the company's offices in Nagasaki. He became a survivor of both atomic bombs.

KAZUO KANEGASAKI: An engineer and a Japanese veteran of the Pearl Harbor attack. A friend of Mitsuo Fuchida, he came to a strange epiphany as a POW under Peggy Covell.

MIZUHA TAKAMA KIKUZAKI: One of only two children who survived in a central Hiroshima school, shock-cocooned but, unfortunately, black-rain-exposed, only seven-tenths of a mile from the hypocenter. Coming from a highly educated family that had already been targeted by the secret police, with a mother who faced torture and murder of a child for the "crime" of being multilingual, Mizuha grew up learning always to question authority, including experts who advised that, as a person exposed to black rain, she must abort her child. She refused, and her daughter, Shiho, grew up as a second-generation *"hibakusha."*

KIMIKO KUWABARA: A seventeen-year-old A-bomb survivor, exposed inside Hiroshima's Central Broadcast Center bunker.

WALTER LORD: An OSS agent and historian who interviewed/interrogated surviving Japanese military officers after the war, including Mitsuo Fuchida.

SHIGEYOSHI MORIMOTO: A champion kite maker who came from a family of "survivor types." Miraculously shock-cocooned in a large mansion very near the Hiroshima detonation point, he departed the ruined city by train, toward a city he believed to be safer. His niece Tomiko, age twelve, also emerged from a shock cocoon, with an important lesson for every child.

ELIZABETH OOKA: Friend of Tak Furumoto. Like Tak's father, who built a camera and produced a family album filled with illegal photographs of life in FDR's internment camps for Americans of Japanese ancestry (and then, photos of post-A-bomb life in Hiroshima), Elizabeth's family preserved a record in both internment camp oral history and photography. Her father is one of the children in the famous *Three Boys Behind Barbed Wire* photo, and her grandfather was business partners with Tak's father of the produce market that was taken away from them by the internment camp Order 9066.

MAMI SAMEJIMA: One of three children and a mother who had survived the firebombing of Tokyo—then, the atomic bombings of both Hiroshima and Nagasaki.

SADAKO AND MASAHIRO SASAKI: Two children caught outdoors in Hiroshima's radioactive black rain. This was the beginning of what would become (especially in the twenty-first century) a worldwide paper crane outreach program—carrying the word *Omoiyari*.

CHARLES SWEENEY: Pilot of *Bockscar*, Nagasaki mission.

LEO SZILARD: Inspired by an H. G. Wells science fiction story, he and Albert Einstein triggered Groves and Oppenheimer's Manhattan Project.

SETSUKO THURLOW: A thirteen-year-old saved from the Hiroshima bomb by a high score on an IQ test—which put her in a bunker with military code breakers. Refusing orders to "shut up" about what she saw, she grew up to win a Nobel Peace Prize in 2018.

DR. SUSUMU TSUNOO: A physician who traveled by train from the ruins of Hiroshima to Nagasaki, where he was exposed to the second atomic bomb—this time, to a lethal dose of prompt radiation.

ALISTAIR URQUHART: A young "hell ship" survivor, sent to the same slave labor camp as John Baxter. Both became witnesses to Nagasaki.

KOICHI WADA: A seventeen-year-old streetcar engineer who, like Haruno of Hiroshima, joined with friends to organize a rescue operation in Nagasaki.

TSUTOMU YAMAGUCHI: One of very few people to survive within the fringe of Hiroshima's "Ground Zero." He left the city, expecting to die with his wife and child in Nagasaki. Three days later, he was describing the bomb's bright flash to a disbelieving boss at the Mitsubishi office when the second atomic bomb blazed forth.

ACKNOWLEDGMENTS

I thank James Cameron for his friendship, and for seeing, and supporting—and Shane Salerno, for taking this massive project up, and guiding it to publication. I want to thank Josh Stanton, my publisher, for believing in this book and championing it. I want to thank Anthony Goff for working hard to ensure *Ghosts of Hiroshima* was Blackstone's lead title. I want to thank Stephanie Stanton for her remarkable artistry with the cover design and Josie Woodbridge for working so hard to make certain the book came together as I imagined it. I want to thank Michael Carr for his fantastic work editing the manuscript. I also want to thank Deborah Randall and Ryan C. Coleman. And Levi Coren and Merry MacIvor.

Hurtling backward through time, I thank John and Jane Pellegrino, Adelle Dobie, and Barbara and Dennis Harris, Agnes Saunders, Ed McGunnigle—and Carole Roble. This project has benefited from conversations with experts and from encounters with eyewitnesses dating back more than five decades to my high school years, beginning with George Appoldt (then of the FBI), who first called my attention to Tsutomu Yamaguchi, Kenshi Hirata, and the existence of double survivors.

In approximately (but not exactly) the order in which I met or corresponded with them about the subjects covered in this book, I am indebted to Don Peterson, Amelia Sheridan, Bob Kessler,

April Riley, Anne Ives, and Michie Hattori Bernstein, to Harold Clayton Urey, Carl Sagan, and Luis and Walter Alvarez (the latter, on New Zealand iridium concentrations and nuclear winter; Luis Alvarez did not speak about the bomb and his flight), Father "Mattias" and Father "John MacQuitty" (whose names have been changed [as in *To Hell and Back*] by request and by contractual agreements going as far back as 1991), James Michener, Norman Cousins, James Powell (Brookhaven National laboratory, head of reactor systems [ret]), Pierre Noyes (Stanford Linear Accelerator), Francis Crick, Senator Spark Matsunaga, Rhold Sagdeev, Father Mervyn Fernando (Subhodi Institute and the Peace Boat), Ed Bishop and Dee Kenealy Bishop, Sir Arthur C. Clarke, Frank Andrews (Carter National Observatory, New Zealand), Sir Charles Fleming (Geological Survey, New Zealand), Edward R. Harrison (Amherst College, Carter National Observatory, New Zealand), historian Walter Lord, William MacQuitty, former Secretary of the Army Stanley Resor, John C. McManus, and philosopher/authors George Zebrowski, Pamela Sargent, Glen Marcus. Among relevant investigations, Haraldur Sigurddson and Steve Carey (volcanology, forensic archaeology, University of Rhode Island), and G. Mastrolerenzo (forensic archaeology, Vesuvius Observatory), and Charles Sheffield: We have worked together in studies of comparative eruptive and explosive force, and what happens to people and objects at temperatures near and above five times the boiling point of water. I also owe Billy Schutt and the three "Pellegrinoids," who have proved to be perfectly consistent with Masahiro Sasaki's command of: "Children! Teach your parents!" (I also owe Mary Leung, who won her bet that I couldn't write a book about Hiroshima and Nagasaki that didn't have the *Titanic* in it; but since Walter Lord conducted some of the primary Japanese WWII veteran interviews, I was bound to lose the bet.) As for the children, it was they who explained to me why thousands of paper cranes were arriving from Japan to a shock-cocooned firehouse (10-10 House) and other landmarks within the deathscape of the World Trade Center's "Ground Zero" in New York. The children were the first to tell me the story of Sadako and the thousand paper cranes, and to bring glimmers of hope from the ashes (in the *Omoiyari* principle).

Huge thanks go out to Miaka Nakao (re: Japan WWII atomic bomb program study, University of Tokyo School of Arts and Sciences), Charles Sweeney, Ken Goldie, Sheldon Stoff, Roy Cullimore, Lori Johnston, Jesse A. Stoff, Bill Broad (*The New York Times* re: the great "downblast debate" of 1996), the family of Nancy and Larry Cantwell, Miko Hatano (Japan Consulate, New York), Hideo Nakamura, Hidetaka Inazuka, Chad Diehl, Mr. and Mrs. Hisao Maegaki, Mr. and Mrs. Masahiro Sasaki and Yuji Sasaki, Yoshinari [Tsugio] Ito, Tokusaburo Nagai, Endo Tai, Hiroshi Takayama, Tsutomu Yamaguchi, Toshiko (Yamaguchi) Yamasaki and the rest of the Yamaguchi family as well, for their remarkable hospitality and support. History is indebted to all of these people—and to Kenshi and Saeko Hirata and their family (and the brother of the lost Setsuko Hirata) for coming forth and providing the rest of the story, along with Akira Iwanaga. And to Hiroshi Fujii (son of Hiroshima nurse Nancy Cantwell's mentor, Dr. Minoru Fujii), Kazuko Kouno, Saito Michiko, Misako Fujita, Reiko Owa, Sigeko Wasada, Saena Magee, Kazuko Minamoto, Nenkai Aoyama, Kenji Kitakawa. Just as many thanks to Mr. and Mrs. Tak Furumoto and family, for revealing another new aspect of unknown history (and in some places, forbidden history); Mrs. John Fuchida; George Takei; and Mitchie Takeuchi. And to Yumi Tanaka (to whom the "Burnt Maria" painting was given by Tsutomu Yamaguchi), Kae Matsumoto and her father Yoji Matsumoto, Frances Kakugawa and Victor Chan, Tomoko Maekawa (Nagasaki University), Steve Leeper (Hiroshima Peace Cultural Foundation), Elizabeth Leeper, Keiji Nakazawa (and his devoted fans, Stan Lee and Jack Kirby), Marc Selden (Cornell University), Hiroko Nakamoto, Akira Setoguchi, Michimasa Hirata (Tokyo Federation of A-Bomb Survivors), Setsuko Thurlow, Shigeko Sasamori, Takehisa Yamamoto, Shinpei Takada, Toshihiro Shiroishi (*The Asahi Shimbun*'s "Messages from Hibakusha" project, along with editors Karen Godshall and Ron Andrews), Shoso Kawamoto, Takashi (Thomas) Tanemori, John Crump, Mark Baraka Strauch, Kenji

Kitagawa, Masahiro Kunishige, Emiko Nakasako, Ari and Eric Beser, Russell Gackenbach, Yasuaki Yamashita, Tomiko Morimoto West, Shigeyoshi Morimoto (via Hideo Nakamura) and double *hibakusha* Sato (re: Kenshi Hirata, via Hideo Nakamura), Kinuyo Fukui, Yagawa Mitsunori, Akira Hirano, Anthony El Khouri, Elizabeth Ooka, and Rev. Dr. Kenjitsu Nakagaki, Shiho (Takama Kikuzaki) Burke.

And thank you to Elaine Markson (wherever exploring has taken you). And Julia Kenny, Gary Johnson, and Jack Macrae. Also to Parks Stephenson and Jon Landau at Lightstorm, to Ari Beser, Clifton Truman Daniel, Paule Saviano, to John Batchelor (at ABC), Ian Punnett and Lisa Lyon (at Coast to Coast AM), Rip MacKenzie, George Greenfield (CreativeWell), Susan McEachern, Audra Figgins, Alden Perkins, Sharon Kunz, Stephen Ryan, and Katelyn Turner (R&L).

SOURCES AND NOTES

NOTES TO PROLOGUE: BY ACCIDENTAL CONNECTIONS, OR BY SPOOKY ACTION AT A DISTANCE?

1. Walter Lord, *A Night to Remember* (R & W Holt, 1955).

2. Lord, personal communication with the author, 1987–2002, Case 2018B.

3. Morgan Robertson, *Futility: Or The Wreck of the Titan* (1898; M. F. Mansfield, 1912).

4. Lord, personal communication with the author.

5. Robertson, "Beyond the Spectrum," in *The Wreck of the Titan; Or, Futility* (McClure's and Metropolitan, 1914).

6. "HMHS 'Britannic': The Brief Life of 'Titanic's' Gigantic Sister," Steamship Mutual, March 22, 2017, https://www.steamshipmutual.com/publications/articles/britannic.

7. H. G. Wells, *The War of the Worlds* (Harper & Bros., 1898).

8. Lord, personal communication with the author. *Beyond the Spectrum* was a series of related stories, tied to one titled "Beyond the Spectrum." The history of Morgan Robertson became of interest after Walter and the author (1987) began reading through everything Robertson had written. Walter then sent a detective friend in search of what could be learned. Also, in 1996, *Titanic* historians/explorers Charlie Haas and Jack Eaton had learned more about Robertson. It wasn't much. Virtually everything known is in these paragraphs.

9. Robertson, "Beyond the Spectrum," in *The Wreck of the Titan*, 210.

NOTES TO CHAPTER 1: SUNRISE

1. Dr. Minoru Fujii's rescue team (including Reiko Owa and Sigeko Wasada), personal communication with the author, 2008. Nurses from Dr. Fujii's rescue team provided the Matsuda boy's identification (as a shadow boy and as the "marble boy" of Hiroshima), and likewise the identification of Mrs. Aoyama as one of the people exposed outdoors and nearest the Hiroshima bomb. Matsuda boy: He received prompt radiation dosing at lethal levels (mostly from deep-penetrating neutrons and gamma rays); but he was a "shadow person" who lived for three days with minimal flash burns. His case corroborated the perplexingly high measure of flash protection provided by thin materials (such as white cloth, a hat, and leaves); "Pigs in Uniform," ORAU, accessed February 3, 2025, https://www.orau.org/health-physics-museum/articles/pigs-in-uniform.html. This was further demonstrated during aboveground atomic tests in which animals (including piglets) were exposed, during tests *Met* and *Gamble*, to varying thicknesses of flash protection.

2. Nenkai Aoyama, personal communication with the author, July 2008.

3. Richard Ned Lebow, The Committee for the Compilation of Materials on Damage Caused by the Atomic Bombs in Hiroshima and Nagasaki, *Hiroshima and Nagasaki: The Physical, Medical, and Social Effects of the Atomic Bombings*, trans. Eisei Ishikawa and David L. Swain (Basic Books, 1981), 32–36. The effects of the flash, including wavelengths of light ranging upward from gamma through ultraviolet, through the visible spectrum and infrared (during the first 0.3–3.0 seconds), and including immediately raised air temperatures at ground level, were determined by studies of "bubbled" roof tiles and other objects in the vicinity of the Aoyama home; Carey Sublette, "Nuclear Weapons Frequently Asked Questions," 4.1, Nuclear Weapon Archive, last updated April 5, 2023, https://nuclearweaponarchive.org/Nwfaq/Nfaq4-1.html. The purity of U-235 in the Hiroshima device had a relatively low-yield effectiveness. Sublette noted that the "Little Boy" bomb was developed with use of less than 90% enrichment: "The actual fissile load was only [approximately] 80%. . . . The explosive efficiency of Little Boy was 0.23kt/kg of fissile material (1.3%) compared to 2.8kt/kg of fissile material (16%) for Fat Man. . . . Use of 93.5% U-235 would have at least doubled Little Boy's yield"; Total yield (Little Boy): up to approximately 12.5 kilotons, upward of 10 kt but no more than 15 kt (Smithsonian and Brookhaven conclusions). Haraldur Sigurdsson et al., "The Eruption of Vesuvius in AD 79," *National Geographic Research* 1 (1985): 332–387. Prompt effects of thermal shock on Mrs. Aoyama's blood and bones, at minimum of five times the boiling point of water in sea-level air, were informed by on-site analysis (2001–2005, 2009) of blood-derived iron deposits on the floor of the Herculaneum Marina; also skull interiors (vaporization of brain matter, steam-jetting apart of skulls, within 1/20th of a second), resulting from 500-degrees Celsius effects of the Vesuvius AD 79 surge cloud on more than 200 individuals; Giuseppe Mastrolorenzo et al., "Herculaneum Victims of Vesuvius in AD 79," *Nature* 410 (2001): 769–770, https://doi.org/10.1038/35071167. That the Herculaneum phenomena are instructive for Hiroshima was a subject discussed extensively with Mastrolorenzo and his colleagues at the Vesuvius Observatory, and with Jim Powell (Brookhaven National Laboratory), personal communication with the author, 1983–2019; 1630 BC surge clouds from Thera (Santorini) and Krakatoa in AD 1883, discussed with Richard Garwin (Fermilab), personal communication with the author, 1995; Charles Pellegrino, *Ghosts of Vesuvius* (HarperCollins, 2004). People in Pompeii's sister city of Herculaneum were dead in 1/200 second; they were disintegrated down to tendon and bone in 1/20 second. This was primarily the effect of contact with hot air and hot dust in motion. Hiroshima: At and in the immediate vicinity of (400, probably up to 800 feet out from) the hypocenter, flash reflective effects on the ground heated the air to significantly higher temperatures (above 500 degrees Celsius) for more than 1/3 second before the blast, implosion, and other disruptive effects of the atomic shock bubble pulled away the hot air. Heated air moving over exposed bodies while covering a distance of only 10–15 feet in 1/10 to 1/20 second greatly magnified the carbonization effect in the manner of superheated air in a blast furnace. This intense heating would have occurred whether or not a flash-desiccated/carbonized person was shock-cocooned (in such cases, the exposed people were sometimes "statuefied" instead of being scattered as ash by the blast).

4. Robert Trumbull, *Nine Who Survived Hiroshima and Nagasaki: Personal Experiences of Nine Men Who Lived Through the Atomic Bombings* (Dutton, 1957), 38–39. Trumbull overstated the detonation point as "almost directly above" Morimoto (38). If this description is taken literally, three tiers of wood and tile (even in a shock cocoon at the bottom of a house full of books) could never have prevented a lethal indoor, ground-floor dose above 600 r (or L-100, Lethality 100% [in the time before bone marrow transplants]). Further details and conclusions about the Morimoto house itself, consistent with Morimoto's temporary illness, arose from discussions with Norman Cousins and George Zebrowski (1987, 1988), and Jim Powell (at various points,

1983–2019). Their analysis of the Morimoto "mansion"—which was filled essentially wall-to-wall and floor-to-ceiling with books—sheds light on the anomalous survival of three people in a region of Ground Zero where essentially no one else escaped death or severe injury: a building large enough to provide adequate shock-cocooning and (just barely) enough shielding from prompt, cumulatively lethal radiation effects. According to aboveground atomic test results, a 3-foot thickness of wood and 3–5 inches of tiles can attenuate prompt radiation dosage by 50%–75% (Ed. Samuel Glasstone, *The Effects of Nuclear Weapons*, [AEC, 1962], 384). The Morimoto mansion provided minimally, and evidently greater than, this amount of shielding.

5. Tomiko Morimoto (West), personal communication with the author, 2015–2016, Case 2016A, 29–32.

6. Kimiko Kuwabara, personal communication with the author, 2010, Case 2018B, 17–22; Kimiko Kuwabara, "I Saw Hell," The National Peace Memorial Halls for the Atomic Bomb Victims in Hiroshima and Nagasaki, Global Network, 2011, https://www.global-peace.go.jp/en/taikenki/en_taikenki_syousai.php?gbID=152&dt=241107084847.

7. Haruno Horimoto, personal communication with the author, Case 2018B, 6A; Haruno Horimoto, "On Duty as a Conductor of the First Street Car after the A-Bombing," The National Peace Memorial Halls for the Atomic Bomb Victims in Hiroshima and Nagasaki, Global Network, https://www.global-peace.go.jp/en/taikenki/en_taikenki_syousai.php?gbID=346&dt=250130140432.

8. Keiji Nakazawa, personal communication with the author, 2010; "NAKAZAWA Keiji," Survivor Testimonies, Hiroshima Peace Memorial Museum Database, released August 1, 1998, https://hpmm-db.jp/list/detail/?cate=testify_en&search_type=detail&data_id=13776.

9. Tsutomu Yamaguchi, personal communication with the author, 2008; family of Tsutomu Yamaguchi, personal communication with the author, 2010–2016; Tsutomu Yamaguchi, conversations with Chad Diehl, 2008–2011; Trumbull, *Nine Who Survived Hiroshima and Nagasaki* (Dutton, 1957), 28–29; Ari Beser, "Tsutomu Yamaguchi, 29 Years Old," chap. 21 in *The Nuclear Family* (pub. by author, 2015), 135–142.

10. Tsutomu Yamaguchi, *I Live to Tell My Story*, trans. Hideo Nakamura (unpub. memoir, 2009). Yamaguchi gave this memoir to the author during the July 2008 filming by Nakamura and Inazaka (at which Chad Diehl was also present); Trumbull, *Nine Who Survived Hiroshima and Nagasaki*.

11. Tsutomu Yamaguchi, personal communication with the author, 2008.

12. Tsutomu Yamaguchi, *I Live to Tell My Story*.

13. Yamaguchi, personal communication with the author, 2008. The description was corroborated in his memoir, *I Live to Tell My Story*.

14. Yamaguchi, personal communication with the author, 2008. Yamaguchi also shared poems about his experiences, written in his own calligraphy (trans. 2009); family of Tsutomu Yamaguchi, personal communication with the author, 2010–2016; Tsutomu Yamaguchi, conversations with Chad Diehl, 2008–2011. All Yamaguchi poems were translated for Diehl and Yamaguchi, *And the River Flowed as a Raft of Corpses* (Excogitating over Coffee Pub., 2010); Diehl, *Resurrecting Nagasaki* (Cornell Univ. Press, 2018); Trumbull, *Nine Who Survived Hiroshima and Nagasaki*, 28–29; Ari Beser, "Tsutomu Yamaguchi, 29 Years Old," 135–142; Yamaguchi, transcript of speech to high school students at the United Nations

(2006), at the showing of the film *Twice Bombed, Twice Survived, Part 1* (dir. Hideo Nakamura, Inazuka Productions, 2006; Part 2, 2010). Nakamura and Inazuka, directors, *Twice Bombed: The Legacy of Tsutomu Yamaguchi* (Inazuka Productions, 2012), film.

NOTES TO CHAPTER 2: BUTTERFLY, BUTTERFLY

1. H. G. Wells, *The World Set Free*, 117.

2. *Britannica*, "Edward Lorenz," accessed January 20, 2025, https://www.britannica.com/biography/Edward-Lorenz.

3. Wells, *The World Set Free*.

4. US Department of Energy, *The First Reactor* (December 1982), https://www.energy.gov/sites/prod/files/The%20First%20Reactor.pdf.

5. Leo Szilard, "We Turned the Switch," *The Nation* 161 (December 22, 1945), 718.

6. Richard Rhodes, *The Making of the Atomic Bomb* (Simon & Schuster, 1986), 307–308.

7. Harold C. Urey, personal communication with the author, 1980. The Japan atomic bomb program; Dr. Yoshio Nishina, Columbia University Conference, November 6, 2009; Dr. Nishina, in John Toland, *The Rising Sun* (Random House, 1970), 794–5. Japan WWII nuclear programs; Roykichi Sagane, "What Happened on This Date?," *The Asahi Shimbun*, August 9, 2005, https://www.asahi.com/hibakusha/english/shimen/happened/happened-02-2.html; "Survey Activities Under the Occupation," (Eizo Tajima), accessed February 4, 2025, https://www.asahi.com/hibakusha/english/nagasaki/.

8. Sasaki family, personal communication with the author, 2008–2018; Masahiro Sasaki and Sue DiCicco, *The Complete Story of Sadako Sasaki*, trans. Naomi Nakagoshi and Anne Prescott (Tuttle, 2020).

9. Endo Tai, personal communication with the author, 2008, Case 2018B, 12–14. The room from which Saito made the only phone call out of Hiroshima has been preserved; Saito Michiko, "Notes on Atomic Bomb Experience," National Peace Memorial Halls for the Atomic Bomb Victims in Hiroshima and Nagasaki, Global Network, 1995, https://www.global-peace.go.jp/en/taikenki/en_taikenki_syousai.php?gbID=166&dt=241107035143.

10. Mitsuo Fuchida, *From Pearl Harbor to Golgotha*, 31, 33–34.

11. Fuchida, *From Pearl Harbor to Golgotha*; Lord, personal communication with the author, 1992–93, Case 2018B, 64.

12. Martin Bennett, "Research and Debate," *Naval War College Review* 66, no. 1 (2013): 110–125, https://digital-commons.usnwc.edu/nwc-review/vol66/iss1/9; Mitsuo Fuchida, in T. McMullen et al., "Appendix on the A-Bomb and Miraculous Find," in Georgia Southern University Archives, 1970.

13. Toshio Nishina, in Toland, *The Rising Sun* (Random House, 1970), 794–5; "Dr. Yoshio Nishina—Japan Scientist Realized at Once that Weapon Dropped on Hiroshima was A-Bomb," *Kondo News*, August 3, 2008.

14. Yasuo Masai et al., "Japanese Expansionism," *Brittanica*, updated January 30, 2025, https://www.britannica.com/place/Japan/Japanese-expansionism. At the time of Fuchida's rescue by a Chinese captain, the enmity between Japan and China was already at a flashpoint, having begun with Japan's 1928 assassination of Manchurian leader Chang Tso-Lin.

15. Keiko Ogura (premonition case), personal communication with the author, April 13, 2018, Case 2018B, 64; "OGURA Keiko," Survivor Testimonies, Hiroshima Peace Memorial Museum Database, released March 31, 2013, https://hpmm-db.jp/list/detail/?cate=testify_en&search_type=detail&data_id=14705; "Atomic Bomb Survivor Testimony Videos Now Available," Hiroshima Peace Memorial Museum, August 6, 2023, https://hpmmuseum.jp/modules/news/index.php?action=PageView&page_id=381&lang=eng; Yuhei Kyono, "A-Bomb Survivor on Discovering Her Life's Calling at Nobel Forum," *The Asahi Shimbun*, December 12, 2024, https://www.asahi.com/ajw/articles/15548640.

16. "TOSHIMUNE Sanae," Survivor Testimonies, Hiroshima Peace Memorial Museum, released March 31, 2006, https://hpmm-db.jp/list/detail/?cate=testify_en&search_type=detail&data_id=14554; Toshimune Sanae, personal communication with the author, Case 2018B, 15.

17. Takashi Tanemori, personal communication with the author, 2010–2015; video interview, November 13, 2010.

18. Yasuko Kimura, *White Town Hiroshima* (Bunka Hyoron, 1983), 12–32; film version by Tengo Yamada, with Shiho (Kikuzaki) Burke, *Shiroi Machi Hiroshima* (1985); Shiho (Takama Kikuzaki) Burke, personal communication with the author, 2024, Case 2024A and B (+); Michihiko Hachiya, *Hiroshima Diary* (UNC Press, 1995), 67, 87; Takiko Okamoto, "Messages from Hibakusha," *The Asahi Shimbun*, 2010, https://www.asahi.com/hibakusha/english/hiroshima/h00-00081e.html.

19. Masahiro Sasaki, personal communication with the author, 2010; Tsutomu Yamaguchi, personal communication with the author.

20. Kenshi Hirata, personal communication of Hirata family to the author, interpreters Nakamura and Inazuka, 2010. The direction of neutrinos through Setsuko Hirata's body is determined not by a straight-line path from the bomb's detonation point and through the Earth's core, but rather by an angle dictated by the location of Setsuko Hirata within the house, relative to the point of the bomb's detonation (Setsuko Hirata's precise location was verified by her husband, 2010).

21. Harold C. Urey, personal communication with the author, 1978–79; Walter Lord, personal communication with the author, 1993; Amand Lucas, "The Overlooked Achievements of Charles Pecher and Edgar Sengier," *Physics Today*, July 16, 2019, https://pubs.aip.org/physicstoday/online/31565. Heisenberg (as unsung hero, internal saboteur of the German atomic bomb); Walter Lord, who sent an assassin to Vienna (who turned back, upon realizing Heisenberg's design, based on a quickly scrawled Heisenberg drawing, was deliberately self-destructive of the German program), and Jim Powell, George Zebrowski, personal communication with the author (regarding declassified recordings of surrendered German atomic scientists, in their rooms), 1986; Thomas Powers, *Heisenberg's War: The Secret History of the German Bomb* (Da Capo Press, 2000).

NOTES TO CHAPTER 3: PROFILES OF THE FUTURE

1. Kenshi Hirata, personal communication with the author, 2010; Trumbull, *Nine Who Survived*; Richard Ned Lebow, The Committee for the Compilation of Materials on Damage Caused by the Atomic Bombs in Hiroshima and Nagasaki, *Hiroshima and Nagasaki: The Physical, Medical, and Social Effects of the Atomic Bombings*, trans. Eisei Ishikawa and David L. Swain (Basic Books, 1981), 73–79.

2. Kimiko Kuwabara, personal communication with the author, Case 2018B, 17–22; Kimiko Kuwabara, "I Saw Hell," The National Peace Memorial Halls for the Atomic Bomb Victims in Hiroshima and Nagasaki, Global Network, 2011, https://www.global-peace.go.jp/en/taikenki/en_taikenki_syousai.php?gbID=152&dt=241107084847.

3. Haruno Horimoto, "On Duty as a Conductor of the First Street Car After the A-Bombing," National Peace Memorial Halls for the Atomic Bomb Victims in Hiroshima and Nagasaki, Global Network, 1985, https://www.global-peace.go.jp/en/taikenki/en_taikenki_syousai.php?gbID=346&dt=250201003226; Haruno Horimoto, personal communication with the author, Case 2018B, 6A, 30.

4. Kenshi Hirata, personal communication with the author via Hideo Nakamura and Hidetaka Inazuka, "Shadow People" and "Statue People," July 2010.

5. Haraldur Sigurdsson et al., "The Eruption of Vesuvius in AD 79," *National Geographic Research* 1 (1985): 332–387; *American Vesuvius*, History Channel and *National Geographic* (2005). On-site research with Sigurdsson et al., University of Rhode Island, 2001–2005 (includes lab video of skull explosion, tendon disintegration of wrists, ankles), Vesuvius Observatory Laboratory, 2005; Mastrolorenzo et al., "Herculaneum Victims of Vesuvius in AD 79," *Nature* 410 (2001): 769–770, https://doi.org/10.1038/35071167; Charles Pellegrino, "Cities in Amber," chap. 6 in *Ghosts of Vesuvius* (HarperCollins, 2004), 205–209.

6. Hirata, in Nakamura and Inazuka, directors, *Twice Bombed Twice Survived, Part II* (Tokyo, 2012), film; Kenshi Hirata, personal communication with the author, 2010.

7. Tsutomu Yamaguchi and Kenshi Hirata, Mitsubishi Records (Hiroshima and Nagasaki), as noted in Trumbull, *Nine Who Survived*, 29, 49–50, 53.

8. Trumbull, *Nine Who Survived*, 24. Kenshi Hirata's prior near miss of the Osaka and Kobe firebombings of March 13 and 17, 1945 (38); Hirata, in Trumbull, 23–27, 34–35, 64–71, 76; Norman Cousins, personal communication with the author, 1987; Hirata and family, personal communication with the author, 2010.

9. Haruno Horimoto, "On Duty as a Conductor of the First Street Car After the A-Bombing," National Peace Memorial Halls for the Atomic Bomb Victims in Hiroshima and Nagasaki, Global Network, 1985, https://www.global-peace.go.jp/en/taikenki/en_taikenki_syousai.php?gbID=346&dt=250201003226; Haruno Horimoto, personal communication with the author, Case 2018B, 6A, 30.

10. Kinuyo Fukui, personal communication with the author via Nakamura, September 24, 2018, Case 2018B, 73–75, communication continues, March 2025.

11. Trumbull, *Nine Who Survived*, 29, 49–50; Nancy (Minami) Cantwell and the Hiroshima nurses of Dr. Fujii's crew, personal communication with the author, 2008. A train picked up speed, fanning the flames as it raced toward a collision with a truck near Dr. Fujii's hospital. Their first rescue effort was in fact at the site of this famous train wreck.

12. Alistair Urquhart, *The Forgotten Highlander* (Little, Brown Book Group, 2010); Walter Lord, personal communication with the author, 1993, Case 2018B, 10–11, 24–29, 36–46. During this interview, Lord refers to the crimes of "Dr. Death" (Seiichi Okada); John Baxter, *Missing, Believed Killed* (Aurum Press, 2010), 124–129.

Baxter relates meeting with an allied submarine commander: "Listening to this account [*Ussuri Maru*] by allied submarines, he fell silent—then told me he had been a submarine commander in the Pacific. When I mentioned the date of the attack [around Sept. 27, 1943] he could not believe his ears. 'I was in charge of that attack on that convoy on that day!' He said, 'We only heard later that many of the boats were carrying POWs and, unknown to us, a number of the boats we sent to the bottom had been packed to the gunwales with innocent men.'" Note on convoy size: Baxter notes a large convoy but *IJA Transport Ussuri Maru Record of Movement* (B. Hackett, 2016) notes that sources may vary on sizes and compositions of convoys.

NOTES TO CHAPTER 4: NEUTRON STAR

1. Charles Sweeney, personal communication with the author, 1999; Ari and Eric Beser (on Jacob Beser and Hiroko), personal communication with the author, 2012–2015; Charles Sweeney, *War's End* (Avon Books, 1997), 106, 172–190; Tom Attridge (Grumman/NASA), personal communication with the author, 1983. "Better is the enemy of best" is often attributed to Grumman Corporation; Gordon Danby, "Siren-on-A-bomb Proposal," personal communication with the author, 1984; Jacob Beser, "The Outlook Interview: Jacob Beser Talks to Bruce Goldfarboln," *The Washington Post*, May 19, 1985, https://www.washingtonpost.com/archive/opinions/1985/05/19/lives/71f72bf0-b1fe-4af4-ac70-cef6ad8b60ba/; Taylor Branch, "Symbols of Guilt and Generosity," *The New York Times*, August 4, 1985, https://www.nytimes.com/1985/08/04/books/symbols-of-guilt-and-generosity.html; Jacob Beser, on *Good Morning America*, August 6, 1985; Beser, in Gordon Thomas, *Enola Gay*, Oral Interview Collection (Thomas, 1975, 1976); Ari Beser, Eric Beser, personal communication with the author, 2013. "Jacob Beser's lecture," Voices of the Manhattan Project, Atomic Heritage

Foundation, September 1, 1985, https://ahf.nuclearmuseum.org
/voices/oral-histories/jacob-besers-lecture/; See Ari Beser, *The Nuclear
Family* (pub. by author, 2015); Theodore "Dutch" van Kirk, Tibbets,
and Parsons, in Paul Wilmshurst, dir., *Hiroshima* (BBC, 2005),
documentary; "Dutch" van Kirk, in Steven Okazaki, dir., *White Light/
Black Rain: The Destruction of Hiroshima and Nagasaki* (HBO, 2007),
documentary.

2. David Elstein, dir., "The Bomb," episode 24, *The World at War*
(Thames Television, 1973), https://archive.org/details/the-world-at
-war-1973-thames-television-world-war-two/24+The+Bomb+(February
+%E2%80%93+September+1945).mp4.

3. Jacob Beser, "The Outlook Interview," *The Washington Post*,
May 19, 1985, https://www.washingtonpost.com/archive
/opinions/1985/05/19/lives/71f72bf0-b1fe-4af4-ac70-cef6ad8b60ba/;
Taylor Branch, "Symbols of Guilt and Generosity," *The New York
Times*, August 4, 1985, https://www.nytimes.com/1985/08/04
/books/symbols-of-guilt-and-generosity.html; Jacob Beser, on *Good
Morning America*, August 6, 1985; Beser, in Gordon Thomas, *Enola
Gay*, Oral Interview Collection (Thomas, 1975, 1976); Ari Beser and
Eric Beser, personal communication with the author, 2013. See Ari
Beser, *The Nuclear Family*.

4. Setsuko Thurlow, personal communication with the author, May
2015, Case 2018A, 18–28.

5. Setsuko Thurlow, personal communication with the author.

6. Charles Sweeney, personal communication with the author,
1999; Ari and Eric Beser (on Jacob Beser and Hiroko), personal
communication with the author, 2012–2015; Charles Sweeney, *War's
End* (Avon Books, 1997); Beser, in Gordon Thomas, *Enola Gay*,

Oral Interview Collection (Thomas, 1975, 1976), Museum of Flight Archives, Seattle, 2011. See Ari Beser, *The Nuclear Family* (pub. by author, 2015); Russell Gackenbach, personal communication with the author, summer 2010. Gackenbach verified "the mathematics"; Eric Beser, personal communication with the author, 2013.

7. Tsutomu Yamaguchi, personal communication with the author, 2008; Yamaguchi, *I Live to Tell My Story*, with the location of key people hand-marked on a US Bombing Survey map, July 2008.

8. Harold Urey, personal communication with the author, 1979–1980; Charles Sweeney, *War's End*, 172–190; Sweeney, personal communication with the author, 1999; Beser family, personal communication with the author, 2013–2014.

9. John Toland, *The Rising Sun* (Random House, 1970), 794–95; Lord, personal communication with the author, regarding Fuchida; J. Record, *Japan's Decision for War in 1941: Some Enduring Lessons* (Strategic Studies Institute, 2009).

10. Haruno Horimoto, personal communication with the author, Case 2018B, 6A; Haruno Horimoto, "On Duty as a Conductor of the First Street Car After the A-Bombing," National Peace Memorial Halls for the Atomic Bomb Victims in Hiroshima and Nagasaki, Global Network, 1985, https://www.global-peace.go.jp/en/taikenki/en_taikenki_syousai.php?gbID=346&dt=250201003226.

11. Mizuha (Takama) Kikuzaki, in Shiho Burke, personal communication with the author, 2024.

12. Walter Lord, personal communication with the author, 1993; Jeffrey Record, *Japan's Decision for War in 1941: Some Enduring Lessons* (Strategic Studies Institute, 2009). In a document from the

Imperial Conference September 6, 1945, success hinged on the hope that Americans would be soft, afraid of losing blood, and after Pearl might sue for peace. Rear Admiral Tasuka Nakazawa said, "A composite of immigrants [that] lack[s] unity, could not withstand adversity and privations, and [should regard] war as a form of sport, so that if we deal a severe blow at the outset of hostilities they would lose the will to fight" (quoted in Record, 30); Admiral Isoroku Yamamoto said, "to fight the United States [shall be] like fighting the whole world. . . . Doubtless I shall die aboard the *Nagato* [his flagship]. Meanwhile, Tokyo will be burnt to the ground three times" (Record, 3).

13. Earl Warren, in "Japanese-American Cases Hirabayashi v. United States 320 U.S. 81 (1943) Korematsu v. United States 323 U.S. 214 (1944) *Ex parte Endo* 323 U.S. 283 (1944)," in *Encyclopedia of the American Constitution* (The Gale Group, Inc., 2000), 1–3.

14. Tak Furumoto and Furumoto family, personal communication with the author, 2022, Case 2018A, 33–58.

15. "History," Tule Lake Committee, 2012, https://www.tulelake.org/history; Furumoto family, personal communication with the author, 2010–2018, Case 2018A, 33–58.

NOTES TO CHAPTER 5: SURFING THE IMPROBABILITY CURVE

1. Tsutomu Yamaguchi, personal communication with the author, 2008. Yamaguchi's arrival in Nagasaki, the calculations of which city might be next; Yamaguchi, *I Live to Tell My Story*; Charles Pellegrino, *To Hell and Back: The Last Train from Hiroshima* (Rowman & Littlefield, 2015), 227.

2. Robert Karl Manoff, "American Victims of Hiroshima," *The New York Times*, December 2, 1984, https://www.nytimes.com/1984/12/02/magazine/american-victims-of-hiroshima.html; Tak Furumoto, personal communication with the author, Case 2018A.

3. Akira Hirano, NHK Archive, testimony regarding Mami Samejima, https://www.nhk.or.jp/archives/en/; Mami Akira Hirano, personal communication with the author regarding Mami Samejima, Case 2018B, 65–68.

4. Trumbull, *Nine Who Survived* (Dutton, 1957), 97–98; Hirata, in Nakamura and Inazuka, *Twice Bombed Twice Survived, Part II* (Tokyo, 2012), documentary; Kenshi Hirata, personal communication with the author, 2010. Hirata, en route to Nagasaki, witnessing the Yawata event that would bring the second bomb to him, the following day.

5. Harold Urey, personal communication with the author, 1979–1980. Events on Tinian as the dawn of August 8 approached; Charles Sweeney, *War's End*, 172–190; Sweeney, personal communication with the author, 1999; Beser family, personal communication with the author, 2013–2014.

6. Alistair Urquhart, *The Forgotten Highlander*; Walter Lord, personal communication with the author, 2018, Case 2018B, 10–11, 24–29, 36–46; John Baxter, *Missing, Believed Killed*.

7. Charles Sweeney, *War's End*; Sweeney, personal communication with the author, 1999; Eric Beser, personal communication with the author, 2013; Beser family, personal communication with the author, 2013–2014.

8. Sweeney, personal communication, 1999. Prison Camp 25, August 10–24, 1945, Case 2018B, 32, 45–48.

9. Urquhart, *The Forgotten Highlander*; Lord, personal communication with the author, 2018, Case 2018B, 10–11, 24–29, 36–46; Baxter, *Missing, Believed Killed*, 163–4, 251–4; Baxter, in William Hollingworth, interview for *The Japan Times*, May 25, 2010.

10. Eric Beser, personal communication with the author, 2013–2014; Ari and Eric Beser (on Jacob Beser and Hiroko), personal communication with the author, 2012–2015; Sweeney, personal communication with the author, 1999; Sweeney, *War's End*; Jacob Beser, "The Outlook Interview: Jacob Beser Talks to Bruce Goldfarboln," *The Washington Post*, May 19, 1985, https://www.washingtonpost.com/archive/opinions/1985/05/19/lives/71f72bf0-b1fe-4af4-ac70-cef6ad8b60ba/; Taylor Branch, "Symbols of Guilt and Generosity," *The New York Times*, August 4, 1985, https://www.nytimes.com/1985/08/04/books/symbols-of-guilt-and-generosity.html; Jacob Beser, on *Good Morning America*, August 6, 1985; Beser, in Gordon Thomas, *Enola Gay*, Oral Interview Collection (Thomas, 1975, 1976); "Jacob Beser's lecture," Voices of the Manhattan Project, Atomic Heritage Foundation, September 1, 1985, https://ahf.nuclearmuseum.org/voices/oral-histories/jacob-besers-lecture/; Ari Beser, Eric Beser, personal communication with the author, 2013. See Ari Beser, *The Nuclear Family* (pub. by author, 2015).

11. Takato Michishita, personal communication with the author, Case 2018B, 63.

12. Charles Sweeney, *War's End* (Avon Books, 1997); Sweeney, personal communication with the author, 1999; Eric Beser, personal communication with the author, 2013; Beser family, personal communication with the author, 2013–2014.

13. Kenshi Hirata, personal communication with the author, trans. Nakamura and Inazuka, 2010; Trumbull, *Nine Who Survived* (Dutton, 1957), 98–119; Hirata, in Nakamura and Inazuka, *Twice Bombed Twice Survived, Part II*; Shinji Kinoshita (on what radios were announcing at Moment Zero), as Kenshi Hirata and his father approached the home of Setsuko's parents.

14. Tsutomu Yamaguchi, personal communication with the author, 2008. Yamaguchi's arrival in Nagasaki, the calculations of which city might be next; Yamaguchi, *I Live to Tell My Story*, trans. Hideo Nakamura (unpub., 2009).

15. John Baxter, *Missing, Believed Killed* (Aurum Press, 2010), 170; Lord, personal communication with the author, Case 2018B, 2015, 43. The sky was clear over the prison camp, clear enough for flash burns from the bomb. The two planes passed overhead at 30,000 feet.

16. Michie Hattori Bernstein and William L. Leary, "Nagasaki Eyewitness," *World War II Magazine* (Summer 2005). Ichiro Miyato, a radar operator, 15 miles away from Nagasaki, was in direct contact with a central Nagasaki, sheltered command center—right up to the moment of its destruction, and subterranean chambers/factories, and facilities inside mountains, and oral histories related to radar operator; George Appoldt, personal communication with the author, 1971–73; Norman Cousins, personal communication with the author, 1987. According to Cousins, the incident became an inspiration for "the Bombing of Moscow Telephone Scene" in the Cold War thriller *Fail Safe*.

17. Koichi Wada, "A Monument to 11:02 a.m.," Nagasaki Peace, accessed February 4, 2025, https://nagasakipeace.jp/en/search/survivors/koichi_wada.html; Wada, personal communication with the author, Case 2018A, 1; "I Killed the King with My Lies," Paule Saviano Photography website, July 8, 2021, https://www.paulepictures.com/blog/tag/koichi-wada/.

18. Charles Sweeney, *War's End*; Sweeney, personal communication with the author, 1999; Eric Beser, personal communication with the author, 2013; Beser family, personal communication with the author, 2013–2014.

NOTES TO CHAPTER 6: ALL THIS HAS HAPPENED BEFORE; ALL THIS MAY HAPPEN AGAIN

1. Michie Hattori Bernstein and William L. Leary, "Nagasaki Eyewitness," *World War II Magazine* (Summer 2005); Urquhart, *The Forgotten Highlander*; Lord, personal communication with the author, 2018, Case 2018B; Baxter, *Missing, Believed Killed*.

2. Urquhart, *The Forgotten Highlander*; Lord, personal communication with the author, 2018, Case 2018B; Koichi Wada, "A Monument to 11:02 a.m.," Nagasaki Peace, accessed February 4, 2025, https://nagasakipeace.jp/en/search/survivors/koichi_wada.html; Wada, personal communication with the author, Case 2018A, 1; "I Killed the King with My Lies," Paule Saviano Photography website, July 8, 2021, https://www.paulepictures.com/blog/tag/koichi-wada/.

3. Kenshi Hirata, personal communication with the author, 2010; Trumbull, *Nine Who Survived*, 98–99, 117–119; Hirata, in *Twice Bombed Twice Survived*, Part II.

4. Tsutomu Yamaguchi, personal communication with the author, 2008; Yamaguchi, *I Live to Tell My Story*, trans. Hideo Nakamura (unpub., 2009).

5. Kenshi Hirata, his daughter Saeko, and Setsuko Hirata's brother, personal communication with the author, trans. Nakamura and Inazuka, July and August 2010; Trumbull, *Nine Who Survived*, 98–99, 117–119; Hirata, in *Twice Bombed Twice Survived, Part II*.

6. Charles Sweeney, *War's End*, 109–110, 176–178, 198, 201–205, 209–218; Sweeney, personal communication with the author, 1999; Eric Beser, personal communication with the author, 2013; Beser family, personal communication with the author, 2013–2014.

7. Case #1, #33, Disk 1, from "Hibakusha Voices" (recordings in Japanese, transcripts in English), *The Asahi Shimbun*, https://www.asahi.com/hibakusha/english/link/.

8. Shigeyoshi Morimoto, in Trumbull, *Nine Who Survived* (Dutton, 1957), 16, 35–36, 38–41, 73–74; Hideo Nakamura, personal communication with the author, 2010.

9. Tatsuichiro Akizuki, *Nagasaki 1945* (Quartet Books, 1982), 67, 78–80; Tokusaburo Nagai, personal communication with the author, 2008; Endo Tai, personal communication with the author, 2008. The doctor who, in the aftermath of the bombings, abandoned his Buddhist upbringing for "irrational" and "murderous" thoughts about one of the unwanted soldiers who robbed a post-bombing hospital of food (but the physician ultimately stopped himself).

10. Witnesses #1, #33, #177, Disks #1, #4, #6, from "Hibakusha Voices" (recordings in Japanese, transcripts in English), *The Asahi Shimbun*, https://www.asahi.com/hibakusha/english/link/; Tatsuichiro Akizuki, *Nagasaki 1945*, 91. Dr. Akizuki on glass in the lungs and other organs; Masao Shiotsuki, *Doctor at Nagasaki* (Kosei Publishers, 1987), 72. At the Omura Naval Hospital, one doctor noted strange objects embedded in survivors' bodies; Case #203, Disk #5; Case

#186, Disk #4; Case #342, Disk #8, from "Hibakusha Voices," (recordings in Japanese, transcripts in English), *The Asahi Shimbun*, https://www.asahi.com/hibakusha/english/link/. Dr. Tsunoo at first seemed uninjured and deteriorated quickly as he was brought uphill to Dr. Nagai's location. Witness #342 reported, "When my daughter died, even her tears were the color of blood." Omura autopsies recorded (in Shiotsuki, 89) the results of bone marrow death.

11. Kinuyo Fukui via Hideo Nakamura and Hidetaka Inazuka, "Messages from Hibakusha," *The Asahi Shimbun*, https://www.asahi.com/hibakusha/english/shimen/; Kinuyo Fukui, personal communication with the author, September 24, 2018, Case 2018B, 73–75; "Woman Who Survived Hiroshima and Nagasaki Bombings Breaks Her Silence, *NHK*, December 11, 2024, https://www3.nhk.or.jp/nhkworld/en/news/backstories/3703/.

12. Akira Hirano, NHK Archive, testimony regarding Mami Samejima, https://www.nhk.or.jp/archives/en/; Akira Hirano, personal communication with the author regarding Mami Samejima, Case 2018B, 65–68.

13. Akira Iwanaga, in Trumbull, *Nine Who Survived*, 54–56, 75, 78; Iwanaga, personal communication with the author, July 2010; Iwanaga, "Messages from Hibakusha," *The Asahi Shimbun*, https://www.asahi.com/hibakusha/english/shimen/; Iwanaga, in *To Hell and Back: The Last Train from Hiroshima* (Roman & Littlefield, 2015) 59–60, 82, 148–149.

14. Yoshitomi Yasumi, lecture transcript, Ministry of Foreign Affairs, Nagasaki, Japan (2002), Nagasaki Museum archive; Yasumi, personal communication with the author, Case 2018B, 5–9B. Tokusaburo Nagai with Endo Tai, personal communication with the author, 2008. Regarding the Children's Crusade and planned Ohka launches from the Urakami Valley's tunnels, and tunnel child "Thunder Gods" who escaped that fate by the ending of the war. Nakamura was researching remaining kamikaze assignees during the year in which the first of the tunnels themselves were being excavated (in Nagasaki, 2008; and also, Nakamura, in 2010); M. G. Sheftall, *Hiroshima: The Last Witnesses* (Dutton, 2024), 112–114, for further reading on the memories and private fears of young Kamikaze conscripts.

15. Joshua Stoff, curator, Cradle of Aviation Museum, https://www.cradleofaviation.org/history/history/heritage.html. Regarding failures in the Japanese rocket program, Ugaki's final attack, and Togo's records; Toland, *The Rising Sun* (Random House, 1970), 836–837, 853–854.

16. Anonymous male nurse, age 16, "2024c," Nagai rescue crew, Case 2018B, 77–78.

17. Masahiro Sasaki, "Sadako's Plan," personal communication with the author, May 2010; Masahiro Sasaki and Sue DiCicco, *The Complete Story of Sadako Sasaki*, trans. Naomi Nakagoshi and Anne Prescott (Tuttle, 2020).

18. Truman letter, read by Clifton Truman Daniel, Truman Presidential Library paper crane dedication ceremony, in "Sadako Crane Donation to the Truman Library," C-SPAN, November 19, 2015, https://www.c-span.org/program/american-history-tv/sadako-crane-donation-to-the-truman-library/421843.

NOTES TO CHAPTER 7: THE FALLEN SKY

1. Haruno Horimoto, personal communication with the author, Case 2018B, 6A; Haruno Horimoto, "On Duty as a Conductor of the First Street Car After the A-Bombing," National Peace Memorial

Halls for the Atomic Bomb Victims in Hiroshima and Nagasaki, Global Network, 1985, https://www.global-peace.go.jp/en/taikenki/en_taikenki_syousai.php?gbID=346&dt=250201003226.

2. Kinuyo Fukui, "Messages from Hibakusha," *The Asahi Shimbun*, https://www.asahi.com/hibakusha/english/shimen/; Kinuyo Fukui, personal communication with the author, September 24, 2018, Case 2018B, 73–75.

3. Koichi Wada, "A Monument to 11:02 a.m.," Nagasaki Peace, accessed February 4, 2025, https://nagasakipeace.jp/en/search/survivors/koichi_wada.html; Wada, personal communication with the author, Case 2018A, 1; "I Killed the King with My Lies," Paule Saviano Photography website, July 8, 2021, https://www.paulepictures.com/blog/tag/koichi-wada/.

4. Stanley Resor and Walter Lord, personal communication with the author, September 13, 1993, File #29 (*Titanic* Expedition files). Regarding Nixon and the questions of leadership; "repeat performance in advance," of drivers, theatre group, as first responders, San Francisco earthquake, 1906: rescuer/actress Anne Ives (b. 1886: *The Producers*, 1967, *The Crucible*, Stratford, 1976)—personal communication with the author, 1976.

5. "Record on the Termination of the War," Post-Nagasaki, Imperial Palace: IMTFEE Doc. #62049, Japanese General Staff; Toland, *The Rising Sun* (Random House, 1970), 810–812, 826; Tatsuichiro Akizuki, *Nagasaki 1945* (London, Quartet Books, 1981), 73–74; Charles Sweeney, *War's End* (1997), 236–237; H. P. Bix, *Hirohito and the Making of Modern Japan* (Harper, 2000), 526 (para. 2), 527–518; Togo, to investigators from GHO Historical Section, in *U.S. Army Statements of Japanese Army Officials on WWII*, vol. 4, May 17, 1949, August 17, 1950, digitalized archive from microfilm [Shelf # 51256];

Lord, personal communication with the author, 1997. Regarding post-WWII interviews, Dr. Nishina, and Dr. Sagane.

6. Tamie Ekashira, personal communication with the author, Case 2018B, 65; Sakue Shimohira, age 10, "My Little Sister Killed Herself," *The Asahi Shimbun*, https://www.asahi.com/hibakusha/english/shimen/nagasakinote/note01-09e.html; Sakue Shimohira, personal communication with the author, Case 2018B, 4. The Nagasaki night glow.

7. Dr. Takashi (Paul) Nagai, *The Bells of Nagasaki*, 60–61, 73–83, 96–97. Nagai remedy details (as Mrs. Yamaguchi was certain the stranger who recommended the remedies was either Dr. Nagai or a member of his traveling aid team; Nagai "From the Ashes," essay in *Leaving These Children Behind*, Nyokodo Hermitage papers (Nagasaki, approx. 1949); Endo Tai, translation and personal communication with the author regarding the Nagai history, 2008; Kayano Nagai, in Takashi Nagai, *We of Nagasaki* (Duell, Sloan and Pearce, 1951), 16–17; Tsutomu Yamaguchi, personal communication with the author regarding Dr. Nagai, 2008.

8. Charles Sweeney, personal communication with the author, 1999; Maika Nakao, regarding Dr. Yoshio Nishina, Columbia University Conference, Tajima, November 6, 2009 (including Dr. Nishina's drawing of San Francisco being destroyed by submarine torpedo launched A-bomb, personal communication with the author, November 6, 2009); Nishina in John Toland, *The Rising Sun* (Random House, 1970), 794–5. Japan WWII nuclear programs.

9. Sweeney, personal communication, 1999, Case 2018B, 32, 45–48. Prison Camp 25, Aug 10–24, 1945; Lord, personal communication with the author, 2018, Case 2018B; Baxter, *Missing, Believed Killed* (Aurum Press, 2010).

NOTES TO CHAPTER 8: IS IT DUSK ALREADY?

1. Dr. Nagai, *The Bells of Nagasaki*, 60–61, 73–83, 96–97; Nagai "From the Ashes," essay in *Leaving These Children Behind*, Nyokodo Hermitage papers (Nagasaki, approx. 1949); Endo Tai, translation and personal communication with the author regarding the Nagai history, 2008; Kayano Nagai, in Takashi Nagai, *We of Nagasaki* (Duell, Sloan and Pearce, 1951), 16–17; Tsutomu Yamaguchi, personal communication with the author regarding Dr. Nagai, 2008; Tsutomu Yamaguchi, personal communication with the author, 2008– 2009. On Yamaguchi's faith in the example of Father Maximilian ("Simcho") Kolbe. Additional clarification of "Simcho's" identity was highlighted in a letter by Brian Taylor, dated March 2, 2010; https://saintmaximiliankolbe.com/biography/; Emiko Nakazako and Keiji Nakazawa, personal communication with the author, August 7, 2010. On the fates of atomic orphans, and the rise of the next-generation crime syndicates from this abused and rejected population; Yamaguchi acquaintance, "On the Beach Bomb," Charles Pellegrino and James Powell, 1984 Valkyrie Sessions (Brookhaven National Laboratory, while designing the world's smallest nuclear detonation systems for interstellar space probes, relativistic velocity), https://charlespellegrino.com/nuclear-propulsion/.

2. Kimiko Kuwabara, personal communication with the author, Case 2018B, 21–22; Kimiko Kuwabara, "I Saw Hell," The National Peace Memorial Halls for the Atomic Bomb Victims in Hiroshima and Nagasaki, Global Network, 2011, https://www.global-peace.go.jp/en/taikenki/en_taikenki_syousai.php?gbID=152&dt=241107084847.

3. Mizuha (Takama) Kikuzaki, in Shiho Burke, personal communication with the author, 2024; Hideaki Ito, dir., *Silent Fallout: Baby Teeth Speak* (2023), documentary. On nucleosynthesis, origins of cosmic rays, carbon, and other heavy elements: F. Hoyle,

"The Synthesis of the Elements from Hydrogen," *MNRAS* 106, no. 343 (1946): 343–83, https://doi.org/10.1093/mnras/106.5.343; Virginia Trimble, "The Origin and Abundances of the Chemical Elements," *Review of Modern Physics* 47, no. 4 (1977): 877–976, https://doi.org/10.1103/RevModPhys.47.877; D. Lynden-Bell, ed., review of *The Big Bang and Element Creation* (Royal Society of London, 1982), *Science* 222, no. 4628 (1983): 1116–17, https://www.science.org/doi/10.1126/science.222.4628.1116.b; Charles Pellegrino, "Compilation of Nucleosynthesis pathways," *Time Gate: Hurtling Backward Through History* (Tab, 1985), 237–248; Pellegrino and Francis Crick, "Genesis and Galactic Blight," *Time Gate: Hurtling Backward Through History* (Tab, 1985), 241.

4. Tak Furumoto and Furumoto family, personal communication with the author, 2010–2018, Case 2018A, 33–58; Colonel Stewart Harrington, *Silence Was a Weapon* (Ballantine, 1987). Harrington was Furumoto's immediate successor. If a Japanese American, in the same manner as descendants of other Axis nationalities (Italian and German), so much as traveled to Japan to learn the fates of relatives trapped behind enemy lines in war-torn countries, only Japanese Americans were singled out for immediate cancelation of passports and revocation of American citizenship, even if their forebears had been Americans for a hundred years; Tak Furumoto served in 'Nam, under the CIA's Operation PHOENIX, with the Japanese American Veterans Association ("Intelligence Officer and Advisor to the National Police CIA-sponsored Project PHOENIX"), July 2024; "As an Intelligence Officer, 1st Lieutenant Tak Furumoto . . . was assigned as an advisor to the Vietnam National Police Chief, during the CIA's Operation PHOENIX. He worked to neutralize VC infrastructures in the district. He was awarded the Bronze Star for actions during the Cambodian invasion by US and ARVN forces in 1970." "Tak Furumoto," 1st Cavalry Division Association, June 27, 2022, https://1cda.org/chapters/new-yorknew-jersey/tak-furumoto/; "Sherrill to bring Camp Survivor and Vietnam Veteran Tak Furumoto as Guest to Japanese PM Joint Address," press release, US Congresswoman Mikie Sherrill, April 10, 2024, https://sherrill.house.gov/media/press-releases/sherrill-to-bring-internment-camp-survivor-and-vietnam-veteran-tak-furumoto-as-guest-to-japanese-pm-joint-address.

5. Peggy Covell, Mitsuo Fuchida, and Kazuo Kunegaski, in *From Pearl Harbor to Golgotha* (Sky Pilots Press, 1953); Fuchida, *From Pearl Harbor to Golgotha*; Lord, personal communication with the author, 1992–93, Case 2018B, 64. References to "Midway" and "The Chinese Captain" are sourced from Fuchida's *From Pearl Harbor to Golgotha* and Case 2018B.

6. Thornton Wilder, *The Bridge of San Luis Rey* (Albert & Charles Boni, 1927).

7. The Sasaki, Yamaguchi, and Hirata families, personal communication with the author, 2010–2018; contemporary letters written by Masahiro and Sadako's mother ("No one is lovelier to a mother than her most miserable child . . . Oh . . . if a medicine . . . exists . . ."), Hiroshima Museum Archive, which also holds Sadako's medical files and copies of letters, including a letter by her roommate, Kiyo; Ishikawa et al, "Meteorological Conditions in Hiroshima"; Richard Ned Lebow, The Committee for the Compilation of Materials on Damage Caused by the Atomic Bombs in Hiroshima and Nagasaki, *Hiroshima and Nagasaki: The Physical, Medical, and Social Effects of the Atomic Bombings*, trans. Eisei Ishikawa and David L. Swain (Basic Books, 1981), 89–91, 93, 101. Masahiro Sasaki, details about bone marrow death in the stages of leukemia, regarding Sadako: Sadako's "plan," and the question of whether she saw what the Omoiyari principle and her paper crane project might become; Masahiro Sasaki, communication with the author, May 2010; Sasaki and DiCicco, *The Complete Story of Sadako Sasaki and the Thousand*

Paper Cranes (Armed with the Arts, Inc., 2018), 21, 30, 38, 57–62, 116–119; Matsu Matsumoto, in Nagai, *We of Nagasaki* (Duell, Sloan and Pearce, 1951), 30–70, 166, 173, 188–189; Tokasaburo Nagai, personal communication with the author, July 2008; Sweeney, personal communication with the author, 1999; Hachiya, *Hiroshima Diary* (UNC Press, 1955), 71.

8. Tak Furumoto and Furumoto family, personal communication with the author, 2022, Case 2018A, 33–58; "History," Tule Lake Committee, 2012, https://www.tulelake.org/history; Furumoto family, personal communication with the author, 2010–2018, Case 2018A, 33–58.

9. Kenshi Hirata, Saeko Hirata, and Setsuko's brother, personal communication with the author, March, July 2015. What happened after Kenshi disappeared (about 1955) to protect his family from anti-hibakusha discrimination.

10. Tak Furumoto and Masahiro Sasaki, personal communication with the author, Case 2018A, 40–58, 59–70 (further on 'Nam and partnership with Mitsuo Fuchida, October 8, 2018); "The Chinese Captain," in Fuchida, *From Pearl Harbor to Golgotha*; Lord, personal communication with the author, 1992–93, Case 2018B, 57–62; Charles Sweeney, personal communication, 1999, Case 2018B, 32, 45–48. Prison Camp 25, August 10–24, 1945; Baxter, *Missing, Believed Killed* (Aurum Press, 2010); Ari Beser, "How Paper Cranes Became a Symbol of Healing in Japan," *National Geographic*, August 28, 2015, https://news.nationalgeographic.org/how-paper-cranes-became-a-symbol-of-healing-in-japan/; Walter Lord, on Moe Berg and the Heisenberg incident, personal communication with the author (with Paul Helou of the *NYT* present), 1991–1992; OSS/MI-5 liaison days (recorded, regarding Fleming) at Lord's memorial service, NYC, 2002. Elizabeth Ooka, personal communication with the author, June 28, 2022; Preeti Deb, dir., *Three Boys Manzanar* (2017), documentary; Setsuko Thurlow, personal communication with the author, May 2015, Case 2018A, 18–28; James Cameron, Toshiko (Yamaguchi) and the President Obama Hiroshima visit, personal communication with the author, May 2016.

11. Mizuha (Takama) Kikuzaki, in Shiho Burke, personal communication with the author, 2024. Mizuha's story (the other child survivor, from the same school): Mizuha's daughter, Shiho (Takama Kikuzaki) Burke, May–September 2024, video interview, August 19, 2024, Case 2024 A and B+; Yasuko Kimura, *White Town Hiroshima* (Bunka Hyoron, 1983), 12–32, film version, *Shiroi Machi Hiroshima* (White City), by Tengo Yamada (Japan), with Shiho (Burke).

12. Leroy "Satchel" Paige, in Joseph Alpert, "Don't Look Back; Something Might Be Gaining on You," *American Journal of Medicine* 122, no. 10 (2009): 885, https://www.amjmed.com/article/S0002-9343(09)00532-4/pdf.

13. Sam Kean, *The Violinist's Thumb: And Other Lost Tales of Love, War, and Genius, as Written by Our Genetic Code* (Little, Brown and Co., 2012).

14. Tsutomu Yamaguchi, personal communication with the author, 2008–2009; Emiko Nakazako and Keiji Nakazawa, personal communication with the author, August 7, 2010; Yamaguchi acquaintance, "On the Beach Bomb," Pellegrino and James Powell, 1984 Valkyrie Sessions (Brookhaven National Laboratory, while designing the world's smallest nuclear detonation systems for interstellar space probes, relativistic velocity), https://charlespellegrino.com/nuclear-propulsion/.

15. Baxter, *Missing, Believed Killed* (Aurum Press, 2010).

16. Haruno Horimoto, personal communication with the author, Case 2018B, 6A; Haruno Horimoto, "On Duty as a Conductor of the First Street Car After the A-Bombing," National Peace Memorial Halls for the Atomic Bomb Victims in Hiroshima and Nagasaki, Global Network, 1985, https://www.global-peace.go.jp/en/taikenki/en_taikenki_syousai.php?gbID=346&dt=250201003226.

17. Kinuyo Fukui, personal communication with the author, September 24, 2018, Case 2018B, 73–75; Yin Tanaka, in "Double A-Bomb Survivor Attends Peace Ceremonies with Deep Emotion for 'Last Time,'" *The Mainichi*, August 11, 2021, https://mainichi.jp/english/articles/20210811/p2a/00m/0na/012000c.

18. "Leo Szilard," The Atomic Heritage Foundation, accessed February 3, 2025, https://ahf.nuclearmuseum.org/ahf/profile/leo-szilard/; Emile P. Torres, "How an H. G. Wells Sci-Fi Novel Predicted Oppenheimer and Atomic Bombs," *Big Think*, July 18, 2023, https://bigthink.com/the-past/hg-wells-novel-predicted-oppenheimer-atomic-bombs/#:~:text=The%20%E2%80%9Catomic%20bombs%E2%80%9D%20in%20H.G.,a%20street%20corner%20in%20London; "H. G. Wells and the Declaration of Human Rights," Univ. of Portsmouth, updated December 10, 2021, https://www.port.ac.uk/news-events-and-blogs/blogs/writing-literary-portsmouth/christine-berberich-hg-wells-whrd.

19. Tak Furumoto, personal communication with the author, 2010–2018, Case 2018A, 33–58; Tak Furumoto, letter, read as recently as the Fred Korematsu Day of Civil Liberties and the Constitution observance, Fort Lee Keynote Address by Tak Furumoto, January 30, 2025.

20. Tak Furumoto and Furumoto family, personal communication with the author, 2022, Case 2018A, 33–58; Ari Beser, "How Paper Cranes Became a Symbol of Healing in Japan," *National Geographic*,

August 28, 2015, https://news.nationalgeographic.org/how-paper-cranes-became-a-symbol-of-healing-in-japan/.

21. Walter Lord, on Moe Berg and the Heisenberg incident, personal communication with the author, 1991–1992 (with Paul Helou of the *NYT* present).

22. Elizabeth Ooka, personal communication with the author regarding Tak Furumoto, June 28, 2022; Preeti Deb, dir., *Three Boys Manzanar* (2017), documentary, https://www.threeboysmanzanar.com/.

23. Setsuko Thurlow, personal communication with the author, May 2015, Case 2018A, 19–24.

24. Kenshi Hirata, personal communication with the author, trans. Nakamura and Inazuka, 2010; Hirata, in Nakamura Inazuka, *Twice Bombed Twice Survived, Part II* (Tokyo, 2012), film.

25. James Cameron, the Yamaguchi family, and the President Obama Hiroshima visit, personal communication with the author, May 2016.

NOTES FOR EPILOGUE: ISLAND IN THE STREAM OF STARS

1. Walter Lord, personal communication with the author, 1987, and the published works of Morgan Robertson, 1898–1908.

INDEX

A

abductions, 15
abortion, 223
acute marrow leukemia, 197
African Americans, 214
Agent Orange, 213
Aioi Bridge (T-Bridge), 32, 92
airburst, 134
air pressure, 134
air-raid alert, 24, 82, 118, 120
air-raid training, 13, 17
Akagi (aircraft carrier), 30, 98
Akizuki, Dr., 148, 156
all stop, 109
Alvarez, Luis, 81
Anami, War Minister Korechika, 31, 93, 155, 167, 171
anemia, 221
animals, radiation effects on, 187
antielectrons, 227
antiseptics, 164

Aoyama, Mrs., 7, 8, 238
Aoyama, Nenkai, 8, 238
Apollo Lunar Module, 257
Appendix, 257
Arisue, General, 97
Armstrong, Neil, 162
Ashworth, Fred, 111, 128, 130
atmosphere, description of, 41
atomic bomb
  altitude settings for, 79
  coincidence and, 146
  complications regarding, 79
  description of, 47
  detonation plan for, 79
  detonation process for, 81, 111, 119, 123, 127
  development of, 77
  geometric formula for, 83
  mystery regarding, 224
  origin of, 22
  prediction regarding, 172

radar system on, 78
release of, 84
testing of, 78
vulnerabilities of, 127
See also detonation
Atomic Bomb Casualty Commission, 197
atomic bomb disease, 184, 196, 232
See also disease X
Atomic Bombing Survey, 220, 222
Auschwitz, 182

B

B-29s
  announcements regarding, 122
  domination of, 16
  as drop-zone suppliers, 173
  firebombings by, 91, 109
  leaflet dropping by, 155
  maneuvers following detonation by, 83
  military information regarding, 12
  at Nagasaki, 123
  speculation regarding, 36
  spotting of, before detonation, 125
  surveillance of, 172
  Tinian Island and, 80
Barefoot Gen (film), 223
Barnes, Philip, 111
barometric fuse, 112
baseball, 239
Battle of Midway, 30
Battle of Spotsylvania, 53
bauxite, 70, 72
Baxter, John
  after surrender, 172
  on Anami, 171
  on British fighter planes, 123
  on hell ship, 70
  Hyato and, 113, 232
  during Nagasaki bombing, 133, 134
  overview of, 257
  speculation of, 167
Beahan, Kermit, 119, 129, 130
Belgium Congo, uranium from, 49
Berg, Moe, 239
Beser, Ari, 237
Beser, Jacob
  on atomic bombings, 90
  background of, 75
  bombing role of, 81, 82, 84, 91, 109, 111, 117, 119, 120, 127
  firebombing raids and, 154
  following Nagasaki bomb drop, 143
  Hiroko Tasaka and, 193
  overview of, 257
  quote of, 132
  on silence of Japan, 90
  on Tinian Island, 170
"Beyond the Spectrum" (fictional tale), 3, 251
Big Stink, 117

Bill of Rights, 236
blindness, 66, 78, 152
blood transfusions, 199
Bockscar, 91, 109, 111, 117, 120, 127, 144
Bohr, Niels, 77
bomb, nuclear chain reaction in, 22
  See also atomic bomb
Bond, James, 240
bonehead maneuver, 83
bones
  projectiles in, 67, 151, 164
  radiation effects on, 8, 33, 44, 96, 150, 158, 167, 187, 227
Boulle, Pierre, 72
bribery, 37
Broadcast Center, 57
Broadwater, Miyuki, xiii
Buckley, Ed, 129
Buddhist traditions, 68
Burke, Shiho Takama, 222, 259
butterfly effect, 21, 53

C

calcium, 97, 187, 227, 229
Cambodia, 215
Cameron, James, 132, 248
camphor trees, 210
cancer, 74, 151, 188, 226, 233, 246
  See also leukemia
Cape Gloucester (aircraft carrier), 175
carbonization, 253

care packages, 189
Carolinum, 22
catechism of war, 29
Central Broadcast Center, 12, 259
Chan, Victor, 20
chaos theory, 21
Cherokee Proverbs of Twisted Hair, 162
cherry trees, 210
chickens, 180
childhood leukemia, 196
children
  activism for, 228
  as bombing survivors, 195
  effects of radiation exposure in, 227
  evacuations of, 36, 38
  radiation discrimination to, 247
  war training by, 38
Children's Crusade, 39, 114
chills, 107
China, hatred against, 29
Chinese Americans, 101, 217
Chinese slaves, 173
Churchill, Winston, 128
Clarke, Arthur C., 162
Clay, Andrew Dice, 217
Clinton, Bill, 234
clocks, detonation effects on, 26, 126
clothing
  as reflective, 19, 66, 107
  radiation effects on, 58, 107, 122

cloud, 13, 14, 19, 32, 55, 85, 134
cobalt-60 radiation treatment, 233
Colby, William, 213
Command Headquarters, 126, 133
Communications Hospital, 86
concentration camps, 182
Confederate sharpshooters, 53
confusion, 186
Constitution, 235
coughing up of blood, 150, 184
Covell family, 23
Covell, Peggy, 27, 97, 191, 233, 257, 259
Crick, Francis, 222
crisis, leadership failures in, 165
Củ Chi (Vietnam), 214

D

dead-alive effect, 60, 168
dead, honoring, 68, 143, 212, 244
Death, Dr., 110
death railway slave camps, 72
death sand, 164, 167
depression, 169, 181
DeShazer, Jake, 192
detonation
   aftermath description following, 42, 46, 53, 54
   altitude settings for, 77, 79
   description of, 8, 13, 17, 20, 25, 33, 39, 43, 57, 66, 108, 133, 136, 137, 167
   as false sunrise, 12
   fire following, 56, 57, 59
   long-term effects of, 20
   plan for, 79
   process of, 81, 123, 127
   sensations during, 13
   as silent explosion, 12, 14
   sound of, 17
Detroit auto industry, 217
discrimination, 209, 247
disease X, 65, 148, 163, 195, 219
   See also atomic bomb disease
DNA, 222, 227
dragon metaphor, 26
dream state, 205
dry heaves, 90
Đức Hòa, 213, 214
Duck and Cover film, 66
Dust Bowl era, 98

E

Eagle, 162
ears, detonation effects on, 67
Earthquake (film), 215
Eatherly, Claude, 82
Ebby, Major, 213
Einstein, Albert, 22, 52, 260
Eisenhower, Dwight D., 104
Ekashira, Tamie, 167
emergency preparedness protocol, 180
emotional withdrawal, 185
Enola Gay, 78, 81, 82, 84, 89
espionage, 37

Executive Order 9066, 100, 189
eyes, in death, 110

F
fail-safes, 111
fatigue, 65
Fat Man (atomic bomb), 119, 128, 153
  See also atomic bomb; detonation
Fermi, Enrico, 22, 48, 49, 77
fetal development, radiation effects on, 221, 224
fever, 65, 90
field-medicine training, 67
Finch, J. R., 20, 178
fire
  description of, 26, 42, 46, 54, 56, 57, 59, 86, 91, 135
  of matter, 47
firebombings, 91, 106, 108, 141, 154, 170
First Amendment (United States), 187
fission, 47
flash
  description of, 10, 13, 39, 41, 44, 45, 66, 84, 86, 88, 134, 147, 152, 250
  strategy regarding, 78, 107, 137, 153
Fleming, Ian, 240
food shortages, 190, 195, 205
forgiveness, 192, 225
formation, strategy, 83
fossilization, 60, 92, 168
FUBAR factor, 109
Fuchida, Joseph, 233
Fuchida, Mitsuo, 28, 91, 97, 155, 190, 233, 258, 259
Fukagata, Echiyo, 20
Fukahori, Kanji, 250
Fukui, Kinuyo, 65, 151, 163, 232, 258
Fukui, Kuniyoshi, 232
Fukuoka coal mine, 112
funeral pyres, 91, 163
Furumoto, Asajiro, 88
Furumoto, Carol, 240
Furumoto, Mary, 208
Furumoto, Tak
  background of, 100
  Elizabeth Ooka and, 241, 260
  on internment camps, 20
  marbles of, 238
  overview of, 258
  PTSD of, 233
  radiation exposure of, 186
  return to America by, 208
  Vietnam War and, 212
Furumoto, Yuku, 88
fusing checklist, 111

G
gamma rays, 150, 151, 188, 227
gangster orphans, 159

gasoline engine, 47
"*Genbaku-O-yurusumaji*" (Never again, the A-bomb), 205
General W. H. Gordon (army transport ship), 187
Germany, 47, 49, 75
Get down order, 13
ghosts, in Japanese mythology, 105
gift offerings, 99
Goodall, Jane, 52
government, control by, 16
Government House, 163
grape seeds, 169
graphite, 48
grasshoppers, 195
Great Artiste, The, 81, 84, 117, 119, 130, 144
Great Confiscation, 209
Great Depression, 98
ground-based radar beam, 78
ground candles, 54
Ground Zero
  nightglow of, 174
  paper cranes at, 235
  peace in, 56
  persons at, 41, 67, 95, 147, 148, 153, 179, 184, 261
  radar station and, 133
  as shock-cocoon, 82
  surveying, 56
  target of, 130
  See also Hiroshima
Groves, Charles Victor, 2
Groves, Leslie, 74, 79
guilt, 181, 247

H

Hachiya, Dr. Michihiko, 104
Hadrian's Wall, 72
Hahn, Otto, 22
Haig, Alexander, 166
hair, radiation effects to, 20, 73, 153, 184
Harper, Henry Sleeper, 251
Harris, Harry Earl, 193
Harris, Hiroko Tasaka, 132
Hata, Field Marshall, 155
Hata, Shunroku, 80
hate, 225
Hậu Nghĩa, Đức Hòa District, Long An Province, 213
heavy water, 47
Heisenberg, Werner, 47, 239
hell ships, 70, 110, 175
Herculaneum, 60
Heston, Charlton, 215
hibakusha, 108, 211, 222, 247, 259
Hirano, Hyato, 113, 115, 172, 174, 232, 257, 258
Hirata, Kenshi
  in aftermath of detonation, 61, 141
  background of, 44
  family of, 193, 210
  grief of, 90, 127
  interview of, 246

Jacob Beser and, 193
  in Nagasaki, 120, 136
  overview of, 258
  as searching for wife, 53, 62
  traveling by, 67, 108
  on Yawata, 119
Hirata, Saeko, 211, 246
Hirata, Setsuko, 43, 54, 62, 121, 137, 142, 210
Hirohito (Emperor of Japan), 15, 155, 166, 170, 171, 180
Hiroshima, 249
  abductions in, 15
  air-raid alert in, 82
  calm in, 163
  communication from, 31, 103
  description of, 6, 7, 16
  fallout-contamination in, 20, 42, 53, 54
  material shortages in, 38
  post-bombing conditions of, 195, 221
  post-detonation fire in, 56, 57, 59
  quiet in, 16
  regrowth in, 210
  schoolchildren evacuations in, 36, 38
  suspicions regarding bombing of, 178
  See also detonation; fire
Hiroshima Castle, 8, 210
Hiroshima Dome, 92
Hiroshima formation, 84

Hiroshima Memorial Museum, 232
Hiroshima Station, 68
Holocaust, 75
hope, 203
Horimoto, Haruno, 14, 58, 64, 93, 163, 258
Hotarujaya Streetcar Terminal, 135
humanitarian perspective, 245
hydrogen bomb, 230
hypercane, 134
hypocenter, 8, 164
  as epicenter, 23
  description from, 12, 14
  destruction in, 148
  dust from, 93
  instantaneous nonexistence effect at, 92
  persons at, 32, 54, 55, 58, 66, 96, 118, 146, 148, 152, 164, 168, 228
  rescue attempts in, 59
  as target, 91
  telephone poles at, 158
  See also Ground Zero

I

Iacocca, Lee, 217
Imani Commercial School, 153
Imperial Palace, 106
Inatsuki, Japan, 232
Inazuka, Hidetaka, 246
Industrial Hall, 8, 15

instantaneous nonexistence
    effect, 92, 253
internees, 187
internment camps, 20, 23, 101,
    102, 178, 186, 234, 242, 260
intestinal upset, 65
  See also atomic bomb disease
invisible radiation, 3
Iran, 225
isotope decay, 221
isotopes, 31, 54, 68, 153, 187
Italy, declaration of war by, 75
Ito, Hideaki, 52
Iwanaga, Akira, 16, 17, 152, 153, 259
Iwo Jima, 82

J

Japan
  attack from, 99
  at Battle of Midway, 30
  complacency of, 83
  declaration of war by, 75
  description of, 80
  destruction in, 80
  deterioration of, 114
  firebombing raids in, 36, 106, 108
  gift offerings to, 99
  hardships in, 15
  loss of control of, 70
  naval power of, 29
  occupation of the Philippines by, 27
  Russian payments to, 29
  suspicions in, 101
  3/11 in, 237
  Truman's viewpoint of, 160
  United States business dealings with, 99, 217
  weapons transport to, 70
Japanese Americans
  assimilation of, in Japan, 209
  bombing deaths of, 107
  care packages for, 189
  deportation of, 186
  discrimination of, 209
  internment camps for, 20, 23, 101, 234
  as outcasts, 189, 208, 209, 216
Japanese Family Association, 189
Japanese POWs, 191
Japanese Zeros, 120

K

Kachidoki Maru, 72
Kaiseizan Park, 237
Kaitaichi, 68
Kai, Yutaka, 132
kamikaze raids, 79
Kanegasaki, Kazuo, 28, 97, 191, 259
Kikuzaki, Futaba, 185
Kikuzaki, Gyoji, 97, 186
Kikuzaki, Kunihiro, 97, 185
Kikuzaki, Mizuha Takama, 33, 66, 82, 94, 184, 218, 259

Kikuzaki, Takama, 36
Kimura, Yasuko, 39
kite men, 9
Kobe, 45, 141
Koi Station, 68, 70
Kokura, 91, 109, 117, 119
Kokura industrial center, 106
Kolbe, Father Maximilian, 181, 226
Konpira Ridge, 135
Korean Americans, 210
Koreans, hatred against, 29
Kuwabara, Kimiko, 12, 57, 184, 259
Kyoto, 106
Kyushin, 65

L

land invasion, fears of, 154
Lax, Peter, 52
leadership, failures of, in crisis, 165
leaflets, distribution of, 155
Lean, David, 72
leeches, 169
LeMay, Curtis, 91
Letter Y, 77
leukemia, 185, 196
   See also cancer
Lewis, Robert, 85
Little Boy (atomic bomb), 131
liver, 169, 180
loans/loan sharks, 196, 204

Lord, Walter, 1, 98, 144, 165, 233, 239, 251, 259
Lorenz, Edward, 21
lungs, detonation effects to, 150

M

MacArthur committee, 190
MacArthur, Douglas, 173, 189
MacKenzie, Rip, 178
Maekawa, Tomoko, 247
maggots, 169, 180
Manchuria, 171
Manchuria incidents, 99
Manhattan Project, 23, 100, 260
   See also atomic bomb; detonation
Manzanar prison camp, 102, 209, 242
marbles, 190, 238
Maria Cathedral, 135
Marquardt, George, 81
marriage, 142, 189
Marshall, George, 170
Mars landers, 257
mass, as converted to energy, 47
mass cremations, 68
mass extinction, 230
Masuno, Mitsuko, 250
Matheson, Dr., 111
Matsuda, Toshihiko, 8, 238
matter, burning of, 47
medicine, 16, 169, 180, 220
Mediterranean diet, 220

Memorial Sloan Kettering Cancer Center, 233
mental absenteeism, 136
Mercurochrome, 93
meteors, examples of, during detonation, 14
Michiko, Saito, 24
Michishita, Takato, 118
microwaves, 150
Mikasa, 216
Miller, Glenn, 176
Minuit, Peter, 49
miracle firehouse (Liberty Street), 235
Misasa Bridge, 42
miscarriages, 221
mist, description of, 41
Mitatake, Toyo, 102
Mitchell, David, ix
Mitsubishi Corporation, 16, 61, 106, 180, 211
Miyajima Island, 194
Miyato, Ichiro, 123, 133
Moment Zero, description of, 8, 10, 14, 39, 43, 57
  See also detonation
monsoons, 221
"Moonlight Serenade" (Miller), 176
Morimoto, Setsuko, 244
Morimoto, Shigeyoshi, 9, 107, 147, 259
Morimoto, Tomiko, 10, 259
Mount Misen, 194
Muslim Americans, 235

N

Nagai, Dr., 150, 156, 163, 170, 198
Nagasaki
  as target, 91, 106, 126, 133
  civilians in, 91
  cloud cover in, 128
  destruction in, 147, 156
  detonation process in, 111
  memorial museum in, 226
  post-bombing description of, 174
  rainbow over, 182
  rescues in, 163
  suspicions regarding bombing of, 178
  See also detonation
Nagasaki Broadcasting Corporation, 211
Nakamura, Hideo, 246
Nakazawa, Harumi, 15
Nakazawa, Keiji, 37, 178, 223
Native Americans, 101
nausea, 107
Necessary Evil, 81
neutrinos, 43
neutron-emitting metals, 22
neutron spray, 150
Newton, Isaac, 144
New York Times, The (newspaper), 75
Nichols, Kenneth, 48

Night to Remember, A (Lord), 1
9/11, 235
9/11 Family Association, 237
Ninoshima, 67
Nishina, Dr. Yoshio, 31, 92, 97
Nixon, Richard, 165, 215
Nobel Peace Prize, 260
nuclear arms, reduction support
    regarding, 166
  See also atomic bomb
nuclear chain reaction, 22
nuclear explosion, requirements
    for, 48
  See also detonation
nuclear fission, 22
nuclear fusion, 230
nuclear testing, 186
nucleic acids, 224

O
Obama, Barack, 248
Ogura, Keiko, 32, 55
Ohka rocket bombs, 114, 154
Oka Produce Company, 209, 241
Okinawa, 79, 155
Omoiyari, 24, 203, 206, 236, 260
"*On the Beach* bomb", 230
Ooka, Elizabeth, 240, 260
Operation Phoenix, 213, 215
orphans, 158, 194
Osaka, 45, 141

P
Paige, Leroy, 226
paper crane outreach program, 260
paper cranes, 23, 199, 235
"Parrot's Beak" III Corps, 213
Parsons, William, 75, 82
Pearl Harbor, 29, 98
persimmon leaves, 169
Philippines, 27
phonograph, 175
photography, 102, 208, 260
photojournalism, 102
piercing hazards, 45, 96, 107, 122, 136, 137, 151, 152, 179, 219
pills, in case of enemy capture, 80
plants, radiation effects on, 187
Pledge of Allegiance, 178
plutonium, 22, 50, 111, 179
political prisoners, 101
positrons, 227
post-traumatic stress disorder, 215, 219
Pot, Pol, 215
POWs
  Chinese, 173
  death of, on ships, 175
  engineering work of, 114
  execution plans for, 111
  holiday for, 167
  instructions to, 173
  Nagasaki expedition of, 174

physical conditions of, 117
testimony of, 191
See also Prison Camp 25
Prefectural Girls' High School, 163
pregnancy, 221
premonitions, 14, 32, 55, 118, 146
Prison Camp 25, 110, 112, 118, 123, 133, 167, 172, 258
Project Apollo, 78

Q
quantum artifacts, 85

R
radar-imaging machinery, 129
radar-triggered altitude sensor, 257
radiation
  description of, 168
  discrimination, 247
  effects of, 54, 62, 65, 74, 90, 94, 95, 96, 105, 107, 108, 150, 153, 184
  prompt effects of, 188
  tumor development from, 227
radiation denial, 178
rain, contamination in, 41, 42, 55, 59, 158, 188, 195
rain of ruin, 159
Ramsey, Norman, 77, 130
rationing, 10, 70, 117
rats, 169
real estate industry, 216, 220, 233
Red Cross, 173

red-stamping, 76
rescue efforts, citizens involved in, 165
Resor, Stanley, 165
rifles, 53
ripple effect, 23
River Kwai, 72
rivers, post-detonation effects on, 61
Robertson, Morgan, 1, 251
Roosevelt, Eleanor, 233
Roosevelt, Franklin D., 22, 48
rose hips, 169
rule of flat, 57
Russia, 29, 225

S
sabotage, 114
Samejima family, 107
Samejima, Mami, 107, 127, 152, 260
Sanae, Toshimune, 32
sand, detonation effects on, 85
San Francisco earthquake, 165
Sasaki family, 23, 56, 85, 187
Sasaki, Fujiko, 194, 197
Sasaki, Masahiro, 42, 158, 160, 188, 194, 198, 203, 236, 260
Sasaki, Sadako, 23, 42, 56, 158, 160, 188, 194, 260
Sasaki, Shigeo, 194
Sedgwick, John, 53
segregation camps, 178, 186

self-censorship, 189
self-silencing, 81
Sengier, Edgar, 48, 49
Septimius Severus (Roman emperor), 72
shadow people, 253
shadow people denial, 178
Shadow People Project, 253
shadows, 8, 10, 88, 136, 164
shock-cocoon effect, 137, 141
shock cocoons, 9
shock wave, 134
skin, detonation effects on, 19, 20, 40, 58, 65, 66, 86, 89, 94, 96
soil, radiation effects on, 187
soot, 88
South China Sea, 72
Special Senate Committee on Atomic Energy, 74
speed of reflected sunlight, 89
speed of sound, 89
Speer, Albert, 239
spirit-lives, drifting of, 64
spotter planes, 166
statues, human remains as, 60
steel "paper crane", 237
  See also paper cranes
St. Francis Hospital, 135
stillbirths, 221, 222
Straight Flush, 82
streetcars, 14, 46, 65, 92, 135, 258
strontium-90, 97, 227

suicide, 171, 186
surrender, 155, 159, 166, 170, 171, 172, 180
surveillance planes, 124
survivors
  conditions of, 64, 65, 67, 156, 163, 164, 184, 219
  as dishonored, 247
  double, 247
  employment challenges of, 188
  medical questioning of, 220
  rebuilding by, 188, 195
  rejection in marriage by, 189
  self-censorship by, 189
  supplies for, 180
Sweeney, Charles
  bombing role of, 81, 91, 109, 111, 117, 119, 128, 144
  overview of, 260
  surrender and, 171
Szilard, Leo, 22, 48, 79, 233, 260

T

Tadako, Father, 95
Tadako, Futaba, 96, 221
Tadako, Mother, 36, 96
Takako, Tamura, 146
Takama, Hidmitsu, 95
Takei, George, 178, 239
talcum, 169
Tamura, Takahiro, 213
Tanaka, General, 171
tariffs, 217

Tasaka, Hiroko, 89, 193
teeth, detonation effects on, 47, 85, 92, 160, 187, 227
Thailand, 110
3/11, 237
Three Boys Behind Barbed Wire photo, 242, 260
Three Boys Manzanar (documentary), 243
thunder gods, 154
Thurlow, Setsuko, 86, 89, 219, 244, 260
Tibbets maneuver, 83
Tibbets, Paul, 76, 78, 79, 80, 81, 84, 91, 109, 144
timing fuse, 82, 112
Tinian Island, 80
Titanic (Royal Mail Steamship), 2, 251
toad venom, 65
Tobata, 108
Tokyo, 106, 155, 171
Tora! Tora! Tora! (film), 213
torture, 80, 113
train transportation, 17, 68, 94, 108, 152, 153
Transportation Ministry, 65
transportation, restrictions to, 17
"Tree of Hope", 249
trees, regrowth of, 210
Tribute Center, 235, 237
Truman, Clifton, 160
Truman, Harry, 103, 159, 170
Trump, Donald, 217, 233
Tsunoo, Susumu, 148, 260
Tule Lake Segregation Camp (No-no Camp), 101
tunnels, 175, 180, 213
2024c (surviving boy), 156
typhoon, 72, 174

U

Ugaki, Admiral, 155
unconsciousness, 25
United Nations, 229
United Service Organizations' concerts, 214
United States
  business dealings between Japan and, 99, 217
  espionage of, 37
  gift offerings from, 99
  hatred against, 29
  hatred for, 38
  uranium in, 49
  war declaration on, 75
Universal Declaration of Human Rights, 233
Urakami, 130, 153
Urakami hills, 167
Urakami Stadium, 130
uranium, 22, 49, 50
uranium-235, 31, 179
uranium-235 bomb, requirements for, 48
uranium bomb, origin of, 31

uranium reactor, origin of, 48
Urey, Harold, 48, 49, 50
urine, 70
Urquhart, Alistair, 72, 110, 134, 175, 261
US Patent 2,708,656, 22
USS *Panay*, 98
Ussuri Maru, 70, 71

V

van Kirk, Theodore, 75
Van Pelt, Jim, 129
veterans, Vietnam, 215
Vietnam War, 210, 213
Violinist's Thumb, The (Kean), 228
vitamin C, 169
Von Braun rocket, 137

W

Wada, Koichi, 126, 135, 148, 164, 261
warlords, behaviors of, 36
War Ministry, 59
Warren, Earl, 100
Watergate scandal, 165
weapons, training and transport of, 38, 70
weather, for the atomic bomb drop, 109
weather planes, 117
Wells, H. G., 4, 21, 47, 233
what-about-ism, 178
White City Hiroshima (film), 223

Wilder, Thornton, ix, 193
World Set Free, The (Wells), 21
World Trade Center, 235, 252
World War II, fictional writings regarding, 2

X

X-ray machines, 96, 188, 221

Y

Yamada, Tengo, 223
Yamaguchi, Hisako, 105, 140, 168, 179, 226
Yamaguchi, Katsutoshi, 140, 168, 179
Yamaguchi, Toshiko, 228, 248
Yamaguchi, Tsutomu
  atomic bomb sickness of, 90, 168, 179
  death of, 246
  detonation and, 14, 67, 84, 137
  at museum, 226
  at Nagasaki, 105
  overview of, 261
  testimony of, 227
  travels of, 41, 61, 85
  work of, 122
Yamawaki, Yoshiro, 74
Yanai, Major, 86
Yangtze River, 99
Yasumi, Yoshitomi, 153
Yawata, 108, 119

NAGASAKI BEFORE